ORGANIZING A LIVING

How to Build a Profitable Career
as a Professional Organizer

By Jackie Tiani, CPO®

Foreword by Barbara Hemphill
Author of Taming the Paper Tiger

**Aspiration
Books**

ORGANIZING FOR A LIVING, 1st Edition; How to Build a Profitable Career as a Professional Organizer by Jackie Tiani, CPO®

Copyright 2008 by Jackie Tiani

All rights reserved. No part of this book may be used or reproduced in any form or transmitted electronically without authorized consent in writing from the author, except in the case of brief quotations embodied in critical articles or reviews.

Organizing for a Living / Jackie Tiani – 1st. ed.
ISBN: 978-0-9785318-0-5
Printed in Canada

 Published by Aspiration Books
Post Office Box 5085
Glendale Heights, IL 60139-5085 U.S.A.
Orders@AspirationBooks.com; http://www.AspirationBooks.com

Table of Contents

Table of Contents iii
Foreword vii
Preface ix
Acknowledgments xi
Disclaimer xii
Part I Understanding the Organizing Profession 13

    Chapter One: Professional Organizing – The Big Picture 15

        What exactly is a professional organizer? 15
        What do professional organizers do? 16
        Advantages (and drawbacks) of being a professional organizer 18
        The evolution of the professional organizing industry 30

    Chapter Two: What it Takes to Be a Professional Organizer 35

        Distinguishing qualities of a successful professional organizer 35
        Determination and self-discipline 37
        Background and experience 40
        Business aptitude and skills 41
        What makes a professional organizer — "professional?" 43

    Chapter Three: Preparing for an Organizing Career 49

        Making the transition from employee to entrepreneur 49
        Technical training and skills development 55
        Credentials and certification 62

Part II Guiding Your Business to Success 67

    Chapter Four: Carving a Niche 69

        Generalists vs. Specialists 69
        Determining your specialties 71
        Exploring opportunities for specialization 74
        Give your niche time to incubate 77

    Chapter Five: Building a Business Plan 79

        Point the direction 79
        Plan your strategy 82
        Analyze your finances 82
        Build your career portfolio 83

Put your business plan in writing 84
Form a support team 86

Chapter Six: Developing Your Business Identity 89

Branding strategies 89
Naming your business 91
Designing your distinctive mark 92
Building your Internet presence 96
Developing your phone personality 100

Chapter Seven: Structuring Your Business Ownership 103

Sole Proprietor 103
General Partnership 105
Limited Liability Company (LLC) 106
C-Corporation 107
Subchapter S-Corporation 108
Other business structure considerations 109
Alternatives to business ownership 112

Chapter Eight: Making It All Legal 115

Getting professional advice 115
Zoning, licenses and registrations 117
Tax issues 121
Writing client contracts and agreements 127
Protecting your name and intellectual property 129

Chapter Nine: Marketing and Public Relations 133

Developing your marketing plan 133
Finding potential clients 138
Advertising 140
Developing promotional tools 145
Networking 148
Getting referrals 153
Getting free publicity 159

Chapter Ten: Setting Your Fees 165

Understanding antitrust laws 166
The psychology of fee setting 166
Calculating your hourly rate 171
Packaging your services 174

Estimating and project planning 180
Getting paid 183
Raising rates 186

Chapter Eleven: Running a Small Business 189

Managing your business 189
Hiring employees and subcontractors 194
Alternatives for increasing revenue 203
Developing your policies and procedures manual 204
Managing your money 206
Protecting your assets 213
Taking care of the boss 218

Part III 221
Working with Clients 221

Chapter Twelve: Cultivating the Client Relationship 223

Converting prospects into paying clients 223
Creating and presenting proposals 231
Laying the groundwork for success 232
Conducting the needs assessment 236
Developing an action plan 240

Chapter Thirteen: Helping Your Client Get & Stay Organized 243

Preparing for client visits 243
Phases of the organizing process 247
Maintaining organizing success 250
Understanding basic organizing principles 252
Teaching organizing principles and skills 261
Managing large-scale organizing projects 266
Understanding clients with special needs 268
Working with business clients 271

Chapter Fourteen: Retaining Ideal Clients 273

Gaining satisfied clients 274
Managing client expectations 276
Treating your clients with dignity 277
Handling difficult situations 278
Ethics and integrity 283
Getting repeat business 285

Afterword 288
Resources 289
Index 295
About the Author 305

Foreword

Finally – the first comprehensive book about how to establish a profitable business as an organizing consultant!

The organizing industry has needed this book for a long time, and I am thrilled that Jackie Tiani has written it. I first met Jackie when I served as President of the National Association of Professional Organizers. After learning about her extensive business and accounting background, I recommended her for nomination as Treasurer of NAPO, which proved to be one of the most valuable decisions I made for the association. She served two terms and put our organization on a strong path to financial stability.

Jackie's insightful advice could only come from years of real-world experience. When I started my business in 1978 with a $7 ad in a New York City newspaper, and a degree in Liberal Arts, I had no idea what I was doing. New and aspiring professional organizers need a roadmap – that is where Jackie comes in. I learned what is contained here through often-painful trial and error because the roadmap did not exist.

Even seasoned professional organizers will benefit from reading this book (I certainly did!). This is the only book on the market that tells professional organizers how to take their dreams and ideas from concept to marketplace, not as a hobby, but as a real, profit-generating business. It is a "must read" for aspiring entrepreneurs who want to build a credible organizing business, but are not quite sure how to get there.

Based on my experience, the organizing industry is still in the "toddler stage." The big reason is that most organizing consultants love the craft of organizing, but know little or nothing about "the business of business." In order for the organizing profession to grow into a strong and viable industry, we need people who understand business to create employment opportunities, for people who do not necessarily want to own their own business, but truly love to help people get organized and are highly competent at doing so. This book is written for the people who want to own a profitable organizing business.

Not only does Jackie provide solid business advice and concrete steps for creating a successful business, but she also inspires people who have forged their own way but are always looking for new ways to grow their business to even higher levels of success.

Thank you, Jackie. We needed this!

Barbara Hemphill
Founder of Paper Tiger Institute
Author of Kiplinger's *Taming the Paper Tiger*

Preface

This book provides the emerging professional organizer with an instruction manual for establishing and operating a profitable professional organizing business. In addition, the book equips veteran professional organizers with tools to assess and enhance their current business practices.

Those that are new to the field of professional organizing will find this book to be a comprehensive guide to the ins and outs of building a profitable business in this market segment. This book addresses the primary aspects of business establishment and many of the pitfalls associated with those efforts. This book provides you with the tools to start your business out on a foundation that will expand in strength as your business prospers and grows.

Those that are veterans will find this to be a tool for assessing current strategies and roadmaps for their existing business as it relates to working with clients, managing finances, setting rates and the ever-important topic of the business expansion process.

Whether you are reentering the workforce, making a career change, embarking on your first career, or reexamining your professional organizing business, you need to be armed with knowledge and tools to assist you in making well-informed choices. As you plan your business, you are likely to have a number of questions about the decisions you have to make. This book is targeted to provide the knowledge and tools needed to plan effectively and make business decisions with confidence. Wherever you are in your professional organizing journey, I believe the ideas in this book will help you achieve something wonderful in your career.

The professional organizing industry is growing rapidly. It is difficult to keep up with the demand for curriculums, structured education and training for the newcomers to this field. I came into this industry with a strong business background, but my own education about the professional organizing industry came mostly through the National Association of Professional Organizers (NAPO). As a newcomer, I joined NAPO and attended a national conference. I quickly discovered that most professional organizers are gracious, unselfish and eager to share their experience and knowledge with beginning organizers. I soaked up information like a sponge and read everything I could about the subject of organizing, consulting and launching a business. It amazed me how quickly I became the person with the answers. It has also amazed me how the industry has grown and evolved since I started.

Today, I am one of the most well fed professional organizers on the planet. A gourmet latte has bought aspiring professional organizers half-hour mentoring sessions. Lunch at the restaurant of my choice, for some of those individuals has allowed them to pick my brain for at least an hour. Being a mentor and assisting colleagues has been one of the most satisfying aspects of my career as a professional organizer. Being able to nurture and contribute to the development of aspiring professional organizers, sharing my experiences, helping them develop their businesses and assisting them in striking a balance between personal and professional priorities has been very rewarding to me personally. I am simply energized by the enthusiasm of new professional organizers taking their place in organizing the world, or veterans driven to achieve more.

This book is a culmination of years of research and interviews with hundreds of professional organizers. Along with my own experience, much of the content in this book specifically pertaining to professional organizing came from the notes I took while attending NAPO conferences and chapter meetings.

In an effort to create a Frequently Asked Questions (FAQ) document, I drafted answers to the questions newcomers frequently asked me. I became aware that experienced professional organizers were also seeking my assistance with various aspects of running their business. I discovered that there were too many questions for me to respond to in sufficient detail using a simple FAQ document. Satisfactory responses to those questions would fill a book. Therefore, against the advice of the publishing experts who warned that the audience was too small, I decided to continue writing and the FAQ's indeed became a book.

The number of phone calls and email messages I receive from people contemplating their own professional organizing business has increased steadily every year since starting my own business. I receive inquiries about the organizing industry. I receive questions about my own business and business model. They ask me if I am hiring. They offer to intern free. They offer to shadow me as I run my business. They ask for my advice about starting their own business. In those conversations, they share wonderful stories about where they are in their life and their business desires. They tell me how they came to realize that they should become a professional organizer and with that enthusiasm, they are looking for answers and direction to get beyond the hurdles at hand. This book provides that support.

I hope that you find this book a helpful resource in starting or growing your professional organizing business. I hope you are inspired from reading this book, and that the following pages provide practical ideas to encourage you to begin your own adventure. Many successful professional organizers were self-taught. You can be, too!

Acknowledgments

I am indebted to those who have generously helped me with this project. I am especially grateful to have a very talented and bighearted family who contributed time, assistance, encouragement, and support.

My copyeditors Karen Schmiedeke and Lynn Tiani cleaned up choppy sentences and more than occasional lapses in word usage and grammar. Thanks for helping to make my book more readable. Thanks to Corey Tiani and Mike Tiani for guidance throughout the process of preparing for print.

My deepest gratitude goes to the National Association of Professional Organizers and the hundreds of professional organizers who have freely shared their knowledge and stories with me throughout my career and especially during years of research. Entwining their experiences with mine has allowed their voices to be heard throughout this book. This book owes much to them for its realistic assessment of the professional organizing industry.

My NAPO colleagues encouraged me throughout the writing of this book, provided valuable feedback, and refused to allow me to put my book on the back burner. Barry Izsak took time from his busy schedule as NAPO President to add his expert technical review. Kate Rhoad lovingly challenged me when I thought my writing task was complete, encouraging me to take my manuscript back to the drawing board to add essential components. Kathi Burns provided a boost to my self-confidence and supported me when I expressed shyness about self-promotion. The Chicago Chapter of NAPO adopted the difficult task of selecting a book title, and Beth Randall offered her keen eye to help with the final proofreading.

My adult children, Bill Tiani, Bob Tiani, and Kathy Dal Pra have always been my source of inspiration and drive for success, as well as my motivation for learning how to be organized. Although they were my first organizing students, they are also my teachers. I am so proud of each of them.

My partner, husband, business coach, and best friend Dan Tiani has been my confidant and sounding board throughout this project. Though he never read a word of this book prior to production, it would not exist without his confidence and constant encouragement. He does not know how to fail, and his belief in my abilities and refusal to let me ever give up has reinforced my self-assurance.

Jackie Tiani
Glendale Heights, Illinois

Disclaimer

This publication contains the opinions and ideas of its author. Its intent is to provide helpful and informative material on the subject matter covered. It is sold with the understanding that the author and the publisher are not engaged in rendering professional services in this book. The reader should consult a competent professional if personal assistance or advice is required. Although the publisher and author have taken every precaution in the preparation of this book, they assume no responsibility for errors or omissions neither is any liability assumed for damages resulting from the use of information contained herein. The author and publisher specifically disclaim any responsibility for any liability, loss, or risk, personal or otherwise, which is incurred as direct or indirect consequence of the use and application of any of the contents of this book.

Rates and figures mentioned in this book are intended as examples only, and may or may not apply to the reader's particular circumstances, region or specialty. It is the reader's sole responsibility to determine how to apply this information to his own use. The author and publisher assume no responsibility for situations that may arise from the reader's application of this information to his own business.

Interviews with hundreds of professional organizers helped to give shape to this book, but the conclusions narrated here are from the personal perspective and bias of the author. Remarks about clients throughout the book alternate between male and female arbitrarily, so as not to show gender preference. Fictitious names have often been substituted to protect the privacy and anonymity of individuals whose stories appear here. Mention of a company name does not constitute endorsement. Links to websites included in this publication are provided for reference to additional information. The author, editors, and publisher are not responsible for malfunctioning links, or for the content of any website referenced in this publication.

Part I
Understanding the Organizing Profession

Chapter One: Professional Organizing – The Big Picture

"The principle mark of genius is not perfection but originality, the opening of new frontiers." -Arthur Koestler

Welcome to the world of professional organizing! Understanding the professional organizing industry and figuring out how you might fit can be tricky. It is a relatively new field. Most business models are still in the forming stages. Professional organizing practices can take shape in many forms that vary in type, specialty, and geographical reach. The first section of this book helps you sort through those details so you can understand what makes professional organizing businesses – especially yours – tick.

What exactly is a professional organizer?

Professional organizers are independent consultants who advise, teach and assist clients in achieving order in their lives. They educate clients on organizing skills, and design systems and processes that use organizing principles. They provide a wide and varied range of services, from household and office organization, to relocation assistance and event planning. They provide expertise in many areas, including de-cluttering, space planning, filing, time-management, preservation of memorabilia, and records management.

Professional organizers serve male and female clients alike, though some do work primarily with one or the other. (Remarks about clients throughout this book alternate between male and female arbitrarily.) Many professional organizers serve the general population, while others work with specific groups, such as families, corporations, students, seniors, and chronically disorganized individuals.

Many professional organizers offer hands-on assistance to organize various aspects of a client's life. Others offer personal services and some provide workshops and seminars. Many professional organizers have drawn on experience from previous careers such as education, decorating, counseling, housekeeping, business management, office administration and accounting to apply their skills and/or passion for organizing to helping people create order in their homes or offices.

What do professional organizers do?

Professional organizers are in the business of transforming lives. They create time, space, and a sense of satisfaction for people. Professional organizers evaluate their client's needs, recommend solutions, assist with implementation, and educate their clients. When clients want to do the work themselves, the organizer acts as a consultant. The following are some of the services offered by professional organizers:

Business and corporate consulting – work with entrepreneurs, executives and business managers to identify and solve their productivity problems

Closet organizing – coordinate closet design, install functional storage systems, clear out and organize closets, cabinets and storage space

Coaching – provide guidance and advice to help clients achieve life and organizational goals, develop and assign exercises necessary to modify behavior and establish supportive habits, encourage and support progress

Computer consulting – train and assist clients in using advanced technology to manage time, organize data, automate tasks, and increase business productivity; recommend hardware and software solutions to help clients become more organized

Clutter control – assist clients in purging and removing excess, unwanted, unneeded or worthless items, and disposing, recycling, or delivering them to consignment/thrift stores or charitable organizations

Estate organizing – help clients record their financial information and create a detailed list of their assets; assist the client's executor or personal representative in sorting and packing items and distributing them to loved ones and charities

Event and meeting planning – assist organizations with planning, venue selection, contract negotiation, promotion, and registration for meetings, conferences and other events; prepare programs and materials; coordinate event services such as facilities, accommodations, catering, signage, printing, audio-visual, transportation and security; monitor progress and budgets, maintain records and prepare report

Feng Shui consulting –apply rules in Chinese philosophy that govern spatial arrangement and orientation in relation to patterns of yin and yang and the flow of energy (chi) to help clients find harmony with their physical environment

Chapter One: Professional Organizing – The Big Picture

Financial and records organizing – assist clients with check writing, checkbook management, bookkeeping and maintain related files

Home office organizing – de-clutter space and set up a functional workspace that is efficient; implement systems to manage paper, personal records, calendars and to-do lists

Household management and organizing – restore order to any room in a client's home; provide household management services; assist in selecting and supervising household help

Garage organizing – clean and organize garages and create efficient work areas and optimize space; mount or install grids, racks, shelving systems and cabinets, develop methods for storing seasonal items, trash and recycling; coordinate garage sales

Image consulting – assist clients in coordinating and aligning the elements that make up the visual and mental representation that a professional businessperson conveys to the world

Kitchen organizing – de-clutter and organize kitchen cabinets, pantry and refrigerator; arrange efficient work areas and optimize space; identify and select proper storage containers; devise systems and routines to help clients stay organized

Memorabilia organizing – assist clients in choosing storage containers and organizing and archiving their collections of photos, memorabilia, and other treasures

Moving and relocations – plan relocation activities and timetable; pack, unpack and arrange belongings; work with employer, realtor, and other services to coordinate activities essential to a successful relocation to a new home

Office organizing – identify problem areas and coordinate solutions; design efficient and functional desks and workstations; implement systems to manage paper, records, and filing systems; instruct office workers in organizing systems and principles

Paper and filing systems – provide solutions for improving paper management; teach clients how to simplify paper flow and eliminate piles of paper; devise systems for keeping track of tasks and activities

Personal errands, shopping and concierge services – provide a variety of personal services for clients, including running miscellaneous errands (dry-cleaning pickup, gift-buying, grocery shopping, etc.); home-care services (mail pickup, pet-sitting, plant care, etc.); make personal arrangements like dinner or concert reservations and travel bookings

Procedure documentation and manuals – evaluate systems and processes; design procedures; research and compile procedure documentation and manuals

Project management – provide leadership to research, coordinate, manage and track a project from beginning to end

Public speaking and training – offer classes, workshops, and seminars to teach organizing skills; speak about organizing principles and techniques to groups at conferences and trade shows; provide corporate productivity training

Records management – help clients identify, organize, maintain, and access needed information in paper and electronic formats; properly dispose of unneeded records; ensure both regulatory compliance and efficiency in records management and storage

Space planning and design – design, plan, and provide guidelines for functional and effective use of space and storage; assist clients in optimizing available space

Time and knowledge management – provide solutions for managing and optimizing time; design and implement business models to increase productivity; help clients harness and document information effectively

Goal setting and priority planning – guide clients through creative thinking processes to help them identify and achieve goals; devise strategies for addressing priorities; assist clients in writing measurable, results-focused plans supported by quantifiable objectives

Virtual assistance – keep small and home-based business clients organized by providing offsite administrative support; organize data into spreadsheets, word processing or database software; organize financial records and provide bookkeeping services; manage desktop publishing and mailings; perform Internet research and Web design

Wardrobe organizing – assist clients in organizing, categorizing, and itemizing their wardrobes; manage seasonal clothing; downsize and optimize wardrobes

Workflow consulting – Review administrative procedures; develop and document procedures for efficient flow of work between staff and departments

Advantages (and drawbacks) of being a professional organizer

It is hard to leave the stability of a secure job, let alone to jump into a profession that is still testing its legs. Evaluating the pros and cons will help you to estimate the risks. The organizing profession is young, but its roots are

Chapter One: Professional Organizing – The Big Picture

firmly planted. Thousands have discovered that a successful career can be built around a passion for organizing, and the numbers are growing every day. The potential for this industry has yet to be fully defined or realized.

Almost every self-employed person has a story about the terrifying leap from working for someone else to self-sufficiency. Those same people ultimately tell a story about the excitement and challenge of starting a business, about the freedom of being the boss, about the chance to really help others and finally reaching the point where they earned the money they needed or wanted. Their success stories usually include a promise never to trust someone else again to control their security. Here are nine good reasons to pursue a professional organizing career.

Independence: The desire for independence usually tops the list of reasons for becoming a professional organizer. Is there an employee that has not dreamed about being on his own? Is there anyone who does not strive for independence? The opportunity to have your own business and work for yourself seems to characterize the concept of "Life, liberty, and the pursuit of happiness."

Whether you practice as a sole proprietor or establish your own corporation, being a professional organizer will indeed bring you independence. If you have worked for someone else all of your life, you will appreciate no longer having someone else telling you what to do. You get to make all of the decisions pertaining to your business, such as working from home, setting business hours, and choosing which clients with whom you will work. You can escape the office politics, petty gossip, and bureaucracy of the corporate world, and take charge of your own destiny. As a professional organizer, you pursue your own vision, follow your own dream, and take full responsibility for the success of the business.

If you have worked 50-60 hours a week, 50 weeks per year to satisfy your employer, you will treasure the option of structuring your own workweek and building generous amounts of time off into your schedule. Independence allows you to work until 2:00 a.m. on days when you are pumped full of energy, or close your office door at 2:00 p.m. on the days when you are burned out. You can be free of the rat race and daily commute of the wage earner.

Solitude can be a mixed blessing, however, and not everyone is predisposed to be independent. Some thrive in solitary splendor, but for others, isolation is a problem. While others leave in the morning for work and structured activities, you may sometimes feel as if you live outside the built-in social system. Working for and by yourself means you will have times when you may wish there was someone on the other side of the cubicle partition with whom to bounce ideas off of or to share a laugh. Isolation issues can be overcome, but if you are social in nature, you may need to create face-to-face opportunities for networking and conversation.

If you are usually self-motivated, you merely need to adjust to being your own boss, set a regular schedule and self-imposed limits, and tell yourself what to do. However, some people lack the necessary discipline to be independent. Without the limits and deadlines imposed by managers, procrastination can become an issue. Without a context for reporting progress or celebrating successes, you may lose enthusiasm. You are responsible for planning your time and pushing yourself to do the less appealing tasks required of a business owner. With no one there to urge you into action, you could end up stalling.

Independence means unpaid vacation and sick days and tackling your own health costs. Without departmental support, you will have to keep your own computer running and clear your own paper jams. You will not have a company supply closet to raid or conveniences like industrial-strength copy machines and support staff to handle mail and phone calls. You will have to find the means to keep basic office supplies stocked, and you are the one who will have to run to the post office and the bank. In addition, you will have to bid farewell to catered lunches and expense accounts.

The definition of independence referred to here is not necessarily financial independence. Having your own business gives you a feeling of control, rather than living in constant worry that you might lose your job. Nevertheless, insecurity inevitably accompanies business start-ups, and initially you will have to learn to live without some of the niceties to which you became accustomed as a wage earner. Once your business is firmly established with a strong base of ongoing clients and bountiful cash reserves, you can begin to realize passive income from diversified investments. You will no longer depend on your business operations for stability and financial freedom will be within reach.

Ample opportunity: You are in demand. There is plenty of work available for a professional organizer who knows how to promote and persuade. Our work as professional organizers is cut out for us. The world is not going to be organized anytime soon, and there are unlimited ways to help people with their organizing challenges. In every city and town, there are homes, offices, commercial buildings and people that need organizing.

Chapter One: Professional Organizing – The Big Picture

Twenty years ago, it might have seemed very irrational to turn a passion for organizing into a career. In the past two decades, however, life has become amazingly complex. The average home in America has doubled in size since the 1950's, yet we do not have enough room to store our stuff. Twenty five percent of garages are used exclusively for storage, while cars are parked in driveways. Nationwide, over 45,000 sheds known as *self-storage units* handle our overflow.

The once immense executive office has shrunk to a tiny cubicle, and the occupant is baffled about what to do with all of the paper, books, binders and files. The promise of a paperless society has been condemned as a myth. We are overloaded with information. The sheer volume of data and the anxiety associated with pursuing, managing and monitoring it can be a source of enormous stress. Communication has become increasingly complex. Technology has contributed tools, toys and time-wasters into our homes and offices.

Today, opportunities abound and our affluent society strives to take advantage of as many of them as possible. We buy more to entertain us, make life easy for us, and make us more comfortable. We travel more, rather than spending vacation time cleaning up and fixing our homes as generations before us. We have more stuff than we need. We have more free time, but too many options for filling it. People are overwhelmed by their calendars, by their clutter and chaos.

We now live in a frightening world where terrorism and job insecurity are harsh realities. There is an emotional yearning to take control, and an increasing desire to live a healthier lifestyle. People are beginning to embrace clarity and purity, as seen in the movement toward cleaner homes and mind-body disciplines such as yoga, Pilates, and meditation.

You can make an important difference with your knowledge, advice, passion, talent and irresistible desire to help others become more organized and efficient. The need for your service is great.

Flexibility: You will be meeting with clients on an appointment basis, which will allow you to maintain flexibility in your work schedule. Your schedule can be arranged to fit your needs, as well as the diverse needs and preferences of your clients. You will have the flexibility to make sure you do not miss the moments and events that matter most to you in life.

You will also have the flexibility to determine the best days and the best times of day, that fit your personal style. If you are a night owl, you might find clients who also work best at night and arrange your schedule to reflect the true biological clock for both of you. Your business and your lifestyle can work in complete harmony.

Many organizers keep traditional business hours, but you do not have to work from nine to five. Some organizers have young children and manage their work schedule during school hours. Working mothers must be on call for unexpected family issues and the working arrangements of professional organizing enable them to attend to those demands. If you need to have an afternoon free for a doctor appointment, you can arrange your schedule accordingly. You will be better able to handle emergencies as they arise.

> One of the greatest joys of my business is the ability to arrange my schedule to spend time with my family. My sons and daughters-in-law are career professionals, and they appreciate the occasional opportunity to call me when they need assistance so that they do not have to leave their office to pick up a sick child on a moment's notice. Sometimes my grandchildren have a day off school or just want a break from the usual daycare arrangements. I am glad to have the flexibility. On client-free days, I jump at the chance to spend time with them!

Flexibility might mean having a chance to get away at the last minute for a week in the sun or travel on business with your spouse.

> When my husband asks me to join him on a business trip, all I need to do is coordinate my schedule with my clients and maintain regular communication while I am gone. I will admit that I sometimes need to work every evening the week prior and pull an all-nighter the night before we leave. You will not hear any objections from me. It is a great opportunity for me to do some writing while in a peaceful, quiet atmosphere as I take a weeklong break from client work. I am writing about *flexibility* as I sit in a guest room in a mountain ski resort in Lake Tahoe, an opportunity I never would have been able to enjoy while working in the corporate world.

Every benefit usually has a downside. The main drawback to flexibility is that your clients may try to take advantage. They may think your availability to handle emergencies was designed for them. If you let your clients know you will be available after hours, expect your phone to ring evenings and weekends. Some clients seem always to have a crisis the day before your vacation. There are always last minute things to take care of the day before vacation, and adding their emergencies to your last minute schedule will put you in turmoil.

Another challenge of flexibility is the need to juggle personal and professional obligations at the same time. The distraction of personal phone calls, last night's dishes or the overflowing laundry basket might get the best of you

Chapter One: Professional Organizing – The Big Picture

when you should be calling prospective clients. Your flexibility allows you to run errands at the least busy times. Yet, personal errands that could easily be put off when you were a wage-earner can end up taking the most productive part of your day. You need to be able to accomplish both your personal and professional tasks without sacrificing either, and you may need to learn to plan your day or week so that you can accomplish both with a sense of balance.

Earnings potential: Aspiring professional organizers want to know if they can really bring in enough money to make a living. There are always risks when you forgo a steady paycheck to start your own business. However, not only can you make a living; you can do very well financially. You can make as much money as you want to make, as long as you have the energy, education, experience, and self-esteem to command premium compensation, along with the creativity to develop additional ways to increase your revenue. Success in the organizing industry requires hard work and persistence. Although most organizers do not become extremely wealthy, some do. Public awareness of the organizing industry is increasing and stimulating the demand for organizers.

An article in the August 8, 2005 issue of *Crain's Chicago Business* featured Cynthia Ivie, owner of White Space, Inc., a Chicago-based professional organizer. The article mentioned that the professional organizing company had 13 employees and spent $20,000 to develop a website. Assuming that one could not incur that much expense without proportional income to support it, you can see that there is clearly profit potential in this industry.

White Space was mentioned in an article published seven months later in the *Chicago Tribune*. The March 13, 2006 article was about a national program to award loans of up to $45,000 plus business advice to women business owners. To be considered for the award, businesses must be at least two years old and positioned to achieve $1 million in revenue within two years. Among those who received the award in 2005 was Cynthia Ivie, owner of White Space, Inc. See *Awardees* at (http://www.makemineamillion.org)

There are many variables and economic factors involved in the earnings potential of a service business. Your earnings potential can be affected by your geographical area, skill level, and the amount of effort you put in to promoting your business. You can expect to command a higher rate of pay if you have your own business rather than working as an employee or subcontractor. (You will have more expenses, too). You have greater income potential if you live in a major metropolitan area. If you have special skills or an extensive business background, you will be able to command a higher rate of pay than a less experienced individual will.

Based on a general estimate that an experienced organizer working as a generalist can charge residential clients $45 to $95 an hour (depending on the size and complexity of the task and your geographic area), you could expect to gross $45,000 to $95,000 per year for hands-on organizing, based on 20 billable hours per week. You may be able to charge anywhere from $75 to upwards of $200 an hour for corporate clients, or $75,000 to $200,000 per year. Specialized skills like estate planning or computer proficiency will further add to that number. If you are business savvy and tap into other revenue sources, such as products, employees, and subcontractors, your earnings potential is virtually limitless. If you are talented, experienced, and have developed a niche, you may blow these numbers through the roof!

> An article in the May 2004 issue of *Fortune Small Business* featured Jeff Smith, an organizer who specializes in helping people manage their wine cellars. His career started when he was between jobs and his father moved to a new house in Beverly Hills. After the move, he organized his father's wine cellar. A family friend saw the results and paid him $500 to help him organize 300 bottles of wine. He built a business by organizing *fermented clutter* and grossed $150,000 in 2003.

Research will produce a wide range of opinions about the potential earnings of professional organizers. It has been estimated by PowerHomeBiz that you can expect to earn annual revenues of $40,000 to $60,000 as a professional organizer; depending on the size of your market, and the kinds of clients you are getting (http://www.powerhomebiz.com/).

The actual earnings average of practicing professional organizers is a tough figure to pinpoint. In a 1998 survey conducted by the National Association of Professional Organizers, 35% of its members said they billed between 20-40 hours per week and 42% said they had a gross income of $30,000 and above. Many of those surveyed were just starting their businesses, and only half worked full-time. In 2005, the Minnesota Chapter of NAPO estimated typical annual gross revenues as $40,000, based on billing 800 hours a year (16 hours per week) at $50 an hour.

When you worked for someone else, your pay was at your employer's discretion. You probably had either a fixed salary or an hourly rate. If you needed to generate more cash flow, you could only hope that a raise was forthcoming or overtime was available. If, on the other hand, you had an

Chapter One: Professional Organizing – The Big Picture

opportunity to earn a bonus or commission, then you had a taste of the control you will have as a business owner.

As a professional organizer, you will be able to control your income directly. You will have the opportunity to determine your own rates and the timing of your increases. You will make the decisions regarding when and how much you will work. If you have subcontractors or employees, you determine what percentage of their pay you will retain for administration and company profit. You can be more aggressive in your marketing and work harder to earn more money.

In order to earn the money you need and want, you may have to work very long hours, especially in the first few years. There may be financial difficulties and you may have to adjust to a lower standard of living until the business becomes profitable, which could take months or even years. Nevertheless, the long hours and hard work will directly benefit you, rather than profiting someone else.

If you are used to living on a steady paycheck, getting irregular income from clients can be a bit unnerving. However, once your bank account starts growing, you will eventually get used to the inconsistency and feel more secure. You will have forgotten your initial discomfort when you reach the point where, rather than worrying about how much you earn, you worry about how much income tax you owe.

Reasonable start-up costs: One of the biggest draws to the organizing business is that it requires very little up-front cash to start. Most organizers start out by using the family vehicle and a home office, and an investment of around $1,000 in equipment. By using office space in your home, you will not have to pay extra for rent, electricity, heating, and air conditioning. In fact, with proper tax structure and record keeping, you may even be able to write off some of those expenses. Your business will not require massive quantities of supplies, and you will have little reason to maintain inventory. Your needs will be modest and you will not have to entertain clients in your office, so you can avoid decorating and remodeling costs. This means that you will not have to borrow money to start or expand your business. The cost to build your business can probably be generated from your operating revenues.

You should plan for some initial set up costs, including:

- Educational materials
- Courses and workshops
- Professional membership fees
- Conference fees

- City, state and federal licensing and registration fees
- Design and printing of business cards, letterhead, and marketing materials

Any business requires a steady flow of money, but unlike many new enterprises, you will not have to learn how to create the convincing business plan that qualifies you to borrow money to start your business. You will not have to purchase or lease expensive equipment, tools, or a fleet of vehicles. You will not need specialized talent for product development or skilled laborers to staff a facility. You will be able to add staff gradually as your client base increases.

Plan to have enough savings to cover your basic business expenses until you get your feet on the ground and cultivate a regular client base. If you have no alternate revenue source, and you do not have savings to support you in the interim, you may need to borrow money to fund the first year or two. If you do not have family or friends to help, you may be able to apply for and receive a Microloan through the Small Business Administration (SBA) to help finance basic business necessities (http://www.sba.gov)

Tailor-made work arrangements: Being a professional organizer allows you to gain exposure to a variety of people, challenges, industries and work environments. In this business, you will have the freedom to seek the type of work you enjoy and select the types of work you want to handle. You can design your business around your own strengths, preferences and personality. You can tailor your business so that you do the work you love and be paid well for doing it.

Maybe you like working with seniors, but dislike working with teenagers. You can choose to help empty nesters downsize their living quarters. Perhaps you like arranging files, but find organizing financial records to be boring or difficult. Your specialty can be filing systems. If you hate to cook but love clothes, you can stay away from kitchen organizing, and focus on closets and fashion arrangement. Simply do not solicit the type of work you do not want to do. You get to make the call.

If you live in the suburbs but like the city, you can target city-dwellers as your clients. If you hate traffic, you have the option of limiting the distance you are willing to travel. The type of person who works best with groups can target businesses and organizations, rather than one-on-one consulting clients. You can control allergic reactions by declining to work in environments with pets or smoke. You set the parameters according to your personality and lifestyle.

Chapter One: Professional Organizing – The Big Picture

Competition: It may seem strange to see competition amongst the positive aspects of choosing the professional organizing industry. However, competition can be an advantage as well as a hindrance. Too much competition can indeed be the cause of death for business. Yet those who are entering the field of professional organizing will find many advantages to having competition. The presence of other professional organizers in your region means that there is a market out there. It means that there has probably been publicity in your geographical area, which might save you from having to explain to people what you do as a professional organizer.

It is essential that you understand two truths about competition. The first is that the best run business wins and keeps the most clients. Be the best you can be, and do not underestimate your competition. The second is that your competitors are not your enemies. They are trying to build their business just as you are. Treat them well, because they may end up working with you or for you. In fact, you may find that by running a good organizing business, you will inspire others to want what you have. If you hire subcontractors, you may be breeding your own competition.

Who is your competition? Simply put, the more specialized you are, the less competition you will encounter. There are probably as many specialties among professional organizers as there are among medical practitioners – maybe more. It is likely that you will be able to find an unmet need and develop a niche around that need, while other businesses are serving their own area of specialization. Rather than compete, you complement their services. They will refer business to you when they discover that their clients or other contacts will benefit most from your expertise.

A good way to evaluate your direct competition is to build relationships with other organizers. Attend local NAPO meetings and get to know your colleagues. Find out who is in your geographical area, what their specialty is, and who their target client is. You will gain more information by talking to other organizers than through any other means.

Much of your competition can end up functioning as your sales staff or being strategic partners. People who look like your competitors may actually be the source of good referrals for you. Many generalists refer business to specialists, and vice versa. Having a close competitor might even mean you will have someone to cover for you while you are on vacation (and vice versa).

Professional organizers in your geographic region may be so diverse that you will find that you may not even compete with them for business. If you organize anyone or anything, you are competing with every other organizer on the planet. You will have to compete based on some other factor, such as geographic location, price, experience, or status.

Some in our field fear competition and actually avoid associating with other organizers. They are concerned about networking with other professional organizers, and make comments like, "I do not want other professional organizers to know too much about me or how I'm doing because I have had jobs stolen from me." I personally have yet to experience the fiendish challenge for clients that people usually imagine when they think of their direct competition. Most organizers that I have met have a congenial and collaborative spirit.

Many veteran organizers embrace competition, and realize its value to the industry. They seek ways to collaborate, helping their colleagues with projects and sharing shortcuts they have discovered. Those who find ways to work together know that our competition moves each of us to a new level of expertise or more clearly defined niches.

During her term as President of the National Association of Professional Organizers, Barbara Hemphill introduced a phrase, *Together, We are Better*, which has become the unofficial motto of NAPO members. There are huge benefits from getting to know other organizers, sharing their associations, working with them, and even competing with them. There are many similarities in the circumstances that aroused our desire to help others become more organized, and you are likely to find camaraderie and synergy in working together with other organizers.

Who, besides other professional organizers, is your competition? Actually, any business that has the potential to fill the organizational needs of your potential clients could be considered your competition. There are many available resources for people to obtain help becoming organized. People relied upon many of these resources long before professional organizers came into existence. The service you provide might be a perfect fit for someone who has sought help from a number of businesses that might be considered your competition, whether or not they were considered organizing specialists. Here are some businesses (not professional organizing businesses) that might be considered your competition:

- Organizing-focused retail stores who offer in-store consultation
- Distributors of closet organizing systems
- Bookkeepers
- Time Management consultants
- Fashion consultants

Chapter One: Professional Organizing – The Big Picture

- Meeting planning services
- Manufacturers of garage organizing products
- Corporate Human Resources Depts. who provide in-house training
- Business consultants
- Event planners
- Self-improvement trainers
- Moving companies
- Computer consultants
- Space planners
- House cleaners, maids and butlers
- Records management services
- Efficiency experts
- Handyman services
- Secretarial services
- Self-storage facilities
- Interior decorators
- Feng Shui practitioners
- Inventory specialists
- Retirement planners
- Property and association managers
- Messengers and delivery companies
- Estate managers
- Stress management services
- Fill in the one that I overlooked. It may be your niche!

Professional organizers have formed strong strategic alliances with many of the types of businesses mentioned here. Our competitors have learned to use the influence we have on our client's purchasing decisions to their advantage. More people need help getting organized than there are organizing specialists to assist them. This industry has a long way to go to reach the saturation point.

Ease into retirement: A survey conducted by AARP found that 70 percent of Baby Boomers plan to work in some capacity during their retirement years. You may be near retirement age, but your need for additional income may exceed what you may bring in from Social Security benefits and what you have gradually saved. You may simply desire the stimulation that work provides. If you are not ready to stop working entirely, helping others become organized can be a great way to ease into retirement.

As a professional organizer, you have more control over your time so that you can enjoy some of those activities you imagined, like working on hobbies or spending days on the golf course. You can choose to accept or decline an engagement, allowing you to work the schedule you choose.

You will be able to put your organizing skills to the test in ways you may not have been able earlier in your career. Instead of retirement being an end to your career, being a professional organizer can reinvigorate your career and provide you with professional, financial, and personal fulfillment.

Personal growth and fulfillment: For most successful organizers, it is a pleasure going to work. It is highly fulfilling to be involved in a profession that is making such a profound impact on people's lives. Being the person to offer an overwhelmed client hope and a chance to get her life back in order is immensely rewarding. Not only will your clients pay you for your knowledge and assistance but also they will thank you for making such a positive impact on their lives. It is awesome to receive so much appreciation for doing what you love.

Not only will you be paid to do what you love, there are many opportunities to learn, and many new experiences to try in this industry. You will find that you are constantly picking up new ideas and tips as you are exposed to a variety of people, places and professions. Your skills will improve with each client. As more and more homes and offices are exposed to you, your ability to see through the chaos and visualize the potential will improve. Your value will grow with your increased wisdom.

Just the idea of owning and running your own business can be more satisfying and fulfilling than working for someone else. Many successful organizers find that they enjoy the respect they earn from their peers for having the courage to start their own business.

If organizing is your passion, working very long hours will probably not discourage you. You will not mind having to adjust to a lower standard of living until you get through the start-up years and your business becomes profitable. You will be buoyed by the opportunity to follow your passion and fulfill your purpose, while making a difference in the lives of your clients.

The evolution of the professional organizing industry

Professional organizing is a relatively young industry, and has been influenced and shaped by many forces during its brief history. The industry is enjoying phenomenal growth, still in its development stages, and gaining exposure and respect worldwide. In fact, professional organizing is one the fastest growing fields, according to U.S. News and World Report. Turn to

Chapter One: Professional Organizing – The Big Picture

Organizing in the Yellow Pages of any major metropolitan area phone book today, and you will find dozens of listings for professional organizing services.

The genesis of organizing as an occupation took place around 1980. Previously, the meaning of *organizer* generally was a person who rallied people around causes or recruited for organizations such as labor unions. Workplace and household organizing consultants were unheard of. Homemakers often became educated in home economics. They were known to scour the pages of *Ladies Home Journal* for suggestions for making their homes more efficient. Commercially, performance standards and time studies were used during the Industrial Revolution to control production and labor costs in factories. As business administration became more complicated and paper-intensive, management began to implement similar concepts to office systems and procedures. Consultants who specialized in business productivity were called time management consultants or efficiency experts.

> When I first listed my business phone number in the Yellow Pages, a category defining our industry did not even exist. After I described the services typically provided by professional organizers, the choices offered by the phone company representative were Business Consultants, House Cleaning, Secretarial Services, Bookkeeping Services and Maid and Butler Service.

During the 1980s, an age marked by material excess and corporate climbing, the employment trend began to shift. Technology slowly began to replace skilled workers and by the late 1980s, long-term employment with large companies was on the decrease, while self-employment and home-based business was on the rise. During the final two decades of the twentieth century, there were close to 50 million layoffs in the United States. Corporations repositioned themselves from being customer and employee-oriented in nature; to being investor-centered, yielding to pressure from stockholders to operate on leaner budgets. Companies reported an increase in profits, but a significant decrease in employee morale. Hard work and company loyalty no longer meant the promise of continued employment. Employees were working harder and longer and feeling less secure.

Two-income families were commonplace and mothers who had taken jobs to supplement the family income became overwhelmed with the demands at home. Unlike their mothers, whose primary jobs were home and family management; these women were having to get their shopping and housework done in the evenings and on the weekends. With less free time and more available income, their lives filled with timesaving conveniences, fashionable wardrobes, luxurious cars, expensive trinkets, and numerous toys to entertain their children. Along with these benefits came complications like commuting, parking, lunches, day care, and credit card bills. Instead of making their lives better, the extra income seemed to add to their problems. Rather than coming home to a retreat from their work lives, they discovered more and more chaos.

As people realized that job security was only a myth, many began to abandon careers where they were unhappy, bored or burned out. People began to look at ways to create their own security and define their own careers. They decided to pursue satisfying work that would enable them to maintain control and balance in their lives. They structured their careers to continuously leverage their natural talents and passions and build upon their experience and skills.

Doing work you love became a movement. The concept of focusing on your natural talents and pursuing your passions replaced the practice of learning skills to mold yourself into the safest career. This paradigm shift moved many people to find successful new opportunities. Moms reentering the job market found it difficult to compete with experienced workers. They began to search for and discover alternatives to low-paying entry-level positions. College graduates had difficulty finding work in their chosen field, and questioned if they had made the right career decision. They identified new approaches to realizing their dreams. Tired of looking for nonexistent jobs, people started creating their own.

Many of us discovered that we loved work that involved organizing. We began to take inventory of those unique talents, skills, experience and interests that would fit that passion, and we began to form careers around helping other people get organized. We combed the want ads (in the 1980's, *Monster* meant a scary creature) looking for the perfect job. From the number of advertised opportunities, one would have to conclude that our talents were not marketable. Yet, strong organizing skills consistently appeared at the top of the lists of skills employers looked for in job candidates. We were driven to find work we loved, and we were convinced there was a need for organizers.

We had proven repeatedly that our unique strengths were in demand. We were the ones people relied upon when they were moving to a new home. We figured out how to fit both vehicles in our neighbor's garage. The church office could not function unless we occasionally volunteered (and overhauled the office). Our friends called us to help them reorganize their closets. We were the ones that coordinated the room mothers, and systematized the hot

Chapter One: Professional Organizing – The Big Picture

lunch program. We managed to fit the entire accumulation of luggage and sleeping bags in the cargo section of the school bus when our children went on a class trip. The classroom never looked as organized as it did after our week of substitute teaching. In our jobs, we transferred from one department to another after streamlining our offices and our positions. Our expertise saved the day when there was an event to plan. So we asked "Why is there not a career called 'organizing'?"

By the mid-1980s, there were already a number of people in the United States operating successful organizing businesses. These trailblazers did not look for organizing jobs; they invented them. They created jobs to fit their passion for organizing. They did not worry a whole lot about what to call themselves. Depending upon their experience and skills, early professional organizers called themselves personal organizers, closet arrangers, relocation experts, personal assistants, record keepers, etc.

When a handful of women in Southern California discovered that they were not alone in this activity, they began to meet regularly to learn more about each other, support each other's businesses, and find ways to get the word out to the public. In 1985, five of these women formed what is now known as the National Association of Professional Organizers (NAPO), the driving force in what has become one of the fastest growing industries in the nation.

The Information Age has shaped new opportunities for those of us who have a talent for clearing up confusion, seeing through clutter, and reducing stress and waste. Information processed through computers has improved our efficiency in many ways, but it has also multiplied the amount of paper and electronic data needing to be managed and organized. The transition to the Information Age has come upon us so quickly that people who have not learned how to be organized now live with confusion and fear. Stress is not only one of the top work-related health problems; it can cause lives to fall apart as it affects relationships and personal values.

The productivity industry is seeing growth in many directions. Sales of PDAs and smart phones are at an all-time high. The Container Store experiences growth at the rate of 18 percent per year. Attendance at time-management seminars is rising. David Allen's *Getting Things Done* and Stephen Covey's *The 7 Habits of Highly Effective People* rate in the top 10 on *The Wall Street Journal's* business best seller list years after publication. The membership in the National Association of Professional Organizers quintupled in 12 years, from 750 members in 1993 to over 4300 members in 2008.

Simplicity has become a consumer trend, giving popularity to expressions such as *quality of life*. The desire for simplicity has intensified the demand for professional assistance. Hiring a professional organizer is becoming a generally excepted practice in our society. In some areas, it is even becoming vogue to hire a professional organizer. Professional organizers can do the job faster than homeowners who are distracted and unfamiliar with suitable solutions. Hiring a professional organizer gives people more time for enjoyable activities and interests.

> In 1995, as Treasurer of the National Association of Professional Organizers, I publicly made a prediction that within twenty years the world would be as familiar with professional organizers as it is of nurses and accountants, and in thirty years *professional organizer* would be a household word.
>
> The growth of this industry has far exceeded my predictions. Just twelve years later, it would be a challenge to find a single person who had not heard of the term *professional organizer*.

In the past decade, there has been a vast increase in public awareness of the professional organizing industry. Professional organizers and organizing projects are frequently featured in magazine and news articles. Julie Morgenstern, former member of the NAPO Board of Directors, gained prominence through her book *Organizing from the Inside Out*, and was featured on Oprah. Television reality shows about organizing and improving living spaces have given the industry vast exposure. The world is fast becoming aware of our profession, and we no longer need to explain who we are or what we do.

Chapter Two: What it Takes to Be a Professional Organizer

"Desire is the starting point of all achievement" Napoleon Hill

Evaluating whether you and professional organizing are a good fit requires that you determine whether the business suits your particular skills and strengths, whether you are adequately motivated, and whether you have a solid chance at profitability. You must judge your ability and desire to handle every aspect of the business. This chapter will help you decide if organizing is the right choice for you.

Distinguishing qualities of a successful professional organizer

There are no rigid requirements for becoming a professional organizer, nor is there a regulatory board or set of criteria to assist a prospective organizing client in choosing a professional organizer. Many organizers have backgrounds in administration, education, or psychology, but a college degree or other advanced credentials will not predict who emerges a success. The number one predictor of success is passion. If you are excited and enthusiastic about your vision of helping others become organized, you are a likely candidate for becoming a professional organizer.

A number of traits are common among successful professional organizers. At the very core, a professional organizer must have impeccable integrity, effective interpersonal skills, understanding of organizing principles, and business knowledge. Certain attributes distinguish the star performers, including the following:

- They are responsible, reliable, and ethical.
- They tend to bring about form, structure, and order in most aspects of their lives.
- They are creative problem-solvers.
- They are constantly seeking to improve efficiency.
- They enjoy helping, teaching and developing others.
- They are open to different approaches for different people.

- They are empathetic and inclined to respond to the needs and desires of others.
- They have the capacity to discern individual preferences and dispositions.
- They are attentive to emotional cues and listen well.

Before you jump in and start organizing professionally, take an honest assessment of where you are now. Compare your own personal characteristics to the unifying traits of the most successful professional organizers. Understanding and cultivating these competencies can be crucial to your success.

Although many professional organizers seem to have a natural talent for being organized, others have asserted that they themselves were miserably disorganized at one time. They found the motivation and means to overcome the chaos and disorder in their own lives and want to lead others to discover similar results. They are proof that one can acquire organizing skills through training and experience, and use those skills to help others get organized.

> I was not born organized. I will admit, however, to having a natural inclination towards avoiding undue exertion. It is almost instinctive for me to identify inefficiencies, document procedures, establish controls and implement follow-up plans. Working myself out of a job by finding ways to do it more effectively has become a pattern in my life. While this has more to do with being lazy than a natural disposition toward organization, it has allowed me to be completely authentic with my clients while satisfactorily advising them how to do more in less time with fewer resources.

Successful small business owners build their businesses around their strengths and find ways to compensate for their weaknesses. Take your inventory and discover where you rise to the top. What are your strongest areas of competence? Evaluate your natural talents and acquired abilities, as well as your preferences and passions. What do you love to do, whether or not you are paid to do it? Determine the areas of your expertise where you are already qualified to advise others. Think about your interpersonal skills from the perspective of dealing with demanding clients and slow providers, and be truthful with yourself about your limitations. Taking a personal and professional inventory will help you to determine the most beneficial way that you can serve your clients by effectively sharing your unique talents.

Although there are qualities that are especially compatible with the field of organizing, organizing skills can be learned. Project management and the ability to perform needs assessments are examples of essential skills that can be acquired through training and practice. Certain areas demand skills that may not be needed for other specialties. For instance, computer skills are necessary if you plan to work with businesses, but not so important for the individual who intends to work with seniors. Launch your practice by taking advantage of your existing knowledge and expertise. Then focus your education and training on areas where you want to increase your value, grow and develop your business, and boost your earnings capacity.

Being an organized person does not necessarily mean that you will make a good professional organizer. The specific skills and abilities required in this profession are as varied as the specialties and needs encompassed in this industry. There are two critical skills that a professional organizer must have. The first is sympathetic understanding. The second is the ability to create customized organizing solutions that work for the client. The greatest ability to organize will not help if you are not open to more than a single solution or have a hard time getting along with other people. If you have a difficult time getting others to like you, you will have a difficult time in any service business. You do not necessarily need experience in customer service, but you are in the business of providing a service, and you must do so effectively to be successful.

Determination and self-discipline

Ambition, resilience, attitude and motivation all contribute to the success of every professional organizer. No matter how much you love to organize or how qualified you are, practical skills and technical abilities alone will not generate success. The ability to self-manage effectively is essential. Hard work and risk are involved in any rewarding endeavor; be prepared for both. You must be persistent, committed, and tough if you want your business to be successful. There will be times when your business drains you, both physically and emotionally. Your determination must be strong enough to challenge you when you are approaching burnout; to energize you when you begin to wear down; to keep you going and help you survive the tough times.

Determination and self-discipline are the key differences between success and failure. Lacking determination, your initial motivation will fall by the wayside when other things come up. Any obstacle will redirect your attention. You will find yourself sleeping late, having long lunches with friends, or going to the mall. When you are truly determined, you get up early, arrange for childcare to eliminate any distractions, and take the time to review your plan every week. You will develop and stick to business-building habits like making client follow-up calls and attending networking events. With determination, you establish priorities that guide you through unforeseen circumstances. With self-discipline, you persist even when you are discouraged.

Why do you want to be a professional organizer? Is it because of a lifelong dream of owning your own business? Is your life situation driving you to pursue this profession? Have you lost a job? Do you fear you may lose your job? Are you disgruntled in your current position or in a career you hate? Are you disillusioned? Are you bored? Have you recently completed school, become empty-nested or divorced? Examine your own situation and be clear about your intentions, the level of your commitment, your true motive and desired results.

I have known organizers who started their business because they loved to organize, but unfortunately their business failed because they just did not want it badly enough to get through the tough times. Be sure that your determination is strong enough to push you to do whatever it takes to succeed. Research has shown that there are two primary motivators, pain and pleasure. Either the avoidance of pain or the pursuit of pleasure will drive us to action. The former, pain is the stronger motivator of the two. Fear of pain creates a sense of urgency. Pain has driven people to achieve great success, as is shown in the following case study.

> Mary is a professional organizer who received an eviction notice and feared she might have to move back to her parent's home. This was a painful prospect for Mary, so she kicked her marketing efforts into high gear. She called her existing clients and surveyed them about her performance to get clues about how she could improve her services. She asked them, "How am I doing?", and listened carefully to their replies. When the responses were positive, she asked for referrals. Mary attended every available networking event and traded her peaceful, solitary lunches for daily face-to-face contact with a client, colleague or prospect. Her stamina was unbelievable. She was relentless in her search for new business. Within two months, she had increased her client base by 50% and her rent was fully caught up. Moving back to her parent's home was a painful consequence Mary could not bear, and it motivated her to succeed in her business.

What is the driving force that will propel you? Do you have a clear vision for your business? Whatever that dangling carrot is, will it keep you pushing toward your goal? How hungry are you for business success? Do you have a real need for money?

> Betty was a retired RN, and her husband was semi-retired. Betty had an inner craving to help others and started her business because of her passion for organizing. Betty derived great pleasure from working with clients and often stayed beyond the billable time to help finish projects. Betty did not have to earn a living from her work, so she had a different attitude than those who must live on their earnings.

Chapter Two: What it Takes to Be a Professional Organizer

> When her business derailed in its second year, Betty was disappointed, but she openly admitted she just was not hungry enough to put in the necessary effort. Betty had already been financially secure when she started her professional organizing business. The pursuit of pleasure was not strong enough as a motivator to drive her business to success. Although her business failed, she nevertheless fulfilled her desire. Betty eventually channeled her passion for organizing and kept her dream of helping people alive by serving as a volunteer on a hospital staff as the resident organizer.

Look at your own situation. What has motivated you this far? What motivated you to buy this book? If your motivator involves a painful situation, you can celebrate the fact that you may actually have an advantage. You must succeed to avoid pain, and you will do whatever it takes. If your motivator involves pursuit of pleasure, there are ways to intensify your motivation, so that you will do whatever it takes to succeed. If you are willing to deal with risk, think about what causes tension for you. Maybe you have a fear of financial insecurity. If so, you can stretch your comfort zone by making a reservation for a cruise or signing a lease on office space.

> Stacy is a professional organizer who started her business in her home when her two children were in high school. Her dream was to become a professional organizer, but years of managing a home and family had formed habits that she had difficulty overcoming. She struggled to stay in her office and work, and found herself doing laundry or cleaning the house instead. At the end of every day, she would make a commitment to work on her business. She did develop a client base, and her income was moderate, but she knew she was not working hard enough to make her business the success she knew it could be. Stacy decided to lease a small office a few miles from her home. Every day that she did not have a client, she dressed and went to the office where distractions were minimal. She believed that she would respond to the pressure of having to pay rent every month. For Stacy, this was the best solution. Her income doubled the year after she moved out of her home office.

If pride is your hot button, and you would rather eat dirt than face embarrassment, make an announcement to everyone you know about each specific intention or goal. Avoiding the pain of embarrassment might be a very effective motivator for you. If you are the type of person who relies on external support and encouragement, enlist the help of an expert to keep you motivated.

> Although I have never been afraid of hard work, I have had many instances of self-doubt that has kept me from doing my best work. Until recently when I hired a

> coach, I relied on my husband as my business coach and advisor. His confidence has seen me through many a discouraging moment. He has no tolerance for negativity or whining. When things got tough and I started to look at the classified ads, I looked to him for approval. He would remind me of my aspirations and provide the needed encouragement to get me back on track.

If you are unsure of your ability to stay motivated, develop a system of accountability and sustained support. Hire a coach or mentor, or form a mastermind group. Do whatever it takes to keep your motivation and performance at a peak level to ensure your success.

Background and experience

Your interest in becoming a professional organizer may have come from the realization that none of the conventional professions available to you has fully taken advantage of your organizing skills. You may have always been passionate about order and have been organizing things as far back as you can remember. If you have organized anyone from babies to executives, if you have organized anything from garden tools to file cabinets, your background can become the springboard for your career in the organizing profession. You may find that as you look back over your life or career, at some point others began to respect your organizing accomplishments. Your unique ability may have been acknowledged even if the economic value has not been apparent.

> My unique ability for organizing was first noticed when I was 21 years old. I was offered an open accounting position for which I was not qualified. I was honest with the employer about my concerns and took the job only after being assured that I would be given adequate training. I compensated for my lack of knowledge and experience by carefully documenting the training process. I redesigned systems and created new forms to make it easier for me to understand what I was doing. Not only did I master the job within three months, but I also received additional responsibility and a pay raise when the corporate office discovered my work and applied my systems to other divisions.

With or without a natural aptitude for organizing, the skills you have developed throughout your career can be the foundation for your professional organizing business. Your expertise will expand from on-the-job training. As you continue to expand your knowledge base and increase your hands-on experience, you will become adept at identifying the nature or cause of your clients' disorder. Your common sense combined with the specialized knowledge and skills you acquire in the course of working with clients will translate into marketable expertise.

Professional organizers come from a wide variety of backgrounds, including:

Administrative assistants	Schoolteachers
Counselors	Office Managers
Corporate employees	Parents
Customer service specialists	Therapists
Psychologists	Home economists
Accountants	Bookkeepers
Interior designers	Information systems specialists
Computer analysts	Real estate agents

Many professional organizers are in their twenties or thirties and embarking on their first career. Others have already achieved their initial career goals and are seeking a change, greater fulfillment, or a more productive work life. You can find your place in professional organizing regardless of your background or experience.

Business aptitude and skills

As a professional organizer, you are a businessperson. This means that you will have to satisfy regulatory agencies and keep your head above water, financially. You are going to manage your office; promote your services; manage your accounting; obtain clients; and solve your client's organizing challenges.

Being a business owner is vastly different from being a wage earner. Along with the skills required to serve your clients, you will need to learn the skills necessary to manage your business. You will wear two distinctively different business hats in your business. The first is the hat of the technician – the person who works together with clients to facilitate amazing improvements in their lives. The second hat is that of the business owner, the person who makes decisions and runs the business. The business owner creates a strategic plan, pulls together a budget, sets fees, interviews clients, promotes services, and much, much more to ensure the well-being of the business.

Many organizers are dedicated and passionate about their work and would rather help their clients than put their energy into the business and marketing of their practice. When thinking about what motivated you to pursue a career in organizing, was it more important for you to do what you love and be on your own, or run a business? Give considerable thought to whether your focus will be on being a business owner (entrepreneur) or a technician (freelancer). Many professional organizers avoid some of the business activities by exclusively working for other organizers.

> A professional organizer in Chicago, Lynn Meyer O'Dowd started her own business simply because there were no other options at the time. "I'm not in this to run a business. If there were a corporation that would pay me what I earn to do what I do as a professional organizer, I would work for them in a second."

If you are driven to pursue innovative ideas, not afraid to take risks, and would rather focus on marketing and running a business, you are suited to being a business owner, or entrepreneur. If your goal is to maintain your independence and concentrate on helping people get organized, you are better suited to becoming a technician, or freelancer.

Carefully choose the principal activity in which you invest all of your hard work and energy. Many talented organizers doom themselves by making the wrong choice; by investing vast amounts of effort into building a business, when they have no business experience or passion; or by working as organizing consultants when their deep desire was to build an enterprise.

Regardless of whether you identify more with the entrepreneur or the freelancer, you *will* be a business owner and need the skills required to manage your business. Whether you operate your business as a sole proprietorship or a corporation, you will have to take care of the typical duties and problems of any business. If you want to limit the extent of business administrative activities you get involved in, you may want to consider narrowing your business structure to that of an independent consultant.

You will be required to promote and sell yourself and your services in order to develop and maintain a successful business. In fact, marketing will become an automatic part of your work. When you first start out, 80% of your activity will be marketing, and 20% of your activity will be revenue producing. Without marketing and sales skills, you will have a difficult time attracting clients. The need to market is greatly reduced if you choose to be a contracted employee or an independent contractor.

You can become comfortable with marketing even if you are not naturally socially adept or persuasive, as long as you are proud of what you do. If you do not possess marketing and sales skills, you can certainly learn techniques that will work for you. Even without experience in marketing or sales, you will find that as you capture new business, you begin to develop phrases and terminology that you can use repeatedly and with confidence. Although most organizers do not find marketing and sales to be the favorite part of their businesses, most of us have become more comfortable with these functions as we implemented new ideas.

Begin now to collect ideas and tips for promoting your business, and plan to implement them one or two at a time. Many periodicals and electronic magazines are devoted solely to the topic of marketing. Bookstore and library shelves are overflowing with books full of techniques for improving your ability to promote and sell your business. Samples of these titles are included in the back of this book.

What makes a professional organizer — "professional?"

An individual does not become a professional organizer simply by knowing how to organize and having a refined image. We are judged by our outward appearance, training and expertise, and by how well we handle ourselves and get along with other people. Your good character, your conduct and attitude, your response time, how you speak, your body language and eye contact, your respect and appreciation for your clients, who you connect with and the groups you belong to, and your knowledge and skill will all reveal your professionalism. You will never have a second chance to make a good first impression, and being professional is the most critical element. Professionalism takes shape in four dimensions — expertise, trustworthiness, demeanor, and appearance.

Expertise: Before you can offer your services to the public, master your craft and build up confidence in your abilities. Your clients will see you as the authority. You are the expert in their eyes. It is critical that you are good at what you do, and you must believe in yourself.

Providing services that you do well for a reasonable rate of pay is professional. The key phrase here is *that you do well.* Clients expect to be charged a reasonable rate for assistance in getting their life in order and will often hire a consultant because she calls herself a Professional Organizer. That is great news for those of you who are new to the field. However, be cautious. You could seriously damage your reputation early on by accepting an assignment for which you are not prepared. The unskilled, inexperienced, unqualified organizer pretending to be polished is soon labeled an imposter.

Client goodwill and word of mouth must be carefully protected, since referrals are crucial to a successful career in professional organizing. Before you offer your services, be sure that you understand your client's expectations and that you can expertly perform the requested services. New organizers often make the mistake of accepting any job that comes their way. Charging your clients for anything they are willing to pay you to do is amateurish. You are the client's advocate— the trusted advisor. Do not accept a job just because a client expresses confidence in you, and never accept a job involving personal conflicts. If you are presented with a project for which you feel it is impossible for you to fulfill the objectives, consider the results. Your success absolutely depends on solid relationships with clients and the ability to obtain referrals.

Volunteer your services or work as a subcontractor for another organizer until you can say, without hesitation, that you will be able to produce the expected results. Attempting to deceive the client could seriously breach your integrity, and discredit the entire industry. Other organizers will gladly hire you to assist with projects to help you learn and begin to earn an income as an organizer.

As you read about the different specialty areas later on in this book, ask yourself what type of organizing you want to do and what type of client you want to serve. Concentrate on learning the required skills for that specialty until your skills reach a professional level. How will you know when you have reached a professional level? You will be viewed as an expert whose views are taken as definitive. You will be qualified to teach others. Your work will be consistently of the highest quality.

Trustworthiness: As a professional organizer, you will be entrusted with sensitive information, personal records, private correspondence, intimate areas of the home, financial records, and secret business deals. Do not betray this trust. A client confides in a professional organizer, and his particular habits and peculiarities are exposed. This is the stuff of the best gossip sessions. Sharing this knowledge is absolutely forbidden! Having a client find that you disclosed confidential information is certain death for your career, or more, if you are sued.

A professional organizer should protect the confidentiality of all information obtained in the course of professional service, and should not solicit private information from clients unless it is essential to providing services. During your initial consultation, discuss with clients your intention to protect their right to confidentiality. Assure her that you will not disclose anything that occurs during your work together. Ask her to share any information that is sensitive in nature of which you need to be aware.

Take extra precautions to protect your clients' anonymity. Disclosing a client's company name is usually acceptable. However, it is wise not to mention an individual's name, unless he has specifically asked that you include him in promotional opportunities. If you teach or train and discuss a client's situation as an illustration or case history, be careful not to disclose identifying information, unless the client has consented.

Trustworthiness extends beyond protecting confidentiality. Honor your word and commitments to your clients. Be forthright and candid when you will not be able to live up to your clients expectations. If clients find that you have deceived or misled them in order to win their business, they will not only discontinue your services, but they will likely tell others that you are dishonest. Your business will flourish if you build and guard your reputation as a person who is sincere, loyal, truthful, responsible and honest.

Demeanor: When people say you are a real professional, they are probably referring to your demeanor, or the way you behave toward other people. Demeanor involves your manner, behaviors, attitude, and nonverbal emotional tone. If you deal effectively with people (especially difficult people), disagree tactfully, and use appropriate language, you are perceived as a professional. You have the ability to disagree or say no without creating resentment. You are emotionally mature and assertive without being aggressive. You are poised and polished, confident and enthusiastic in any situation. You willingly accept obligations and complete them on a timely basis. You are punctual and prepared. You have integrity and your actions speak louder than your words.

You can inspire the opportunity for others to trust you with your positive attitude and pleasant conduct. Whether or not you are aware of it, this is your business presence. You may or may not be conscious of all of these behaviors. However, they affect the way you are perceived by others, as well as your ability to influence others to your point of view. Weaknesses in the area of professional demeanor can make others feel uncomfortable and hold you back in business dealings. A powerful business presence conveys professionalism on the nonverbal level: "I am levelheaded and capable of handling any situation; I can manage and inspire other people."

Your smile is one way you can communicate your business presence. Genuine smiles are an empowering method of communication. They can break the ice and communicate that you are approachable. An insincere smile, however, can make you look nervous, sarcastic, or give the impression that you are self-righteous.

It takes practice to learn to maintain your emotional balance regardless of the circumstances, and always come across as calm, cool and collected. Be aware of the components of business presence, and learn how to use them to your advantage. Your mannerisms, body language, and posture can convey confidence. Your smile, eye contact, handshake and business courtesies communicate that you are a person with whom it is easy to do business.

Appearance: Unless you plan to restrict your practice to phone consulting, virtual organizing, or organizing financial records from your home office, a professional appearance is important. A professional should be aware of his appearance and behavior at all times whenever in a public setting. You are risking your integrity if you show up to your condominium association meeting in a jogging suit or go to the grocery store with uncombed hair. You may not think of yourself as high profile. The paparazzi may not catch you on film, but you never know when you will be in the presence of a potential client or business associate.

A favorable first impression is critical. Clients will make a connection between your appearance and your ability to help them become organized. If your appearance looks out of date, clients may think your skills and attitude are as well. Your appearance will give your clients clues as to whether you are prepared and dependable. People notice things like your untidy car, your overflowing briefcase, and your wrinkled shirt. They will question how an organized person could lose his car keys or show up late for a meeting. You need to look so successful that a client would be reluctant to hire anyone else.

Since you are your own boss, no one can tell you what to wear. However, you do have a dress code, and it is established by your clients. No matter what is your usual style, the way you dress for work is more than a fashion statement. Consider what your style might be saying to your client. Your appearance should reflect the subliminal promise of the service you offer. Self-expression is of little importance if you do not fit your client's expectations. Study your client's style and dress accordingly. Your appearance should convey your assurance and capability without intimidating the client.

When meeting with a first-time client, assume that he will hold you to a high standard, and always err on the side of being over dressed. With residential clients, dress professionally and neatly casual. If your client wears jeans, dress in khakis. With business clients, assume more of a corporate look. This does not have to be a constricting suit and tie, or a tailored skirt. A coordinated jacket and pants would be appropriate. The information you gain in the preliminary meeting typically reveals the person's background and style, and you can adjust accordingly.

Your area of specialization also helps to determine the appropriate way to dress. Clients will expect a person who organizes garages to dress much more casually than a person who specializes in home offices. Even so, clean jeans or khakis and a polo shirt leave a better impression than dirty, torn jeans and a sloppy T-shirt. It is okay to be informal, just keep in mind that being too casual when business attire is expected can possibly sabotage your career.

A uniform personalized with your company name, logo, and tag line is quite appropriate, and may help to build recognition for your business. Apparel such as oxford shirts, blazers, polo shirts, and sweaters can be individualized with embroidery to give a professional appearance.

Pay attention to all aspects of your appearance, including:

- Your clothing selection, including shoes
- Your use of accessories, such briefcase, pens, technology tools, etc.
- The style, color, condition, and length of your hair
- Your grooming and overall cleanliness
- Jewelry — use and overuse
- Fragrances — use and abuse

Be aware of how you appear anywhere that you could meet a potential contact. The way that you dress, your personal hygiene, hairstyle and posture all reflect what you think of others. Let others know that they are worth the time and effort it takes for you to look good.

Chapter Three: Preparing for an Organizing Career

"Luck is a matter of preparation meeting opportunity" - Oprah Winfrey

As you venture into a career in professional organizing, you may discover areas needing additional training or experience. An adjustment in your specialties might compensate for areas where you may be less proficient. This chapter will help you plan your transition and arrange for the training and development that will increase your value and boost your profits.

Making the transition from employee to entrepreneur

Studies show that 75 percent of the population has a strong desire to be self-sufficient, but only a small number actually make the transition from employee to entrepreneur. If you have relied on a steady job and the paycheck and benefits that go along with it, getting beyond the dependencies associated with full-time employment can be both terrifying and liberating!

> When I left my corporate job, my colleagues reacted as if I had found a serendipitous lifestyle. They asked, "Is there really life after corporate employment?" They were not joking; they could not imagine any life but their own.
>
> Honestly, it was scary to give up a secure, well-paying job. I had drawn much self-esteem from working in the corporate environment. I was just hitting my career stride, and I felt needed, competent and in control as an employee. I had worked with senior management in lead roles on a variety of projects, and I had earned their trust, confidence and wide visibility. Until I was on my own, I did not realize how much I cherished the recognition.
>
> Sometimes I thought I must have been crazy to abandon this connection to start my own business. I have never been much of a risk-taker, but making the transition from corporate manager to entrepreneur was dramatic. It allowed me to take a fresh look at myself. I was fortunate in that I had the support of my family and friends. I had a business plan that I believed in, which gave me the courage to step

away from a perceived security that was actually holding me back. The fear of starting a new business was no big deal, once I had overcome the fear of departure.

Evaluate your time and resources. Before you leave your regular job, evaluate your current savings and make a decision about how long you will be able to pay the bills until a regular clientele is established. If you are not blessed with a generous financial cushion, you may decide that leaving your regular job is too great a risk. There are many options for making the transition without bankrupting yourself.

First, it is important to understand that you will not be able to spend 40-50 hours per week performing income-producing activities as you do as an employee. You will need extra time to do the non-billable tasks in your business. Running your own full time business requires at least three hours a day in the beginning to attend to marketing activities and follow up on leads. If your goal is to bill 30-35 hours per week, you will actually be working 40-45 (or more) total hours each week. If you plan to work 30-35 hours per week, you will probably only be able to commit to 20-25 hours of actual client work that you are paid for.

When you are not scheduled to be with clients, you will be spending the majority of your time focusing on growth or maintenance work for your own business. Figure time in your schedule to build your resources so that you can be more effective in what you offer your clients. There are always bills to pay, bank statements to reconcile, credit card charges to record, Web pages to update, thank you notes to write, and plenty of other things to organize in your own office. Even when your practice is booming, you must continue your marketing efforts. You will also need to devote serious time and effort in developing your skills and knowledge.

Consider your options for remaining employed. Some organizers just take the plunge into full-time consulting, relying on savings or another family member's income for survival. Others risk it all to pursue their dreams.

> One organizer lost her patience with the corporate world and quit her job on impulse. The next day, she settled on a name for her new business. She poured herself into her professional organizing business and never looked back. Ten years later, she is the highest paid organizer in her state.

If quitting your job is not an option for you, do not despair. Many organizers start out by combining regular employment with part-time consulting. You may be able to work your regular job during the day and run your consulting business in your free time. Professional people are sometimes the most in need of organizing assistance, but their careers tie up their weekdays.

Chapter Three: Preparing for an Organizing Career

They can afford your services and will be pleased to find a professional organizer who is willing to work weekends and evenings.

On a part time scale, keeping up with the demands of a business along with a full time job can be overwhelming. If you held a job while going to college, you already know how tough it is to keep up your energy for two such taxing endeavors. Once you have established a client base and are generating enough revenue, you can resign from your regular job. If you must combine regular employment with part-time consulting while getting your business off the ground, be reassured in knowing that the long hours and hard work required to launch your professional organizing business will directly benefit you, rather than profiting someone else.

You might be able to work out an outsourced arrangement with your present employer. You essentially give up the security of employee, and gain the freedom of an independent contractor.

One professional organizer convinced her employer to hire her as an independent consultant to handle his organizing needs. As part of the arrangement, he provided office space and covered her telephone and supplies expenses while she launched her business. By the time his projects were just about completed, she had built a solid client base.

Another option that will help you obtain organizing experience while remaining employed is to work for a company that provides services, or sells products that closely match your intended specialty. For instance, you might get a job with a home services business. If you want to get experience with organizing closets, look for a job with a company that sells closet organizing systems. If you plan to help people with organizing photos and memorabilia, you might seek employment with a company that sells scrapbook supplies. Large organizing stores that sell containers and other organizing products frequently offer great compensation, product discounts and extensive training programs for part time employees.

Do not become discouraged if you are not yet in a position to leave your present job or company in order to start an organizing business. More and more organizers are finding full-time employment in the corporate world. If you are dissatisfied with your current job, ask yourself if it is the job, the company, or the industry with which you are unhappy. Perhaps your current company needs organizing. Perhaps you are just the person to do it! There may be a possibility of initiating a project that will be exactly what you need, to motivate yourself and find pleasure in your current company. Just as you must sell your services to new prospective clients, you may be able to convince your current employer of a need and create a new job in your current company. What better way could you find to gain the experience you will need to launch your own business?

Evaluate your capacity to furnish money for your business. The cliché "it takes money to make money" does not necessarily apply to professional organizing. It may take some creativity, however. You do not need much start-up capital because you can work out of your home and use your own vehicle. Your equipment needs will be minimal. There are many creative ways to get revenue trickling in, even if the type of business you select is not your long-term goal. Once your business is off the ground, you can be more selective about the type of work with which you get involved.

A study conducted by the National Federation of Independent Business found that one out of three new businesses start with $10,000 or less. Many professional organizing businesses launched for a great deal less. Since you need minimal funding to get started as a professional organizer, your main concern is to keep up with your living expenses while you build your business. It helps to have an alternate source of income since it may take you some time to build your client base.

Your credit rating contributes greatly to your ability to secure funds (as well as your company image), so begin immediately to build good business credit. A good credit rating will help you to qualify for accounts with suppliers, enabling you to conserve your cash for living expenses. Establish business accounts with suppliers as soon as possible, and pay your accounts promptly. At first, you will probably have to rely on your personal credit history, but you should be able to build company credit quite easily.

If you do not like the idea of people probing into your affairs, asking questions, and demanding answers about your business and its profitability, do not borrow money from friends, relatives, or in-laws. If you do, be prepared to surrender some of your personal control. Once you involve them in financing your business, expect to have them looking over your shoulder and advising you.

The first place to seek financing is with you. Look at your assets and evaluate what you have of value that you could use to finance your business. Your main options are savings, investment portfolio, mortgage refinancing, home-equity loans, and employer buyouts. If you own your home, the equity in your home may be a source of capital. Your home may have appreciated more than you know, or you might consider a second mortgage to finance your business. Borrowing against the cash value of your life insurance policies at low interest rates may be an option for funding your business startup. Perhaps you have an expensive collection you could sell.

> As crazy as it sounds, one organizer cleaned out her house to get cash to start her business. She took her stereo equipment, excess furniture, sterling silver, and unused jewelry to a pawnshop. Then she sold the rest of unneeded items in a garage sale. When she was finished, she found that her house was larger than she needed and she relocated to a less expensive home. The entire process not only financed her business startup, it was like getting a degree in professional organizing.

You can contribute the money from your own savings, but be careful not to use contingency savings (you may call it an emergency fund or rainy day savings) to start a new business. If you use your savings and require more money down the road, you will have no advantage with your financing institution. If you do have money in a CD or savings account and a decent credit rating, ask your banker for a loan. (Home improvement loans typically have a higher rate of acceptance than loans to start a business.) Even if your bank does not require your savings as collateral, the existence of a balance in savings will help you acquire the loan. Make an appointment with a senior or regional loan officer, rather than a branch loan officer. Working with a loan officer of a higher rank increases your chances of getting a loan without the involvement of a committee.

Financing your business start-up on personal credit cards is tempting. It is not advisable if you already carry a large balance. If you are broke and deep in debt because you have not been able to manage your money in the past, you will probably not be able to make it in business. Being weighed down with obligations like monthly payments and heavy interest is not an optimal start for your business. Borrowed money is just another bill.

You may qualify for a loan through your bank guaranteed by the Small Business Administration, if you meet certain criteria. The SBA guarantees loans through private lenders to small businesses who are unsuccessful at securing financing through normal lending channels. The application process is no more difficult than applying for a mortgage. You can afford to start a professional organizing business if you have enough money to establish the business and sustain its operations over the first two to three years. You will need to have sufficient funds for your personal needs until your business starts producing enough income to sustain its operations and provide a profit for you. Determining how much you need to take care of your personal needs is the first step in estimating how much you will need to start your business. Set up a personal budget, as in Figure 3.1.

Personal Finances	Monthly $	Annual $
Mortgage Payments		
Power (electric, natural gas, etc.)		
Property Insurance		
Property Taxes		
Personal Loans		
Water		
Telephone		
Car Payment		
Car Insurance		
Car Expenses		
Health Insurance		
Life Insurance		
Food (groceries & dining out)		
Entertainment		
Credit Card Payments		
Retirement Fund Contribution		
Education		
Clothing		
Travel		
Gifts		
Other		
Total Personal		

(Figure 3.1)

The next step is to determine how much money you will need to establish your business. Make a list of startup expenses, as in Figure 3.2.

Business Startup	Cost $
Computer	
Copy Machine	
Fax Machine	
Printer	
Scanner	
Furniture	
Telephone	
Organizing Tools	
Educational Courses	
Licensing & Registration Fees	
Marketing Materials Design & Printing	
Association Membership Fees	
Basic Office Supplies	
Other	
Total Business Startup	

(Figure 3.2)

Business expenses must be taken into consideration when determining set up costs and monthly disbursements for your business (see Figure 3.3). Over time, you may have additional monthly expenses, such as payroll expenses, worker's compensation, office rent and utilities.

Business Expenses	Monthly $	Annual $
Accounting Fees		
Auto Expense		
Equipment Lease/Payment		
Insurance		
Legal Fees		
Licenses & Registrations		
Marketing Expense		
Office Supplies		
Organizing Supplies		
Owner's Draw		
Printing & Photocopying		
Postage		
Taxes		
Telephone		
Travel Expenses		
Other		
Total Business Expenses		

(Figure 3.3)

Technical training and skills development

Just as in any career, you will need to devote serious time, effort and money in gaining new skills for becoming a professional organizer. You will need to learn both the skills required to serve your clients, and the skills necessary for managing your business. In this young industry, resources for gaining skills are emerging at a rapid rate. Curriculums are evolving in educational institutions, and education is provided through professional organizing association programs, regional seminars and chapter programs. Some veteran professional organizers also offer customized training programs for professional organizers.

Join a professional organizer association. The need to join and support your local and national professional organizer associations cannot be stressed enough. They represent the conduit through which information about the professional organizing industry flows. There are many ways professional associations can help you, such as public relations and advocacy, continuing education, and even legislative efforts. By joining a professional association, you will be able to:

- Make others aware of you and your business
- Learn about qualities needed to be successful in your profession
- Establish professional credibility in the eyes of your clients
- Meet and interact with those who already are where you want to be
- Expand your knowledge base and stay current in your field
- Be informed about ongoing industry trends
- Take advantage of affinity programs and member discounts
- Minimize the trial-and-error process of learning the business

National Association of Professional Organizers (NAPO): NAPO, whose tag line is *The Organizing Authority*, is the original and premier national association dedicated to the field of organizing. The growth and development of this profession have been deeply affected by the National Association of Professional Organizers. NAPO was founded in 1985 to promote awareness of the organizing industry, educate the public about the field of professional organizing, and encourage the education and development of member organizers.

NAPO is a nonprofit 501(C) (3) organization dedicated to sharing information about the growing organizing industry, its trends, and its concerns. NAPO works to set and define quality standards for the organizing profession. NAPO's members include organizing consultants, speakers, trainers, authors, and manufacturers of organizing products.

There is only one requirement for membership in the National Association of Professional Organizers – you must be an individual representing yourself or a company who is doing business primarily in the field of organizing services. NAPO has members throughout the world and chapters across the United States.

Joining the National Association of Professional Organizers can help you introduce your company. As a member, you can use the NAPO Member's logo to demonstrate to your clients that you are committed to the industry. You will learn more about the organizing industry through NAPO than through any other means. For more information, visit http://www.napo.net.

National Study Group on Chronic Disorganization (NSGCD): NSGCD, a group of professional organizers and psychiatric professionals, is an affiliate of NAPO. The mission of the National Study Group on Chronic Disorganization is to educate professional organizers and related professionals on the issues relating to Chronic Disorganization. NSGCD accepts applications from professional organizers and individuals currently working or employed in the following occupations:

Chapter Three: Preparing for an Organizing Career

Planning and Zoning – Code Enforcement
Psychiatrist/Psychologist
Medical Doctor (MD) or Registered Nurse (RN)
Social Worker
Health Department Professional
ADD/ADHD Coach
Cross-Field Association Executive Board

NSGCD is a valuable resource to professional organizers for dealing with clients, and many of the most accomplished and highly respected individuals in the field of organizing belong to this group. For more information, visit http://www.nsgcd.org.

Professional Organizers in Canada (POC): POC is also an affiliate of NAPO. POC was incorporated in February 2001 as a Not-For-Profit Organization. POC is a self-monitoring association run by and for its members.

POC's mission is to provide a supportive environment for professional organizers, promote networking, share ideas, encourage referrals, and increase public awareness of the field of professional organizing in Canada. Membership in POC is open to individuals currently working in the field of organizing or dedicated to pursuing such a career. For more information, visit http://www.organizersincanada.com.

Nederlandse Beroepsvereniging van Professional Organizers (NBPO): NBPO was formed by a merger of two associations, the European Professional Organisers (started in 1997) and the NPO Dutch Professional Organisers (started in 1998). For more information, visit www.nbpo.nl.

Australasian Association of Professional Organisers (AAPO): AAPO was incorporated in November 2005 as a non profit organization comprising members from Australia and New Zealand. For more information, visit http://www.aapo.org.au.

Association of Professional Declutterers and Organisers (APDO) UK:
APDO was founded in 2004. For more information, visit http://www.apdo-uk.co.uk.

Take advantage of community opportunities. Seek out areas where you can get involved, contribute and learn new skills at the same time. Do a self-assessment and review your skills. Look at your entire professional history and document the work experience that you already have. Evaluate your strengths and build an informal resume that includes your education, talents, jobs and skills. In which projects have you been involved? What special training have you had? What processes have you implemented? What awards or certificates have you earned?

Next, take a good, hard look at the gaps and identify the skills you would like to develop or master. Actively look for opportunities to gain the skills you will need in order to excel in the specialty you plan to pursue. You can gain new skills by serving on a committee or holding office in your professional association, a chamber of commerce, homeowners' association, or community groups. You may be able to gain skills by participating in a local project or organizing a special event.

Read pertinent books and professional journals. If only I knew when I started my business what I know now. If only I had the resources that are now available. The wise man learns from other people's mistakes, and the bookshelves are chock full of information about how to organize. Rely on books for knowledge about being a professional organizer. Read everything you can about organizing, especially in the area you intend to specialize. Rely on books to help you decide your specialty. Rely on books to stimulate your own belief system. Rely on books to teach you organizing techniques and concepts. When you think you have read it all, keep reading and learning to fill the holes in your knowledge bank.

If you join NAPO, you will find many interesting and educational articles in its newsletter to help you stay abreast of current industry news and standards. Your local chapter newsletter is another valuable source of information, and exposes you to the perspective, experience and ideas of other professional organizers. In addition, your local chapter of NAPO may have a library of books, recordings, and other resources that you can borrow.

Many organizers obtained their education from NAPO and from library books. A librarian can help you locate specific information you need in reference books. Most libraries have a variety of resources that cover many business topics, such as trade association directories, manuals on small business, and business and professional magazines. The resources at the end of this book include a list of books to get you started. Keep in mind that books and periodicals can become tax deductions.

Take classes and workshops. Classes are offered at community colleges, evening adult schools and national seminars on topics such as getting organized, clearing clutter, time management and business management. As someone who is highly organized, you may believe that you cannot learn much from these types of seminars, but even the most experienced organizer comes away with new ideas and fresh perspectives. Take classes to develop a greater understanding in the areas where you are weak. Take classes to help build your business, such as accounting, proposal writing, business development, or marketing.

Associations such as NAPO and NSGCD offer extensive educational opportunities in the areas of organizing skills and business development at their annual conferences and chapter events. Classes and workshops instructing new professional organizers are offered across the United States, Canada and Europe by veteran professional organizers. NAPO members can call NAPO's headquarters and request to be added to their electronic mailing list to be notified of these educational opportunities.

Seminars and educational classes can be a tax deduction. Besides education, they can also be valuable opportunities for networking with other professionals and possible clients.

Find a mentor (observe a master). Ask just about anyone who has achieved professional success, and chances are very good that they will tell you that they had some guidance. Successful entrepreneurs invite mentors to play an important role in their business life. If you are fortunate enough to find a professional organizer who is already successful in her business, is willing, and has the available time to advise you, invest in yourself and pay her fee.

Mentors are different from business advisors. Business advisors can help you in specific areas such as accounting, legal, or marketing. A mentor is intrinsically interested in your personal and professional success. A mentor understands your ambition and passion and will play an important role in your career and your life and help you find balance as an entrepreneur. Your mentor has a unique advantage and can help keep you grounded as you embark on new challenges. Having a mentor can inspire you, guide your professional development, and show you the possibilities of moving ahead in the industry.

Mentors can balance the peaks and valleys of your journey and help you navigate the uncharted waters where you have little or no previous experience. Mentors can provide a fresh perspective, rein you in when you are off balance, and help you focus. Mentors can share technical experience and guide you to resources for improving your skills and acquiring more knowledge. A formal mentor arrangement will offer coaching and assignments to challenge your capability.

The best education to be found in this profession is in working with a seasoned colleague, no matter how full your resume or how stellar your academic credentials. A mentor will help you gain business knowledge and ease your transition from employee to business owner. Working with someone who knows the ropes can help you understand the business environment, as well as your clients and their challenges.

If you are willing to devote serious time and effort, you may even find a local organizer who will let you observe. The key to making this type of relationship work is to ask, "What's in it for her?" What advantage would there be to the experienced organizer to involve you in her project? If you can ease her workload and provide some additional labor, your assistance may be welcomed. Ask if you can work as an intern to gain experience and learn from her. A professional organizer in a non-competing specialty will be your best option, since most entrepreneurs are not open to the idea of training their competition.

You will receive sound advice from a veteran in exchange for your time, and you may even be able to get some experience helping to organize a client. The time spent with someone who has an established career as a professional organizer can give your business a real boost. This is a great way to get training and build confidence, and the feedback you receive from a seasoned professional is priceless! A mentor can help you deal with the challenges of life and business, lift you up when you are down, and provide insight when you are out of balance.

Once you have established a relationship with a mentor, be respectful of your mentor's time. Do your own thorough research and do not expect your mentor to have all of the answers. Make sure you are knowledgeable about your options before you seek your mentor's advice. Do not forget to show your appreciation, and make sure to keep your mentor updated on your progress. Share the credit with your mentor when you achieve your goals. Be sure to let him or her know when the day comes that you are able to pay it forward by serving as a mentor to someone else.

Offer a free sample. It is common for new organizers to get their feet wet by getting people to try their services by giving a free sample of what they offer. Offering free services can help you to establish a record of accomplishment, generate testimonials and get referrals. In theory, if the client likes it, he will want more.

In practice, though, giving away business can become a trap since it does not fully convey the message of value. A free sample may give a taste of what you can do, but it does not communicate to a client the value of your services. The value of something free is zero. The value of your time and energy, as well as that of your client's should never be underrated. Be sure to let your clients know that you are offering them a one-time special arrangement. Let them know your regular fee and make sure to ask them if they would like to make an appointment. Follow up later with those who sampled your services but were not ready to buy. Make sure that *free* means money or time well spent for you and your business.

Volunteer in a nonprofit setting. One of the best ways to gain experience is to volunteer for an organizing project in a charity setting. Volunteering your services enables you to identify areas of interest and measures your sense of satisfaction from this type of work. Through volunteer work, you can pinpoint any skills deficiencies that you may need to address in order to become marketable.

Your church, synagogue, community center or organization will probably not be choosy about your credentials, and will be grateful for whatever help they can get. In this setting, you can experiment with different organizing methods, tools and products. You can practice new techniques and learn ways to work with different personality types. You can learn a great deal from planning and completing an entire project. What you give away may come back to you a thousand times.

> Tom, a new organizer volunteered to organize the storage room at his church in order to practice planning and estimating a project. Two members of the Board of Trustees were so pleased with his work that they hired him to organize the supply rooms of their own businesses, resulting in $5,500.00 in revenue.

Another benefit of volunteering is that the experience will prepare you to quote jobs in the future. Documenting every aspect of a free job, as if it were a trial run, will better position you to estimate a job when a similar opportunity arises. Keep track of all of the variables:

What is the scope of the project? Is it a 2-car garage, a small office, a walk-in closet, a storage room or a large kitchen?

What was the condition of the space when you started? Did the space need to be de-cluttered, or did it simply need rearranging? Was there enough space to achieve the desired result? How did you get rid of excess?

How much help did you have? How many people participated in the project? Did the project involve anyone with organizing experience? Did the project involve anyone who obstructed the progress?

What tools and supplies did you use? Did you shop for supplies, and how much time did that process consume? What tools would you put on your wish list?

What obstacles did you encounter? What took more or less time than you anticipated?

How much time did the project take? Break the project down into phases. How much time was devoted to each phase?

Each time you volunteer your services, be sure to get testimonials and save photos for your sample file. Try to get a letter of thanks or recommendation that you can use in promoting your services.

Hire a business coach. A great way to jump-start your business is to hire a coach. For a reasonable consulting fee, you can contract for an ongoing coaching arrangement with a business coach or professional organizer coach. This is a one-on-one arrangement with someone who knows a lot about what you need to learn and where you are trying to go. This arrangement can save literally years in your process. With the individual attention, guidance and encouragement you receive from a coach, you can avoid serious, even deadly mistakes. A business coach can assist you with setting goals, identifying obstacles, and holding you accountable to your intentions. Hiring a business coach is the fast track to success.

Credentials and certification

Whether formal or informal, having credentials is evidence that you are an expert. Building credibility will convince your clients that you are capable of providing their desired results. Credentials include your degree, formal training, and career and life experience.

Even if you do not have a formal degree or professional designation, you can demonstrate expertise through your accomplishments. For example, one professional organizer gained credibility for her estate organizing business through the passing of her parents. She depicts the experience in her brochure and on her website, and her clients feel confident in hiring her.

Be prepared to list your accomplishments, both personally and professionally. Show your resume and qualifications on your website, and display any past examples of your work. Include any volunteer work you have done, articles you have published, news items that included you as the subject, anything you have learned from self-study and testimonials from your clients.

Get involved in your community. One of the best ways to increase your profile and credibility as a business is to lend your time, talent and influence to help your community. The more involved you are in your community, the more others will trust you. We all have times in our lives when we need the support of our community, and we have a responsibility to help make the

Chapter Three: Preparing for an Organizing Career

community a better and stronger place to live. If your community thrives, your business will benefit from a larger client base.

There are plenty of opportunities to get involved in your community. Because of your extraordinary organizing skills, you can assist in planning, organizing and directing fund-raising activities in your area. You can serve on the board of directors for nonprofit organizations. Join planning committees or donate your time and expertise to help with annual charity events, like golf outings, health fairs, and walkathons. Adopt a highway, sponsor a sports team, organize a blood drive, offer high school students an intern program, help organize clothing for a homeless shelter, and provide mentoring for young people. The list is endless.

Chamber of Commerce events will introduce you to various community organizations that work together to benefit the community and its residents. Join them. Your skills and capabilities will become well known in your community. Community work is meaningful and rewarding. It will help you to integrate yourself into your community as a respected professional organizer.

Get involved in professional organizations. Membership in professional organizations can provide credibility and demonstrate your commitment to your profession. Membership in professional organizations generally represents strong standards and industry ethics, which can influence potential clients to place their trust in you.

Do not just join; get involved. Be an active participant and take advantage of the education and other benefits offered by your organization. Get ideas and resources that will help you in your practice. Serve on an association committee or give a talk at a local or regional conference. Read your association newsletter and contribute articles. Read other magazines related to your work. Become published in your area of expertise, to add more emphasis and gain more exposure for your industry.

Being active in your association will enhance your credentials and improve your resume. Attending meetings and networking with other professionals can be a valuable time for you. This activity gives you a chance to compare notes on what others are doing. Networking with colleagues gives you the opportunity to air out your concerns and do a reality-check.

Being involved in a professional organization does much more than adding to your credibility. You will find educational and marketing opportunities through professional organizer associations such as NAPO, NSGCD and POC. You will be kept up to date on news and trends in the organizing industry. You will also meet some wonderful colleagues and learn more about being successful as a professional organizer at NAPO's chapter meetings, regional and annual conferences and organizing expos.

In addition to those specifically related to the professional organizing industry and your community, there are thousands of other organizations you might consider joining. For more information about opportunities for conventional membership, industry partnership and strategic alliances, see Membership Opportunities at http://www.organizingforaliving.com/docs.

Become certified as a professional organizer. Certification demonstrates that you have met certain minimal training and experience to be included in a list of qualified practitioners. A board or association of similarly qualified practitioners administers the process, and the criteria are generally accepted standards by the profession. The strongest argument for certification is that to be considered a true professional in our culture, a professional must be certified.

Being certified as a professional organizer will do a lot to increase your credibility. Several options have emerged for obtaining national certification in the field of professional organizing, and each provides an opportunity for an individual to learn and grow in his profession. As additional opportunities become available, further training and endorsements will serve to enhance an individual's competence, especially if specialty-based certification becomes available. Multiple certification certificates say that a person has worked very hard to learn his trade and meet the highest standards of the industry.

Through the initiative of the National Study Group on Chronic Disorganization (NSGCD), five levels of certification specifically designed to qualify and prepare individuals to serve chronically disorganized clients are available to professional organizers. In addition to other requirements, an organizer must pass a Peer Panel Review in order to be presented with NSGCD Certified Professional Organizer® *CPO-CD* Credential. For eligibility requirements and other information, contact NSGCD:

National Study Group on Chronic Disorganization
http:// www.nsgcd.org

The National Association of Professional Organizers (NAPO) began exploring the feasibility of certification in 1996 with the urging of a few very forward-thinking organizers who believed that professional certification would provide a career advantage. With the support and financial backing of NAPO, many volunteers worked diligently over a period of ten years to build a strong foundation for a certification program. NAPO's goal was to have a certification program viewed as the industry standard, a goal that was reached (after a few stops and starts) in April 2007.

The Certified Professional Organizer® program is independently managed and operated by the Board of Certified Professional Organizers (BCPO). The CPO® examination is based upon a properly conducted Job Task Analysis, which empirically defines the necessary competencies for the successful practice of organizing. BCPO will eventually seek accreditation by the National Commission for Certifying Agencies (NCCA). NCCA accreditation means that the certification has been reviewed by a panel of impartial experts and found to comply with applicable accreditation standards. Membership in NAPO or any other organization is not a requirement of certification. For eligibility requirements and other information, contact BCPO:

The Board of Certification for Professional Organizers
http://www.certifiedprofessionalorganizers.org

Part II

Guiding Your Business to Success

Chapter Four: Carving a Niche

"Discoveries are often made by not following instructions, by going off the main road, by trying the untried." -Frank Tyger

You may notice two distinctions the first time you are in a room with a group of professional organizers. The first is an uncanny passion and enthusiasm for organization. This group of people embraces your irresistible desire to help others become more organized. The passion you share will enable you to relate to these people as you probably have with no other group.

The other distinctive quality is that although these people seem to have so much in common, each has a unique skill set, background, and interest. No two of these individuals perform the same type of service in the same way. Your unique abilities will differentiate you from other organizers, and will enable you to carve out a specialty that will appeal to a different group of clients. In this chapter, we will look at the limitless ways to define you as a unique professional organizer.

Generalists vs. Specialists

Some professional organizers call themselves generalists, meaning that they organize just about everything for everyone and make themselves available for popular requests for organizing services. Others differentiate their practices and focus on specific areas of organizing. They devote their practices to a narrow audience or a particular need.

What is a Generalist? No challenge is too big or too small; no project is too grimy, heavy or complicated. The practice of a generalist is similar to a series of part-time jobs, and the variety helps to prevent burnout. Being a generalist offers almost unlimited areas of income.

An advantage of being a generalist is that you are more likely to be recession-proof. There will probably always be work for the generalist. If you are willing to take on just about any challenge that is presented to you and variety in your work and clientele is your definition of success, then being a general practitioner is for you.

Many generalists have done remarkably well through shrewd business strategies and creative marketing. Many organizers have started out as generalists, and then defined their specialties as they progressed. You might consider that option if you are unsure how to design your business or until you acquire specialized skills.

The main drawback of being a generalist is that generalists all look the same to potential clients. The services appear to be equivalent, and the quality seems to be uniform. With nothing to differentiate you from other generalists, clients may perceive you as having no clear benefits. They may have no special reason to choose you, unless you offer the lowest rate.

In this age of specialization, people are generally willing to pay top dollar for services provided by an expert. Popular opinion holds that the person who is able to do a variety of different jobs acceptably well cannot do any particular job exceptionally well. For that reason, organizers without specialties seldom reach a high level of financial success. The abundance of general professional organizing services could dilute your value. Be careful that you do not try to offer so much that you are not perceived to be proficient at anything.

What is a Specialist? Specialization means narrowing your focus to a precise range of services when marketing yourself and your business. Packaging yourself as a specialist enables you to highlight your expertise and strengths and target your marketing efforts so that prospective clients will want to choose you over anyone else. Specialization not only attracts your ideal clients, it also drives away unsuitable prospects, the ones that waste your time and cost you money.

Specialization opens up more opportunities to find clients. Although there is plenty of business for everyone, something must differentiate us if we are all using the same vessel to find business. Using the bakery business as an analogy, let us assume that all of the bakeries in town are competing for wedding business, and they all advertise in the Yellow Pages under *Bakery*. To the bride looking for a sweet table for her wedding, the one that specializes in European style pastries will arouse interest. That bakery will stand out, have more opportunities to reach its client base, and be able to develop marketing strategies for not only bakery customers, but wedding customers as well.

If you establish yourself in a specialty where you can excel, you can charge accordingly. A specialist has a greater perceived value and can demand more money than a generalist performing the same services can. In the eyes of the client, the harder it is to find the type of service you offer, the higher your value. Clients equate the discovery of the right specialist to finding a rare gem or a valuable work of art. The client base of the specialist is typically higher quality and more affluent than that of a generalist.

When you specialize, you get good at what you are doing and can serve a greater number of clients in less time at a higher rate. By learning one specialty thoroughly, you will improve your knowledge and skills. You will become more efficient and be able to fit more jobs into your day. You will establish yourself as an expert in your niche and attract more business. Your skills will be in demand and you will be able to charge more for your services. You are also more likely to get client referrals if your services are more specific.

Limiting the types of clients you choose to serve will help you to market more effectively. Many business owners target a market that is too large because they are afraid of limiting their opportunities to gain clients. In reality, you expand your chances of getting clients if you do not spread yourself too thin. Focusing on helping seniors transition from a lifetime of work and responsibility to a period of relaxation in their golden years, for instance, enables you to get to know that group and better understand their needs. This improves your ability to solve your client's problems and gain their appreciation. As a specialist, your clients will see you as the expert, and influence others to do the same.

Specializing does not necessarily mean that you limit the scope of what you do. You may occasionally be offered a business opportunity that is outside of your area of specialization. If the job is lucrative and your skills can back it up, there is no reason not to take it. Just be careful not to dilute your marketing message. Persist in directing your marketing efforts on your niche. Resist any temptation to branch out or promote additional areas of expertise, so that you continue to be perceived as a specialist.

Determining your specialties

To ensure a steady flow of revenue, most new organizers will offer to take any type of work in the initial months of operating their business, and gradually shift into a specialty. Specialties are ways that you can tap into your talents, be competitive, and grow professionally. Specialties are limited only by your imagination. You may already have a very good idea about the type of organizing in which you want to specialize. If you are unsure, try a variety of different projects, including offices, garages, closets, paper management, kitchens and pantries, basements and storage areas, children's rooms, etc.

At the most elementary level, most organizers differentiate their services by specializing in either residential or business organizing. Residential, or household organizing spans a wide range of services, from organizing rooms, garages, and attics, to running errands and performing other personal services. Business or commercial organizing specialists are usually involved in office organizing and time management, as well as storage and production areas.

Your niche may be right under your nose. As you work with different clients in different settings, pay attention to what you enjoy, and what annoys you. Ask for feedback from your clients about the experience. Pay attention to the areas where people ask for your advice. Constantly listen for the answer to the question, "what is my niche?" The following questions might help you zero in on the type of organizing that is perfectly suited to you.

Who are your target clients? Whom do you intend to serve? Will you be helping young moms, busy executives, students, seniors, entrepreneurs, or clients with special needs? Who has the money, or who controls the money that will pay you for your services? Before you set your rates or market your business, have a clear idea of whom you will serve.

Where are your target clients? Will your clients live in a particular geographic area or work in a specific industry? If you have not defined a limit to the range or scope of your audience, how will you direct your marketing efforts? You may want to be national, but consider that it is far easier to expand a local niche than to narrow a national niche. If you have spent your marketing efforts targeting a national audience, you might have difficulty attracting clients in your local area.

What services will you offer? How do you create value? If you want to provide a service that clients will buy, talk to potential clients. Too many entrepreneurs plunge into their business without first talking to likely clients. If you build it first, they might not come. However, if you find out what potential clients want and what they are willing to pay for before you expend marketing effort (and dollars), you will better know with whom you will compete and how you will differentiate yourself. Find an unmet need and offer a service that fills it. When you interview people who fit your target client profile, ask what types of services they would be interested in if they were to hire a professional organizer and how much they would be willing to pay.

What existing capabilities do you have that you can build on? What skills have you mastered? Are you compassionate? Do you have good interpersonal skills, analytical skills, oral and written communication skills, motivational skills or public speaking skills? Do you have the ability to write policies and procedures? Are you computer savvy? Do you know how to sew? Are you handy with tools? Consider your work, volunteer and personal experience.

What are your deepest strengths? What is your thinking style? What are your interests? What proficiencies enable you to deliver unique value to clients? What differentiates you and gives you a competitive advantage? What is it about you that your competitors could not copy?

What existing relationships can you tap? Are you involved in an organization? Are you connected with specific groups? Do you belong to a health club, church or card club? What types of relationships have you developed that might lead you to potential clients?

What do you like to do? What floats your boat? What are you enthusiastic about? What do you do really fast? Where do you see the most dramatic improvement in your work? When do you feel content? What makes you lose track of time? When do you not mind working extra hours? No matter how much in demand your skills are, or how profitable a certain job can be, do not do it if you hate it. If it does not fit your personal desires, find something else.

Who is your competition? In order to focus on specialization, which is the key to your success in dealing with competition, plan to do some market research. Figure out where you fit in and how you might differentiate yourself from the others. Look to find out what services are being offered in your area, so that you can find a hole and fill it.

If you are like most new organizers, you will be surprised to learn that your real competition is not necessarily another professional organizer. Your potential clients are finding many ways to spend their dollars in an effort to get organized. Look in your Yellow Pages directory under any category where you would find the services you might provide, and you will get clues about the types of businesses who compete with you for clients. Go to your local library or telephone company office and obtain Yellow Pages directories for all of the neighboring communities. Do your homework and know what your challenges are.

Your competition may be another professional organizer, and of course, you will want to know who is already doing what you plan to do. If you suspect you will be competing with a professional organizer in your area, call that individual and introduce yourself. Explain your intentions and ask if they would be open to a discussion about how you might compliment each other's services and avoid competing for clients. They may already be overworked and delighted to have another professional organizer to whom to refer business.

Another way to do this type of research is to attend local NAPO meetings and conferences and get to know your colleagues. Organizers who attend these meetings are continually sharing insights about how to organize clients better. You will gain more knowledge and information by talking to other professional organizers than through any other means.

Exploring opportunities for specialization

The image that the public has of professional organizers is most likely formed by the media and from contact with people who have had experience with professional organizers. The public's view of a professional organizer is a consultant who works hands-on with clients to help them get their home, business or life organized. There are, however, multitudes of ways to put organizing skills into practice, beyond this basic understanding of the profession. Professional organizers can create all kinds of specialties in response to trends like cocooning, ergonomics, small indulgences, and technology.

Notice the current trends as you watch TV or listen to the radio. Opportunities are created as the world revolves. Home staging is a hot business, as well as silent auctions. Military personnel have businesses and families that they have left behind who need organizing assistance. As the Baby Boomer population ages, creative people in all industries are sorting out the best way to meet the needs of this generation. The ever-growing senior population represents a huge opportunity for organizers, who can assist with transitioning to smaller homes. Professional organizers have already built flourishing businesses around this group.

Most entrepreneurs pursue the hot business of the moment and chase the same markets everyone else is going after. They pay attention to what is working for others and then either duplicate it or try to improve on it. It is not necessarily sensible to reinvent the wheel, but you may miss opportunities by limiting your thinking to what has already been done. Your industry peers may be ignoring obvious markets. Consider going where the other person is not. Your rivals may be going after the big fish and missing the school of fish that just swam by.

If you can find a niche that few organizers are serving and cultivate it, you can swiftly become the expert in your specialty. Identify a market that nobody else wants to pursue, and you may have a goldmine. Opportunities for specialization exist in many different areas, and the list is growing at a fast

Chapter Four: Carving a Niche

pace. For further up to date information, you can find the Specialization Opportunities booklet, at http://www.organizingforaliving.com/docs. The document will help you to brainstorm ideas and discover some of the many ways that you can refine your own skills to create a business that has the most potential and fits you best.

If you have worked in the trenches of the corporate world, you may be drawn to that arena when defining your organizing business. You have seen large companies spend exorbitant amounts of money on outside consultants to avoid increasing head count and related costs, so you know the advantages of approaching a company as an independent contractor. Your familiarity with the ins and outs of the corporate world can be an advantage when pursuing corporate clients, especially if you have broken bread with upper management or played golf with top executives. You may be able to take advantage of your connections when seeking corporate clients.

Vast opportunities exist for professional organizers in the corporate arena. The stress and anxiety on the faces of your corporate friends and the long hours they work are evidence of the need for organization in their world. A large corporate contract could make a significant impact on your business. Just one corporate contract could potentially double (or triple) your revenues. Once you have contracted with a large firm, you have a good chance of having continued assignments, provided the company is satisfied with your work. The respect you gain within a corporation is likely to secure you as the first choice the next time that company is looking for a consultant.

There are barriers, however, to working with large corporations. There are some subtle differences between working with small privately held companies and large public firms that you must understand before deciding to make large corporate clients your specialty. Cracking the big business market is usually a slower (often frustrating) process. This discussion is intended to make you aware of some of the barriers you might encounter before you undertake a venture of this kind.

> One of the most frustrating experiences of my career was when a deal with a large corporation went sour and a good business relationship came to an abrupt end just as it seemed the contract would be finalized. After spending months developing relationships, preparing mandatory proposals and following up with executives in a large corporation, I suddenly had my phone calls go unreturned for no apparent reason. Four months later, I learned that the company had been a victim of a hostile takeover.
>
> Although I have had some very lucrative and satisfying experiences with large corporations, I have also spent a great deal of time and energy pursuing contracts that

never transpired. Sometimes it has been impossible to figure out what went wrong. Other times it was absolutely clear what happened, just as clear that the whole situation was completely unpredictable, and out of my control.

Common belief is that the big money is to be found by working with large corporations. True, you can usually command a larger fee from a company with deep pockets. Keep in mind, though, that you may spend considerable time and effort getting a large firm to actually sign a contract and hire you.

A common barrier most organizers run into is difficulty in getting to the decision maker. Unlike a small company, where the client is generally the one who authorizes payment, a large corporation has many levels of authority with a gatekeeper for each level. Unless you can get to the decision maker, it is unlikely you can get a corporation to pay for your services. A manager who is completely convinced that he needs your services might not be willing to propose the concept to the hiring authority. Doing so can be political suicide. You must get to the decision maker, which takes skillful perseverance and tenacity.

Once you reach the decision maker and develop rapport, you may find that the deal is broken after weeks or months of work on your part, simply because the person you were dealing with got promoted, transferred, or fired, and his replacement is not interested in your proposal.

Another roadblock is the nature of the decision making process in a large corporation. Policies intended to protect the company and ensure efficiency, often cause lengthy delays in finalizing a consulting contract. Unless the situation at the company is extremely urgent, it may take many months or even years to get a contract signed. Payment of your invoice could also be delayed in large companies that have standard buying contracts. Many large companies have policies prohibiting them from paying an invoice until it has reached an age of 60 days or more.

You are one of the fortunate individuals who have avoided the gatekeeper issue, if a large firm actually approached you. However, if a friend, client, or another professional organizer has not specifically referred you, beware. Being sought after by a well-known company can almost be an intoxicating experience. Be prepared and protect your interests, and do not forget the important aspects of bidding and negotiating.

Large corporations usually have stringent policies and expectations with regard to consultants and other service providers. It is important to understand the risks of working with big corporation decision makers, who are confronted with different pressures than those in small companies.

- They are accustomed to meeting with sales representatives and interviewing employees. Your initial consultation may be viewed as such a meeting.
- They are usually required to obtain multiple bids, so they are probably interviewing several of your colleagues, as well.
- They often must adhere to a policy stating that a consultant cannot be hired without a written proposal. It can take many hours for you to draft and perfect a written proposal, and you may be under pressure to divulge your best ideas in order to compete with other consultants.
- There is no guarantee that your written proposal will be reviewed or even seen by the decision-maker, who may not even have the time to take your calls.
- Corporate decision-makers are under extreme pressure to achieve company goals and stay within budget. You may ultimately lose the job to the lowest bidder.

In today's economy, big companies are constantly changing, as shareholders demand more sales and higher profits. When they are dissatisfied, the company shifts its strategy and cuts costs. The project you are bidding on may be delayed or even cancelled. Reorganizations are commonplace and changes in leadership could easily mean a change in your would-be client. These changes could be happening behind the scenes and your prospective client might not have a clue. The executive who championed your contract might find him/herself in a new job, or even jobless. Your alliance might be doomed from the start and neither of you would have any power to stop it.

A method of protection is to insist on a written request for proposal. Tell the company that you want to be sure you clearly understand its needs and expectations. If the company is not willing to provide a written request for proposal (RFP), then explain that your alternative is to charge a fee for the needs assessment and an additional fee for a written proposal. If you follow this recommendation, the worst thing that can happen is that you have spent a few minutes on the phone attempting to gain a new client who will respect you for being clear and firm about your business policies. Alternatively, you might receive a written RFP, allowing you to submit a fair bid and gain a valuable new corporate client.

Give your niche time to incubate

Once you choose your niche, drive a stake in the ground. It takes time to grow your niche, so concentrate on the conditions that promote its development. Maintain your focus, be patient and allow time to become known in your target market. Write a slogan or tag line that captures the essence of your specialty. Work your specialty into your marketing message with every opportunity. Look for creative ways to identify you with your niche. Be consistent.

New organizers often seem to be bothered by a nagging voice that says, "The other guy's specialty looks more interesting and attractive than what I'm doing." When new business people are preoccupied by thoughts such as, "the grass is greener," or "opportunities are passing me by," the tendency is to chase every opportunity that comes along. You can become obsessed with trying to figure out why the other person seems to have more clients or a better practice. From my experience, it takes time to nurture and develop a niche, and I urge new organizers to be patient during this process.

Being perceived as the person with special knowledge in your niche can be a great help in getting referrals. As you learn your trade and develop your niche, your recommendations will become increasingly valuable. Clients will come to depend on you for good advice and resources. Over time, you will come to have preferences with regard to organizing products, time and space-saving devices, and services. Keep pertinent information in a file so that you will be able to make recommendations to your clients, and be perceived as the expert.

Build a resource library that includes books, catalogues, print materials and websites that you can use to provide your clients with resources to get and stay organized. Keep a list of vendors and suppliers that you can refer to your clients to meet their organizing needs. Request catalogues from stores or manufacturers. Take them with you for client visits so that you will be able to order supplies and tools when your clients have the need. In addition to your paper files, make a folder in your browser bookmarks called *Resources*. As you find products or services to recommend to your clients, add the Web page to the Resources folder.

As you get into the flow of business, you will be aware of more and more possible jobs relating to organizing. However, over diversifying or leaping into new ventures without proper training and experience can wear your expertise thin and dilute your profits. The best way to overcome competition is to focus your energies and strengthen your own specialty.

Chapter Five: Building a Business Plan

"Vision without action is a daydream; acting without vision is a nightmare" - Japanese Proverb

Making the transition from worker to entrepreneur requires that you do the work of business planning. Build a strong foundation for your business by creating a model and getting support from every resource available to you. Planning to ensure that your business is successful is the most gratifying part of the transition, and allows you to open your mind to opportunities. This chapter introduces you to the phases of creating a functional business plan and the resources to support it.

Point the direction

A business plan lays out your key objectives and gives your business a track to run on. As Cheshire, the cat in Alice in Wonderland said, "If you do not know where you are going, any path will take you there." You would not dream of taking a road trip without a map and an itinerary. Set your business up for success and build a business plan to give your business the fuel, power and direction to achieve your deepest desires for your business.

Clarify your business vision and mission. Your journey as a business owner can be very challenging. While life as an employee can broaden your skills and perspective, someone else ultimately holds the responsibility for ensuring that the business endures. As a business owner, you are the holder of accountability for your business. All responsibility for the business rests with you. You are the primary investor, risk-taker, and decision-maker.

A clear vision will keep you on course. It forecasts the journey you are about to take and establishes a destination to reach. To clarify your vision, ask yourself, "What will it look like when I get there?" Just as you need inspiration in your personal life, you need a vision for your business. The vision you hold for your business forms the basis for you to implement your business and to overcome the obstacles of business ownership. Being clear about your desired outcome will help to shape the direction for your business.

Imagine that you have no limitations and that you can create your business any way you want. What is your vision for your ideal business? How would you describe your perfect business? What words do you want your employees and subcontractors to use to describe you and your business activities? What words or phrases would you want your clients to use in describing your business to other potential clients?

If everyone around you described you and your business with the words "dependable, gracious, superb quality, great service, high integrity" and so on, would this be helpful to you? If so, how could you direct your business activities to assure that these are the words people use when they talk about you? Here is your chance to create a self-fulfilled prophecy. The greater clarity you have with regard to this ideal description, the greater probability your business will evolve according to your desires.

With a clear vision, you can create a mission statement for your business. An effective mission statement should clearly explain why your business exists and what it hopes to achieve. Before you begin your journey into professional organizing, ask yourself "Why do I want to do this?" There are many avenues to choose from to achieve such desires as gaining independence, making more money, having your own business or finding more free time. Why professional organizing? What is your intention?

Begin the process of drafting a mission statement by answering these three key questions:

- What opportunities or needs do we address? (What is our purpose?)
- What are we doing to address these opportunities or needs? (What is our business?)
- What principals or beliefs guide our work? (What are our values?)

When developing your mission statement, be clear about your purpose. Think about what you want to accomplish with your business for your clients. Your purpose drives your mission statement and contains a measure of some kind that you can use to evaluate whether or not you have completed your mission. For instance, the initial mission statement for Bill Gates (billionaire, philanthropist, and founder of Microsoft) was "a computer on every desk and in every home." Walt Disney's mission statement was "To make people happy. Disneyland will never be completed as long as there is imagination in the world." Mary Kay's mission statement was "To give unlimited opportunity to women."

Many entrepreneurs say the purpose of their business is to make a profit. According to Peter Drucker, author of The Effective Executive, "The

Chapter Five: Building a Business Plan

purpose of a business is to create and keep a customer." This deeper concept focuses on the idea that all of the profits you make are a result of creating and keeping an adequate number of clients and serving them in a manner that produces profit for your business.

As you think about your business purpose, develop an acute client focus. Put yourself not only in their shoes, but also inside their hearts and minds, and see everything you do from your client's point of view. Your clients must be at the center of your thinking in all business activities, and they must be the focus of your business plan. Your purpose is not about you, but the client. What truly is your purpose in becoming a professional organizer? Your purpose may be to bring order into households, help people find more free time or eliminate stress in the workplace. Individualize your mission statement and make it meaningful by defining your true intent as a professional organizer.

In defining your purpose for your business, ask yourself the broad questions of how you can make a difference, contribute in a unique way and leave the world a better place. Your purpose should satisfy an inner desire. When you read your own mission statement, you should be inspired. Stephen Covey said, "The key to the ability to change is a changeless sense of who you are, what you are about and what you value." The Franklin Covey website www.FranklinCovey.com offers a wizard that takes you systematically through the process of creating a personal mission statement. This tool might be helpful in creating your business mission statement, as well.

Microsoft's current mission statement is, "To enable people and businesses throughout the world to realize their full potential." A computer on every desk and in every home might have seemed like reaching for the stars at one point. As your mission becomes more and more possible, you may look for new mountains to climb. I have already achieved several business missions in my career. The mission that inspired this book is to "provide every emerging professional organizer with the information he or she needs to implement a successful organizing business." Everything I do, from strategic planning, to marketing, to policies and procedures all have a central focus that makes it much more likely this mission will be accomplished. What is your mission for your business and your clients?

Set specific goals. The purpose of goal setting is to give you measurable guidelines and keep you from straying from the path on your journey to your success. Your journey cannot begin until you answer the question "Where do I want to go?" If you do not have well defined, written, specific goals and time-lines, there is no way to determine if you are on the right path. Be clear about what you want from your business. What does success look like to you? How will you know when you are there? Setting goals is not a complicated process. There are a number of simple questions that you can ask yourself to help you evaluate your current situation and determine your next steps. Here is a partial list:

- How much do I want to earn?
- What is important to me in terms of work-life balance?
- What values do I want to honor?
- What are my strengths that I want to build on?
- What skills do I want to develop, or master?
- In what type of environment do I want to work?
- Who do I want to work with (who is my ideal client)?
- What obstacles do I need to overcome?
- Who can assist me in achieving these goals?

Plan your strategy

A strategic plan defines the model that drives your business. It guides you in all of your decisions, from choosing your market and services, to determining major purchases and with whom you will work. Your strategic plan will help you manage your time and resources by knowing what opportunities to pursue and what offers to decline. Any decision that does not support the strategic plan is discarded.

A detailed strategic plan will help you to focus on what to accomplish that will keep you moving forward. Determine what is needed to achieve each objective and outline the specific steps of your strategic plan. Identify weaknesses to overcome and include them in your plan. If you need to take a course or attend a seminar, include that in your plan. If a mentor could provide the information and encouragement that you need, put that in your plan.

Your strategic plan should include ways to improve your services and performance continuously. Seek out ways to get feedback, both externally and internally. Create measures of performance, such as doing a job faster, or making more money. Be sure to include a time-line to keep you on schedule and provide milestones that will help to boost your morale.

Analyze your finances

How much do you have to spend and how much will it cost? Every business plan should include a break-even analysis, a screening tool for setting fees that will be explained in a later chapter. Even if your break-even analysis shows you will make more money than you need to break even, you still need to do a complete analysis before you start investing money in your business. You will need to figure out how much profit your business will generate, and whether you will have enough available cash to pay your bills when they are due.

The following are additional financial projections that should also be part of your business plan, to round out your business's financial picture.

- Profit-and-loss forecast – a month-by-month projection of the net profit your business will generate.
- Cash flow projection – a month-by-month picture of how much actual cash you will have to meet your expenses.
- Start-up cost estimate – an estimate of the total expenses you will incur before launching your business and beginning to generate revenue.

Build your career portfolio

Clients will not come knocking on your door, so you will have to build a foundation for creating your promotional materials. Gathering information and developing a portfolio is time-consuming and may not seem worthwhile now, but you will discover its value in years to come. Keeping it current and up-to-date is simple.

Set up a three-ring binder with tab dividers, and include the following information:

- Goals and interests
- Professional philosophy and guiding principals
- Resume – summarize education, achievements, work experience, skills
- Degrees, certificates, awards and honors
- Anything you have learned from self-study
- List accomplishments, both personally and professionally
- Past examples of your work
- News items that included you as the subject
- Articles you have published
- Client testimonials, glowing reviews, survey results and recommendations
- List workshops and seminars you have participated in
- List professional associations and conferences attended
- Describe volunteer or pro bono work you have completed
- List references
- Before and after photos

As your strategic business plan evolves, it is critical that you regularly evaluate your own personal and professional development. While maintaining your current proficiencies, track your efforts and make sure that you are reaching your peak potential.

Keep focused on your own professional growth. Keep learning new skills and gaining new knowledge, so you have more to offer your clients. Update your resume and keep track of your growth. What classes have you attended? Have you learned new software or tried new systems for doing things? With what professional organizations have you been involved? You should have at least two or three significant things to add to your resume every year. Set personal and professional goals and create an action plan so that you are continually developing yourself and building your value.

Put your business plan in writing

Writing an organized business plan increases the odds that you will succeed as an entrepreneur. It will help you compete in the marketplace and anticipate potential problems so you can solve them before they become catastrophes. Writing down all of the information that makes up a business plan may seem unnecessary, and you may be tempted to skip this exercise. The more care and attention you devote to your business plan, the more successful your business will be. Thoughtful planning and research will save you from having to reinvent your business down the road.

The main purpose of this plan is to define the roadmap for your business journey. It does not matter whether you handwrite this information in a journal, capture it in an electronic document, or print and bind it in a binder. Choose a format that works best for you. Since sharing this information with bankers or other business partners probably will not be required, do not worry too much about proper wording or grammar. Pay closer attention to what you want to see happen in your business this year and in the next five years. Evaluate your plan on a regular basis and use it to build your action lists. Your business plan will keep you focused and help you to stay on track.

What goes into a business plan? The body of a simple business plan can be divided into four main sections:

- Description of the business
- Marketing plan
- Financial management plan
- Management plan

Chapter Five: Building a Business Plan

Use the following model as a guide when developing the business plan for your business, or use the Organizing For A Living Workbook, which can be found at http://www.organizingforaliving.com/docs.

Business description: Answer the question "What business am I in?" How would others describe you? When describing your business, explain the business form (sole proprietorship, partnership, corporation) and the licenses and permits you will need. Describe your services and their benefits. What is different about your services? Why will your business be profitable? What growth opportunities exist? Why do you want to be in business? Identify where you will locate your business, why, and how the state and local laws affect the location of your business. Clearly identify goals and objectives.

Marketing plan: Develop a strategy that you can use as an ongoing initiative to market and promote your services. Identify the clients who are most likely to purchase your services by their age, gender, income, educational level, residence, interests, etc. Describe how you will attract, hold and increase your market. Define your pricing strategy. Devise a plan for promoting your services. Develop short descriptive copy with catchy phrases to arouse the interest of your clients that clearly identifies your services. Start a file of each of your five nearest direct competitors. What are their strengths and weaknesses? How will you distinguish yourself? What sets your business apart from your competition? Include their promotional materials and pricing, describe their strengths and weaknesses, and explain how they operate their businesses.

Financial management plan: Your financial management plan has several components:

- **Start-up budget** – Plan a realistic budget by determining the actual amount of money needed to open your business and keep it open, including equipment costs, deposits and down payments, licenses and permits, insurance, membership fees, supplies, promotions, etc.
- **Operating budget** – Reflect your priorities in terms of how you will spend your money, the expense you will incur, including insurance, promotions, legal and accounting, supplies, dues and subscriptions, repairs and maintenance, etc.
- **Gross revenues** – Describe how you will meet those expenses (income). Do not skip this step or wait until your business is going well to think about gross revenues. Without a goal and a plan, it probably will not get to that point. If you are clear about how much you want to make, you can make things happen. Take control of your business and be specific

about how much your gross revenues and business owner's compensation will be.

- **Balance sheet** – List assets (cash, bank accounts, anything of value that is owned or legally due the business, equipment and furniture) and liabilities (debts, monetary obligations, accounts, loans and notes payable), and include your personal financial statement.
- **Break-even analysis** – What is your break-even point? How is it calculated?

Management plan: Describe how you will manage your business. Managing your business requires more than just the desire to be your own boss. How well you manage your business is the cornerstone of every successful business venture. It demands dedication, persistence, the ability to make decisions and the ability to manage finances. Set the foundation and facilitate the success of your business by answering questions such as: How will your background and/or business experience help you in this business? What are your weaknesses and how will you compensate? How will you obtain assistance? Will you hire employees or independent contractors? How will you compensate them? How will they acquire the necessary skills and training? Address the accounting system you will be using. How will you handle daily administrative details? Begin to capture and document operating procedures in this section.

Form a support team

Powerful people have help in every area of their life, and they surround themselves with the right resources. When planning for your business success, be sure to ask yourself "Who will I take with me?" and "Who will help me get to my desired destination?" First, get the cooperation of your spouse and children. Plan to get them involved in the business and reward them accordingly with payment.

It is wise to form an informal advisory board for your business that you can draw upon when needed. Concentrate on the gaps in your skills and knowledge, and recruit advisors that will fill them. Your advisory board will probably include someone with financial, legal, marketing and general business expertise. Advisors do not have any legal responsibilities to your company. They simply provide advice. Do not be too concerned about compensating your advisors, because they will probably enjoy mentoring you as a spare-time activity. You can usually persuade advisors to join your advisory board by offering them a free lunch or dinner, or providing a retreat setting for your meetings.

Chapter Five: Building a Business Plan

You can start with your current brain trust, or you can find advisors through SCORE (Service Corps of Retired Executives).

> Figen Genco is a professional organizer who was featured by SCORE in one of their Success Story articles. Formerly from Turkey, she moved to the United States and launched her organizing business, Genco Organizes, in 2001 with the assistance of SCORE volunteer counselors. Besides helping her register her company name, secure insurance, and develop brochures and business cards, the SCORE volunteers provided encouragement and support.

Another great way to get advice and support is to join or start a mastermind group or action team of like-minded individuals to facilitate brainstorming, support and accountability. In his book, *Think and Grow Rich*, Napoleon Hill introduced the concept of a mastermind group as "The coordination of knowledge and effort of two or more people, who work toward a definite purpose, in the spirit of harmony." Participants in a mastermind group challenge each other to create and implement goals. The group gives you feedback, helps brainstorm ideas, and sets up structures to hold you accountable and keep you focused.

If you plan to form a mastermind group, choose people who have a similar interest, skill or success level, have the desire to reach their goals, and are passionate about their business. You will be sharing your successes and explaining how you achieved them. You may not want to include anyone in your group that you see as competition. You want others to celebrate with you and encourage your success, and not to feel jealous or steal your ideas. The more you are able to share freely with others, the more you will benefit from the group.

Determine the number of people to allow in your group (3-4 is a good minimum; 5-8 is a recommended maximum). New members should only be allowed into the group by unanimous consent of the existing members. Make sure every member is committed and willing to give and ask for help and support. One slacker or inactive member will kill the energy level for the entire group. Be prepared to ask a member who is not fully participating to leave the group.

The mastermind group can have a face-to-face meeting or meet via a teleconference. You can meet once a month, once a week, or once a quarter, although meeting every week or two is optimal to keep the momentum going. You can take turns chairing the group; all you need is a regular agenda. The function of the chairperson is to enforce the rules established by the group. Here are some examples of group rules:

- All discussions must be treated as confidential
- Crosstalk is not allowed while another is sharing

Examples of agenda items are:
- Each person reports on his progress since the last meeting and gets feedback from the group
- Each person tells what he has done in his business that has been effective
- Each person commits to something specific that he will do before the next meeting
- Each person can ask the group for help, in terms of leads, encouragement, resources, ideas, etc.

When you participate in a mastermind group, you will give and receive support from your accountability partners. You will get the unique perspectives of each member of your group, and you will gain enormous insights for improving your business.

Chapter Six: Developing Your Business Identity

"Nothing succeeds like the appearance of success" - Christopher Lasch

Your identity or *brand* tells your prospective client whether he will approve of you before he even meets you. Your professional identity can be defined in very simple terms:

- Your background: how you were trained, your credentials, your education
- Your conduct: how you meet your obligations, how you follow through on your promises
- Your appearance and mannerisms: how you present yourself to the public; the way you walk, talk and dress
- How you work with and treat your clients: your presentation skills, the way you negotiate
- How you appear to other professional organizers

Your prospective client really does not care how you look, how many awards you have won, or whom you have worked with. What is of importance to the client is whether you are successful, whether he can trust you, whether you will understand his needs, and whether you will do a good job for him.

Branding strategies

A brand is the way you are identified and recognized. It is not your name and logo, but the perception that comes to mind when a person hears your name or sees your logo. It is the impression people have of you. It is the way you convey your values, benefits and personality. Branding is more than a buzzword. Your brand is your unwritten covenant with your client. It is about the expectations people have when they hear your name. When people hear *Disney*, they expect wholesome entertainment. If you read a *For Dummies* book, you expect a lighthearted, down-to-earth approach to an otherwise complex topic.

Branding is not just for large corporations. It is for small businesses and solo practitioners, as well. As a business professional, you are your own brand. Your style, character, predictability, and sense of purpose all contribute to your brand. Your brand involves the values that make you love your business. Your brand is impossible to communicate quickly, but it has clear and lasting implications about how you conduct business.

Brand development is not a requirement for starting your business, but neglecting to develop a brand can have serious consequences. The brand that evolves without your awareness may not be the identity you intended. If you do not brand yourself, others will. It is human nature to typecast. Cultivating a strategic brand statement and building your business around it puts you in the driver's seat, so that everything you do in your business forms the perceptions others have about you.

A strategic brand statement provides guidance for your business. Work on developing your brand before you develop your service, alliances, communications, etc. Focus on visibility and impact, not relevance. When developing your brand, ask your friends, colleagues, and clients how they see you. When you get a referral, ask what the person who referred the client said about you. Make a list of your strengths, skills, and professional traits, and compare them to what others have said about you.

One of the most important questions to ask about branding is, "Who cares?" besides you, of course. Keep in mind that in addition to your expertise, your clients are investing in the sense of security you give them through your sense of confidence. As you envision your brand, include your prospective client and your client's needs. List the values that are and will always be associated with your brand. Develop a strong personal identity based on what you stand for, what you stand against, your talents and skills, how you are unique, what you believe in, and what you do not believe in, what you will do, what you will not do, etc. Ultimately, this translates into how other people will feel about your capabilities, attributes and performance and how they judge your worth.

Self-branding can make the difference between a professional who is doing relatively well and one who is doing exceptionally well. A strong brand helps you to be noticed and remembered, and helps you stand out in a crowd. Once you define your brand strategy, stick to it. Consistent and repetitive exposure to a brand tells prospective clients that you are successful and professional. Each time they see your name, hear you speak, or come across your website, your message will work its way into their hearts, forming positive impressions.

Chapter Six: Developing Your Business Identity

Naming your business

Your business name is usually your first introduction to potential clients. It should reflect the purpose and nature of your business. You can use your given name (Suzie Smith, Professional Organizer); of course, but using a business name rather than your own appears more professional to many potential clients. Give careful thought to selecting a name for your business, and consider the following:

- Choose a name that is easy to spell, pronounce and remember.
- Choose a name that is descriptive and captures the nature of your business; eliminate any doubt about what you do.
- Choose a name that appeals not only to you, but also to the kind of clients you are trying to attract.
- Choose a name that distinguishes you from your competition and features a benefit of your niche.
- Choose a name that gets clients to respond to you on an emotional level.
- There are riches in niches but be wary of a title that is overly specific – Ruth's Pantry Organizing may be problematic if Ruth decides to branch out into general kitchen organizing.
- Give considerable thought to adding a geographic tone to your company name. Geographic names can sometimes be limiting. A name identifying you as a local business can sometimes give you more credibility with clients. Violet Canyon Professional Organizers is a great business name if you plan to limit your practice to the Violet Canyon area. However, before choosing a name such as Violet Canyon Professional Organizers, think about whether you might ever want to expand your business beyond the Violet Canyon area.
- Looking big has advantages, especially to vendors when you are trying to establish credit.
- A dry, corporate-sounding name might imply you do not personally care about your clients' needs.
- Avoid long or complicated names that can be difficult to remember.
- It is okay to make up a word or combine two words or partial words to make a name (it worked pretty well for Bill Gates), but check out the spelling and pronunciation with a few trusted friends to make sure it will be correctly interpreted.
- Unless your target market is children, avoid cutesy names.
- If you are certain you will be working solo, you can include your own name in your company name.
- Use *Inc.* in your name only if you are incorporated.

Finding the right name can be challenging and it is quite common for organizers to change their business name a year or two after they have started their business and figured out their niche. Changing your name can be expensive and sometimes awkward. Select your name and try it out for a few weeks to see how it feels before registering it and ordering business cards.

Test your name with friends, family, colleagues and potential clients. Ask people what they think of the name you have chosen for your business, and notice how you feel about the name as you go through this process. If the name you select for your business does not cause pride or excitement for you, do not force the issue. It would be better to operate as a sole proprietor under your given name for a while until you are sure of a name.

Before deciding on a name for your company, check to see if a matching domain name on the Internet is available. Once you settle on a name, check with your state governing agencies to avoid duplicating an existing name or using a trademarked name. Along with a name, you might want to choose a tag line or slogan that further describes or draws attention to your business. For instance, the tag line for my business, Organizing Systems, Inc. is *Our business is organizing your business.*

Designing your distinctive mark

Choosing your business colors: Make sure the colors you choose are consistent with the image you are trying to convey. Choose colors that fit your business and the audience you would like to attract. Some colors carry an air of power and authority, while others signify peace, encouragement, confidence or success. To learn the meaning of your favorite colors, try an Internet keyword search on the words color, meaning, and association.

> From what I learned about color associations at a Chamber of Commerce meeting many years ago, I chose the colors red, black and gray for my business — red for strength, black for authority, and gray for balance.

The use of bright colors goes a long way in business, but only in small doses. The use of too much color or many different colors may lower your perceived professionalism.

Printing stationery in full color (four-color printing) can be very expensive. Two colors can look great, so if you are on a budget, try to build your color scheme around two colors. Whatever colors you choose, make sure that a black and white reproduction will look good in print, such as newspapers or the Yellow Pages.

Chapter Six: Developing Your Business Identity

Designing your business logo: A logo is a special symbol that identifies and distinguishes your company. Your logo is your visual identity. A logo may be quite influential if it conveys a professional image. The benefit of a logo is the unique look you can create for your business that makes you stand out from the crowd. Your logo goes on everything, including:

Business cards	Web site pages
Advertising	Projected presentations
Polo or t-shirts	Invoices
Letterhead and envelopes	Brochure

A logo could simply be your company name in a special font (like Coca Cola). In fact, your name portrayed in an elegant font may be the most desirable logo. You may have an idea of a graphic design that depicts your style or service, or your company name may have characteristics that resemble a certain graphic. Do not get too hung up on the design. You can easily change your logo, as long as you do not go overboard with stationery and other logo products.

Generic symbols are available through companies that print business stationery and forms. Although they are free, it may be difficult to find a generic symbol that accurately portrays what you do. Consider also that the purpose of a logo is to provide a visual identity, and generic symbols do nothing to differentiate your company.

Consider hiring a graphic designer or a graphic design student to help you design a logo. Your local printer may know a graphic artist who can help you with a design, or he may have a graphic designer on his staff. Alternatively, try searching on the Internet for a designer. If you cannot afford to pay a designer, try playing with a design on your own. My own company logo came about one day when my son, Bill and I were tinkering around with Microsoft Paint. We created a prototype in about twenty minutes. I sent it to my cousin's husband, a graphic designer, who finalized the design.

Most graphic designers will offer you several logo designs from which to choose. Be sure to get both a camera-ready copy and a digital copy of your final choice, and ask for color separation if your logo uses two colors, in order to save money when printing in quantity. Make sure the images are in a format that your printing company can handle. Ask the printing specialist in what format you should deliver graphics files. If you are scanning images, ask what resolution should be used.

Take special care to protect your artwork. A printed copy of camera-ready art will not produce good quality printed materials unless you are prepared to pay extra for the printer to clean up and manipulate the reproduction. Keep your artwork in a safe place to keep the print quality high and the prices low.

Be prepared to live with your business colors and logo for a long time. When you get tired of it, celebrate. Your boredom with your business logo, letterhead and business card is an indication that it is becoming familiar and recognizable. That is a very good thing when it comes to your business identity

Designing business cards and stationery: Avoid being too elaborate and presenting too much detail when designing your stationery. In this industry, the image you want to convey is one of organization and simplicity. Make sure your letterhead is uncluttered and professional looking. Be consistent in the way that you present your image to the public. If any piece looks like it came from a different company, your prospective clients will not easily recognize you.

Make sure your business card reflects your business purpose and identity. Your logo, if you have one, or an eye-catching graphic illustrating what you do, can make your business card memorable. Alongside your name, include a clear, concise positioning statement or tag line.

Keep your card simple, legible and informative. Overcrowding your business card with information might cause your potential clients to wonder about your ability to help them with their clutter. The most important information to include on your business card is your name, company name, phone number (including area code), URL (yourname.com) and email address. If you include other phone numbers on your business card, such as your fax or mobile phone number, be sure to put your main number in larger, bold text, so that it stands out.

- Maximize the functionality of your business card and look for creative ways for turning your business card into a mini-brochure. There are many ways to vary the look of your card, make it unique, and add to its functionality. Here are a few ideas (but do not try to use them all):
- Fold-over cards work well as mini-brochures; use the inside to describe your services.
- Do not waste space. Take advantage of the backside for additional information about you or your company. List your services, useful tips, your guarantee, client testimonial, your philosophy, etc.
- Add graphics that illustrate what you do.
- Modify the shape of the card, use a nonstandard size, use unusual material, or print your information vertically if your audience is likely to transfer your contact information into a computerized address book. (If

your audience is likely to keep and file your business card, stick with a standard card and a horizontal design.)
- Add your portrait or a photo of you at work.
- Have some sort of an enticement or coupon printed on the back of your business card.

Choosing a printing company: Do not rush into printing large quantities of business cards, or spend so much on your printed materials that you do not have enough money to publicize your business. It is easy to allow yourself to become wrapped up in looking like a business. Before you end up with boxes of useless stationery, take the time to complete your business plan and be clear about your niche. It is also wise to get an Internet domain name established before having business stationery printed, so that you can have the URL printed on all of your materials.

In the interim when you need something visual to give your clients and prospects, create brochures, letterhead, and business cards on your computer and print small quantities. Stationery templates can be created in your word processing software. You can design and print flyers and brochures from your own computer using inexpensive software, like PrintMaster®. You can also have business cards printed for free (www.vistaprint.com, and others).

When you have settled on your niche, color scheme and logo, registered your URL, and created a website, you are ready to order professionally printed materials. Although it may seem economical to do it yourself, outsourcing the printing of your business cards and stationery may turn out to be the best option. Unless your expertise happens to be commercial printing and you own a high-end printer, the expenses of a print shop could be cheaper in the end than the costs of equipment and the time you spend learning on the job. Commercial printing produces high quality, an essential component when you are trying to make a good impression.

You can search for a printer through the Internet or Yellow Pages, or ask for recommendations of reputable printers from your friends and associates. Printers can specialize in many areas. Some printers specialize in stationery, brochures and postcards, while others focus on books or newsletters. Some printers are suited to handle many different print jobs, while others outsource jobs when they do not have the proper equipment. Giving all of your print jobs to one printer may not be the best option. Your main goal is to match your print job to the printer who gives the best quality at the lowest price.

Setup costs have always remained the same regardless of the quantity, with the first copy costing almost as much as printing thousands. However, today's advanced technology has made it possible to produce small quantities of high-quality color products at affordable prices. Companies are now offering reasonable pricing for short runs, allowing you to reap the benefits of digital printing and only pay for what you need.

Online printers are more convenient to choose than local printers are, and they can save you money because they only do business online. You send your printing requirements and specifications online, and they deliver the printed outputs directly to your homes or offices. Even though online printing companies can offer affordable prices, local printers are more preferable when you are concerned about quality.

When using local printers, always visit the printers and talk to their representatives about printing rates, turnaround times, etc. If you visit the print shops in person, you can get a feel for the people and the service. You can show them what you want to produce and view actual samples. Proposals vary when shopping around by phone, because your order is subject to interpretation (unless you know printing terms and jargon). To get good quality printing without spending a fortune, get printing quotes in person. The quotes you end up with will be more realistic.

Develop a relationship so that you feel confident asking your printer for recommendations. Your printing company knows what costs extra and what produces about the same result at a lower cost. Ask for advice about paper size and type, and the number of inks being used. Get explanations for terms like bleed, offset lithography and gravure printing. Whatever your desired result, ask about the most efficient and cost-effective way to produce it.

Your stationery and business card may be the first impression of your company, so do not skimp on quality. Use good quality paper with the right weight and texture to express the integrity of your company image. The feel of the paper is often the first thing noticed. Paper is the largest part of a printer's expense, so always ask about reducing paper waste. One color is always going to be least expensive to print, so if you are planning on a two-color print job, ask whether having your work printed on colored stock would save money.

Building your Internet presence

Almost every viable business today has a website, and there is no more powerful way to convey your business image than through your presence on the Internet. Taking full advantage of everything the Internet has to offer you as a small business takes careful planning.

Choosing your domain name and email address: If you want people to notice you, you need the right domain name, or URL and email address.

Chapter Six: Developing Your Business Identity

The right domain name can make the difference between being memorable and being lost in cyberspace. Registering a domain name (yourcompany.com) is the first step in creating your website. You can ask your Web designer to help you with this, but it is easy to do it yourself. You do not need to know anything about HTML or Web page design to register your domain name. When you register a domain name, you specify the person to contact and assign a password. Doing it yourself ensures you will have complete control.

Registering your domain name is similar to purchasing a product on the Internet, and costs are minimal. Go to www.netsol.com, or type *domain names* in your search engine (Google, Yahoo, etc.), to find dozens of companies where you can register a domain. If your business name is not an available URL, choose a URL that will get attention and be easy to remember. Most domain registries have tools for searching for a suitable URL.

Once you register a domain name, you will be able to set up a dedicated email account to use exclusively for your business. This makes it easier to separate your personal email from your business email and gives a better impression to your clients. Do not use yourname@hotmail.com if you want your clients to take you seriously.

Designing your website: Your website can be your most effective marketing tool. Even though your business may be small, the Internet helps to level the playing field. In fact, you have an advantage over large companies, since your website is more personal and interesting than the big corporate site. You may assume that the Internet has little value to you because you must provide your services in person, but a website does not have to have an emphasis on e-commerce. Even if you do not process business transactions over the Internet, your website can be a virtual brochure that you can continually update without spending a lot of money. Your prospective clients can have unlimited access to information about you and your business.

A compelling website for a professional organizer will grab attention, create interest, and get the visitor to take action. Your website design can be as simple or as complex as you want to make it. The more advanced the site, the more it will cost in money and time to create and maintain. Your website can virtually be a business card, a brochure, or part of your sales team. It can give more information than a static brochure, and can allow your readers to select the information they want to see. Your website can provide your contact information and verify you are in business, or it can pre-qualify prospects, present solutions and close sales. It can do just about anything in between.

If you collect a deposit for your services or offer products, you can set up your site so that clients can pay by using a variety of payment methods. If you do set up your site to take private information from your clients, like charge cards or phone numbers, make sure that you can process the information reliably. Ensure that your site and the information sent to you are secure, and make sure the visitors to your site are aware that it is protected.

If you do not want to learn how to build your own site, you can hire a professional to develop your website, or check with your local community college to find students who are learning to build websites. Another option if you do not want to learn HTML is to find someone who can create your website in Adobe (formerly Macromedia) Dreamweaver, and then maintain the content yourself using Adobe Contribute software. Contribute lets you keep you website content current and relevant with up-to-date information without having to be a Web design expert.

If you develop your own site, you will be using Web authoring software to write HTML, the code that formats Web pages. Creating a website is easier than ever with several options available to build your own basic website on a budget. Your ISP as a part of your contract may offer site building software that is easy to use and makes learning HTML unnecessary.

You can use free Web authoring software like Netscape Composer. If you are comfortable with Microsoft products, you may prefer Microsoft FrontPage. If you have used graphic design software before, you may prefer Adobe Dreamweaver. FrontPage has a shorter learning curve, while Dreamweaver writes cleaner HTML code.

Plan your site: You will actually need two plans for your website. The first plan defines how your site will look and feel to your visitors. The second plan defines what information the site will contain and how it will be arranged. Unlike printed documents, a website will constantly change and grow, so carefully plan your initial design to allow for expansion. Storyboard your site, or draw a flowchart of all of the pages you intend to have on your site.

The first page or *homepage* creates the first impression and matters the most. The homepage sets the tone for the rest of the site and introduces your business to your visitors. Design your first page to load efficiently for all connection speeds. Make sure your visitor does not have to wait too long for flash animations or graphics to load.

To be effective, make your site pleasant to look at, easy to understand and fun for clients to navigate. You can get your creative juices flowing and learn how to use the Internet to your advantage by surfing the Internet to see what other organizers and consultants are doing. Type the words that describe your niche into a search engine. For example, if you specialize in closet organizing, search for the phrase *closet organizing*. Spend some time reviewing the websites you find, and take notes about what you like and do not like about the sites you visit.

Try to create an interesting and involving site to give visitors a reason to return. Make their experience both educational and interactive. Provide basic and essential information, along with a clear explanation of your service that makes it unique. Include success stories or case studies to help your visitors relate to your services. Imagine that you are giving your visitor a chance to see you in action and include information that will impress them.

Do not be a copycat. Using another website to get ideas for developing your own is okay, but copying someone else's words (or graphics) and using them as your own is plagiarism. Besides, you want to be the leader, not the follower in your specialty. Use your research to get ideas, and then do some serious strategic planning to build your own unique site.

Once you decide on the initial design for your site, determine how your visitors will navigate it. Navigation is a group of links or buttons that lead to other pages of the site, and back to the homepage. It should be easy to understand and important pages should be easy to reach with relatively few clicks.

However you design your site, make sure that it is consistent so that your visitors will easily find their way around. Pick a palette of colors and a theme. Choose from typefaces that are available on the Web. Once you have ideas, sketch each page of your site on a separate piece of paper. Lay all of the pages out on a table or the floor and imagine you are a visitor. Can you find your way around?

Choose your website host: Once your website is complete, you will need to find a host. Be choosy about who hosts your site. Find a reputable Web host or Internet Service Provider (ISP) to ensure that your site will be up and running 24/7 without fail. If you know a computer professional or small business owner in your area, ask who is hosting his website and whether he is satisfied. You can compare dozens of host servers by typing, *Web hosting* in your search engine. The cost involved with hosting your website varies (as does the quality of service), and it is usually billed on a monthly basis.

You will need to update and maintain your website. Again, you can hire a professional to do this or do it yourself with a little bit of training. It is best to do it yourself so that you can easily update your website periodically without having to go through a third party. It is important to communicate timely and accurate information about your business to your potential clients.

Optimize your site for search engines: A key factor in the effectiveness of a business website is making it easy for clients to find you. Many clients search online for local merchants they can buy from in their geographic region. Make sure that your website is showing up on Internet searches for your potential client's location.

Using your browser, do a search and make sure that your information is accurate and up-to-date. Search for your business, the services you offer, and any other keywords that you think potential clients may search. Consider adding your business listing to a local search engine to make sure your services get noticed. Some local search engines offer options to enhance your listing for better placement, which may be worth the nominal fee. A list of local search engines is available at www.localsearchguide.org/index.html

Developing your phone personality

A popular topic of conversation today is phone etiquette. Everyone seems to have a complaint about automated attendants, cell phone jabbers and abuse of the hold button. Who has not been stuck in *voicemail jail* at one time or another? Have you ever placed a call from your cell phone and been greeted by, "Will you please hold?" Have you ever been placed on hold, despite the fact that you did not even have a chance to respond?

The call you receive from a potential client may be your only chance to make a good first impression. Anyone who answers your business phone should be trained in phone etiquette. A cheerful hello followed by your company name and your first name helps callers feel welcome and makes it easy for them to initiate a conversation with you. If you are sharing your residential line for both business and personal calls, instruct everyone in the household to answer "Good morning/afternoon. How may I help you?"

As your business grows, you will find that you seem to be answering the same types of questions repeatedly, including:

- What do you do?
- What do your charge?
- How do you work?
- How long will it take?
- Do I need to prepare anything?
- Do you throw things out?
- Do I need to be there when you are working?

Chapter Six: Developing Your Business Identity

Preparing an FAQ sheet (frequently asked questions) may help you and anyone who answers your phone respond to client inquiries. Have your schedule available, and be prepared to describe your services and discuss your rates. It may also be helpful to create a form to use with callers while on the phone with them. A form will help you to remember to collect critical information, such as a caller's email address.

Courtesy and efficiency of employees is often overlooked in business. The way employees deal with clients over the phone may some day be a concern for you. The importance of how your company is represented over the phone cannot be overemphasized. My relationship with a longtime client was seriously jeopardized when my employee mishandled a phone call. I had been very satisfied with this employee, and she was always cheerful and cooperative with me. I was stunned when my client reported to me that she did not seem to be concerned about his problem. He said she did not follow up as she had promised to do, and was rude when he called to check on the status. It was embarrassing to me to discover that my client doubted how valuable he was to my company.

Teaching an employee to greet callers properly is only the beginning of training. Each employee must be equipped to give the caller what he needs. Employees must have an understanding of your products and services. They should learn to distinguish between a valuable prospect and the time hog that never books an appointment but takes up precious time getting free advice. Employees should be equipped to refer a client elsewhere if appropriate. They should be trained to inform callers properly when their call will be put on hold or transferred, and to give them an option to leave a message in voicemail, call back or receive a return call. Any follow up agreed upon must be completed – messages delivered, research finished, callbacks noted, appointments scheduled.

Chapter Seven: Structuring Your Business Ownership

"Only those who dare to fail greatly can ever achieve greatly" - Robert F. Kennedy

Before you open a bank account, choose a name, or sign an agreement for phone service, decide how you will legally structure your company. The type of business entity you choose will depend on three primary factors: liability, taxation, and record keeping. Your form of business determines your level of personal liability and your ability to raise money. This decision will also have an impact on which income tax return form you have to file and the amount of paperwork your business will be required to do.

Proper business entity structuring minimizes your risks and maximizes tax strategies. Protecting your business is important and choosing the proper business entity is not a decision to make without sound counsel from business experts. Your attorney or CPA will be able to answer any questions that you have and help you determine the best business structure for your business. While I am neither an attorney nor a CPA and your own advisors should guide you, I will give you a brief overview of the basic differences between the forms of business ownership to get you thinking about your options. The information in this chapter will help you make an initial evaluation of different options available.

Sole Proprietor

If you will be operating your business and performing services by yourself, the simplest and most common form of business structure is a Sole Proprietorship. A sole proprietorship is a business that is owned by one individual and that is not registered with the state as a corporation or limited liability company (LLC). No organizational documents are needed in a Sole Proprietorship, and the owner has the freedom to operate the business in whatever way he or she chooses. The Sole Proprietorship is useful for consulting and service-oriented businesses. An independent contractor who is not on an employer's regular payroll is automatically a sole proprietor.

As a sole proprietor, you may have to comply with local registration, business license, or permit laws to make your business legitimate. All you need to do is register your name with the appropriate local, county or state office, pay any required fees, and obtain a local license (if required). Once you have obtained the necessary permits and registered your business name, you are in business.

As a sole proprietor, you own the assets of your business and profits or losses are considered part of your personal income. In the eyes of the government, you and your business are the same; the business has no existence apart from you, the owner. You report the income and expenses of the business on your own personal tax return. The Sole Proprietorship does not protect you from personal liability. You undertake the risks of the business for all assets owned, whether used in the business or personally owned.

When you are a sole proprietor, you work for yourself, and you alone control the business. You usually work by yourself as well, but you do have the option as a sole proprietor of hiring employees or subcontracting freelance organizers. Sole proprietorship is the simplest and least expensive way to run a business. An attorney is not required to file papers on your behalf. Funds can easily be transferred between business and personal bank accounts. You do not necessarily need an accountant to do your taxes, and bookkeeping requirements are simple. If your business is home-based, there can be tax advantages to being a sole proprietor.

You will have to handle all of your own income taxes as a self-employed business owner, which means you will have to set aside money to pay your tax bill each year. Since you will not have taxes withheld, as you did when you worked for someone else and filled out a W-4, you must pay estimated taxes on a quarterly schedule. If you pay less than you owe in any quarter, you may owe a penalty, even if you pay the difference before year-end. Your income may be unpredictable, so it may be wise to work with a tax advisor to do your calculations.

At tax time, you fill out a (one-page) profit and loss statement (Schedule C) and a statement of your company's property (Form 4562) and attach to your federal income tax return. The SIC code you will use is 738936 – Organizing Services-Household and Business. You will pay quarterly estimated taxes (Form 1040-ES) on your expected income, because you will not have an employer to withhold and pay the taxes for you. You must pay self-employment taxes (Social Security and Medicare) on top of regular income taxes (Schedule SE). If you are currently employed, your employer pays half of your Social Security and Medicare, but as a self-employed person, you will pay the full amount. You will not have an employer to pay unemployment insurance on your behalf, nor would you qualify to collect unemployment.

Dissolving a sole proprietorship is easy. When you want your business to stop functioning, if you become seriously ill and stop working, or when you die, your business simply ceases to exist.

Federal tax form requirements for a Sole Proprietor:

- Pay estimated taxes on Form 1040-ES Estimated Tax for Individuals
- File Schedule C, Profit or Loss From Business, with your Form 1040 tax return
- File Form 4562, Depreciation and Amortization, with your Form 1040 tax return
- File Form 8829, Expenses for Business Use of Your Home with your Form 1040 tax return
- File Schedule SE, Self-Employment Tax, with your Form 1040 tax return

General Partnership

A Partnership is formed when two or more persons contribute money, property, labor, or skill, and share in the profits or losses of a business. Partnerships are like Sole Proprietorships in that no written documents are required and each of the partners has unlimited personal liability for all business transactions and obligations. Partners in a General Partnership must come to an agreement with regard to the operation of the business. In addition, each partner has unlimited liability for all partners and for the acts of each partner.

Next to Sole Proprietorship, Partnerships have the simplest tax structure. A Partnership must file an annual information return to report the income, deductions, gains, losses etc., from its operations, but it does not pay income tax. Instead, it passes through any profits or losses to its partners. Each partner includes his or her share of the Partnership's income or loss on his or her tax return.

Compared to a sole proprietorship, it costs significantly more to form a Partnership, due to attorney and accounting fees. An agreement must be written covering all of the details of the Partnership. A Partnership can be formed by a verbal agreement, but a written legal agreement is preferable for several reasons. Each state has its own uniform rules governing Partnerships.

Your state will control many aspects of your Partnership unless you set out different rules in a written Partnership agreement. A written legal agreement establishes guidelines for working together and making decisions. A partner may eventually want to separate from the business, and a legal agreement detailing the provisions for dividing assets can save a lot of aggravation. Your attorney can create, or at least review your Partnership agreement to assure that the agreement protects all parties.

The following issues should be considered when creating a Partnership agreement:

- The amount of equity to be invested by each partner, i.e., who is going to contribute cash, property or services to the business
- What ownership percentage each partner will have
- How profit or loss and draws will be divided and distributed
- Compensation levels and associated details for each partner
- Authority for payment of expenses and disbursement of profits
- How business decisions will be made
- How the business will be managed, who will deal with clients, who will deal with vendors and suppliers, who will deal with the government, who will keep the books, who will supervise employees and subcontractors
- Guidelines for admitting new partners
- Procedures for settling disputes
- Guidelines for modification, disillusionment, death or incapacitation of a partner

Except in rare cases, partnerships should be used only when an LLC cannot be established.

Limited Liability Company (LLC)

A Limited Liability Company (LLC) is a relatively new business structure allowed by state statute. An LLC provides personal liability protection from business debts without the complexity and expense of forming a corporation.

LLCs not only help separate your business from your personal property and money, they also provide some flexibility with management and taxes. By operating as a Limited Liability Company, you have less personal liability than a Partnership, and a more flexible tax structure than a Corporation. An LLC is similar to a standard Partnership from a tax perspective, in that owners report income and expenses on their personal tax returns. It is a separate entity for asset protection purposes.

An LLC is more flexible and easier to establish than a Corporation, but more complex than that of a general partnership. LLCs must file articles of organization. LLCs are popular because, similar to a corporation, owners have limited personal liability for the debts, actions, and obligations of the business. The law provides owners of LLCs with what is called *limited personal liability* for business obligations. This means that owners of LLCs can normally keep their houses, investments, and other personal property even if their business fails.

Other features of LLCs are more like partnerships, providing management flexibility and the benefit of pass-through taxation. LLCs can only have two (or less) of the four corporate characteristics (limited liability to the extent of assets, continuity of life, centralization of management and free transferability of ownership interests).

Participants (owners) in an LLC are called Members, and all are on equal footing. Since most states do not restrict ownership, members may include individuals, corporations, other LLCs and foreign entities. There is no maximum number of members. Most states also permit single member LLCs; those having only one owner. Check your state's requirements and federal tax regulations for further information.

C-Corporation

A C-Corporation is a legal entity that is completely separate from you, the owner. The corporation can own assets, incur liabilities, and provide goods and services to the public. A corporation is managed and controlled by the board of directors. Every Corporation starts out as a C-Corporation and remains so unless it makes a Subchapter S-Corporation election. The primary reason for incorporating is usually to limit personal liability and protect personal assets. Normally, you as an owner can keep your house, investments, and other personal property if the business fails.

There can be other advantages of incorporating. Some companies will not hire a sole proprietor, because they do not want to get involved in the issues and risks associated with employees versus independent contractors. If you have to raise capital, incorporating may ease this process. Corporate shares are more attractive to investors than unincorporated businesses. Because it is a separate legal entity, a C-Corporation can continue even after your death.

In forming a C-Corporation, prospective shareholders exchange money, property, or both, for the corporation's capital stock. A C-Corporation generally takes the same deductions as a sole proprietorship to figure its taxable income. A C-Corporation can also take special deductions. The profit of a C-Corporation is taxed to the Corporation when earned, and then is taxed to the shareholders when distributed as dividends. Except for dividends, shareholders are not taxed; however, shareholders cannot deduct any loss of the C-Corporation.

Incorporating is the most complex and expensive business structure to form and manage. Your business name cannot be the same as another corporation in your state, so you will have to reserve your name. A Corporation must elect a board of directors, file written rules or articles of incorporation, draft and adopt written bylaws, issue stock, and hold shareholder and director meetings. Bookkeeping and other record keeping requirements are more complicated, and the services of an attorney and an accountant would most likely be required.

With a C-Corporation, you will file taxes based on the Corporation's income, and personal taxes based on your personal income and dividends. Federal and state authorities impose regulations on C-Corporations. You will be paid as an employee, and your company will have to pay unemployment taxes.

Federal tax form requirements for a C-Corporation:

- Pay estimated taxes on Form 1120-W Estimated Tax for Corporation
- Deposit payroll taxes, withholding, and corporate income taxes using Form 8109B, Deposit Coupon
- File Form 4625, Depreciation, with your Form 1120 Corporate Income Tax Return

Subchapter S-Corporation

A Subchapter S-Corporation starts out as a C-Corporation. It is then converted by filing of form 2553. By filing this election, instead of paying taxes on business income, the income and expenses are passed through to the shareholders and reported on their personal tax returns.

S-Corporations were designed for small businesses, and the number of allowable shareholders is restricted. A C-Corporation and a S-Corporation are identical for non-tax purposes. An eligible domestic corporation can avoid double taxation (once to the shareholders and again to the corporation) by electing to be treated as an S-Corporation. Generally, an S-Corporation is exempt from federal income tax other than tax on certain capital gains and passive income. On their tax returns, the S-Corporation's shareholders include their share of the corporation's separately stated items of income, deduction, loss, and credit, and their share of non-separately stated income or loss.

Other business structure considerations

Sole Proprietor Versus Corporation/LLC: If you do not have many assets, you may want to file a DBA as a Sole Proprietor to start. The cost is negligible, but paperwork is more complicated with corporations and LLCs. Most professional organizers start out by operating as a sole proprietor, as it is the simplest form of business organization to start and maintain. If you want independence and the opportunity to work for yourself, it may be your best option.

Liability is one of the main drawbacks of a Sole Proprietorship. As a sole proprietor, you have full exposure and unlimited liability in the event of a legal suit. You can be held personally liable for any business-related obligation, including that involving your employees and subcontractor. If you accidentally drop a box and break pieces of an expensive collection that is impossible to replace, a client can hold you liable. If a hard drive crashes while you are organizing a client's computer files and he loses all of his company data, he can sue you for damages. A client or a creditor can legally come after your house or other possessions if you default on a debt or lose a lawsuit. Although these events are unlikely, as a sole proprietor you assume full liability.

If you are one person with a home or expensive car, incorporating or forming an LLC will generally better protect your assets. A corporation or LLC is a separate and distinct business entity that limits the personal liability of the owners. The shareholder/owner's assets are not at stake if the corporation is sued. On the other hand, legal experts have cautioned business owners not to create a false sense of security by incorporating. Although a legal suit would be directed at the corporation, it might also be directed at you as the principal.

Corporations enjoy more tax savings than sole proprietors do. A corporation can take special deductions not permitted for sole proprietors. A tax expert can help you plan tax strategies to avoid overpaying taxes, allowing you to keep more money to continue to build your business. Other tangible benefits of incorporating include employee benefit plans, such as fully deductible medical insurance, profit sharing, bonuses and tax-sheltered retirement plans. You can be included in them as an employee of your company.

There is also a significant intangible benefit of incorporating, that of the perceived stability of a corporation. Presuming that only those who are serious about the future of their business would go through the effort and expense, incorporation is, to many, a symbol of commitment. The perceived value of corporate status may especially appeal to business clients who are particularly concerned with continuity. In fact, you may even invite your star clients to serve on your Board of Directors. In addition to the skill and wisdom they will add, you can use this opportunity to assure them that you value their judgment.

Your individual circumstances will determine which form is best for you, but do heed this word of caution. If you are ambitious and committed to building and growing your company beyond working solo, you may be thinking about starting out as a sole proprietorship and then incorporating when you are ready to expand. If you are in the middle of a growth spurt, the last thing you will want to be doing is establishing a new business structure. Making the transition from sole proprietor to corporation can be quite disruptive to your business. Make the decision right at the start. If your intention is to be a corporation, take the time and form your corporation from the beginning.

Corporation versus LLC: Both the Corporation and the LLC are entities that limit the personal liability of all the owners; however, the Corporation offers more personal liability protection than any partnership form. Because of its simplicity and flexibility, an LLC seems to be the best choice for most professional organizing businesses. Your situation would be an exception if you would like to provide extensive fringe benefits to yourself and any other owners, since you could also be an employee of your corporation, making you eligible for benefits. Your corporation can deduct the cost of these benefits and they are not treated as taxable income to you as an employee. You would not receive such favorable tax treatment as an LLC.

S Corporation versus LLC: As a shareholder in an S Corporation, you may pay less self-employment tax than an LLC member with similar income may. You will have to weigh the advantages of the potential tax savings vs. the advantages of the LLC, such as simplified record keeping; flexibility is distributing profits and losses, and flexibility and management structure

Partnership risks: Professional organizers occasionally team up as partners in business. If you are the type of person, who prefers to work collaboratively, a partnership may work well for you. Working in partnership gives you the benefit of sharing creative ideas and financial resources to create mutual profit and solve problems.

Partnerships can also be risky, since partners must consistently agree on control, managerial responsibility, workload distribution, and allotment of profits. Partners are responsible for other partner's business actions as well as their own. No matter how compatible the personalities, it is common for partners to encounter misunderstanding or confusion about key business issues.

A partnership requires commitment and a willingness to work through tough issues, just like a marriage. The dissolution rate of partnerships is also about the same as marriage. Partnerships have been known to cause an end to lifelong friendships. If you decide that a partnership is right for you, give serious thought to what would happen to your company if a co-owner:

- Goes through a divorce
- Wants to retire
- Goes through personal bankruptcy
- Wants out of the business
- Wants to sell their shares to someone else
- Passes away

Whatever good intentions you and your business partner may have, sometimes life just gets in the way. Before you seal the deal on a business partnership, be sure to include a buyout agreement, which will govern what happens when a partner leaves the business.

Changing or closing your business: If you should decide to change the form of your business or close your business, there are actions you must take. You must file an annual return for the year you go out of business, or for the last year, you do business in the old structure. If you have employees, you must file the final employment tax returns, in addition to making final federal tax deposits of these taxes.

You will also file returns to report disposing of business property, reporting the exchange of like-kind property, and/or changing the form of your business. Below is a list of typical actions to take when closing a business, depending on your business structure:

- Make final federal tax deposits
- File final quarterly or annual employment tax form
- Issue final wage and withholding information to employees
- Report information from W-2s issued
- Report capital gains or losses
- Report partner's/shareholder's shares
- Issue payment information to subcontractors
- Report information from 1099s issued
- Report corporate dissolution or liquidation
- Consider allowing S corporation election to terminate
- Report business asset sales

- Report the sale or exchange of property used in your business

Alternatives to business ownership

Self-employment is not for everyone. Rather than providing your services directly for clients, you may choose to work for a professional organizing business. For some people, the security of working for someone else outweighs the advantages of having a business of their own. There are two distinctly different ways to work for someone else, as an employee, or as an independent contractor.

Employee of a Professional Organizer: If you work for someone else as an employee, you will probably receive hourly pay. Your employer will be responsible for withholding federal and state income tax and FICA taxes from your wages. Your employer will pay a matching amount of Social Security and Medicare, and will be required to contribute toward unemployment insurance on your behalf. Liability insurance and worker's compensation are also the responsibilities of your employer.

You will likely have little control over the details of how your services are performed and for whom. You may be required to participate in a training program in order to learn the methods used by your employer, and you will be expected to abide by his standards.

Independent Contractor: If you choose to operate as an independent contractor (also referred to as a subcontractor or freelancer), your legal business structure will be a sole proprietorship. Even if you only work a few hours and only have a few clients, when you work for someone else as a subcontractor, you will need to run a legitimate business. As a small business owner, you will need to learn bookkeeping basics and record keeping. You will register your business and pay taxes as a sole proprietor.

If you plan to work for others as a subcontractor, you must also comply with government rules pertaining to independent contractors. You must meet certain requirements in order to qualify as an independent contractor. Choosing and registering a business name, charging by the contract or project rather than by the hour, and paying estimated taxes could help to fill basic requirements of independent contractor status.

Unlike employees, whose income taxes and self-employment taxes (Social Security and Medicare) are withheld from their paychecks, independent contractors must handle their own taxes. All independent contractors who make more than $400 per year on business activities must report their business income to the IRS. If you make $600 or more performing services for one employer, you will receive a Form 1099-MISC, Miscellaneous

Chapter Seven: Structuring Your Business Ownership

Income, and this information will be reported to the IRS. If you earned it, report it, even if you do not get a 1099. Then take every penny of the deductions to which you are entitled.

Chapter Eight: Making It All Legal

"Law is order in liberty, and without order, liberty is social chaos." - Archbishop Ireland

Failing to make it legal right from the beginning is one of the most common mistakes new entrepreneurs make. You may not be surprised that Uncle Sam and your state want to know about your new business. Many entrepreneurs, however, forget to check in with their county and city governments. As a business owner, you need to be aware of who has jurisdiction over your business, and you must comply with the laws of each. You can also avoid headaches by learning how to protect your identity and set legal guidelines right up front for how you will deal with others.

Legal and regulatory issues are probably the easiest part of getting your business started, yet many people start without registering their business, getting a license, or filing a tax form. You could just start working without writing a contract or dealing with legal requirements or policies, and you might never be caught or run into conflicts. However, you will feel more confident and gain greater respect if you take the time to build a solid foundation.

Getting professional advice

Consulting with a trusted professional is always advisable before starting a new business. Professionals can simplify legal language and ease your frustration and uncertainty while making crucial decisions.

If you do not already have a trusted attorney, as a business owner, you will most likely need to choose an attorney with whom you can work at some point. An attorney will be able to help with various business needs, such as zoning regulations and employment practices. It is important to retain a lawyer if you are applying for trademarks because many legal issues arise during the application process. Knowing a good attorney in the event of a dispute is critical.

Check with your local lawyer referral service if you need legal advice. When you are seeking professional help in setting up your business, you will specifically want to consider tax experts. There are attorneys who specialize in tax law. These attorneys act as advisors, rather than tax preparers. They are experts in tax interpretation and litigation, and they can represent you before the IRS and in court, if necessary.

Certified Public Accountants (CPA) are experts in tax preparation and can represent you during audits. In addition to preparing tax returns, CPAs often assist clients throughout the year with financial statement preparation, and advise them on tax planning matters. Most accountants offer a free initial consultation. Take advantage of this opportunity to determine whether the accountant is a good fit for your needs.

How do you choose an advisor? It is preferable to find someone who has experience in service or consulting businesses. Ask professional organizers, business associates or other people you know to recommend someone they trust. Choose an advisor as you would choose a doctor. Research your options and pay close attention to specialties and experience. CPAs without a business specialty may not be familiar with the complexities of the different kinds of business structures.

An attorney's fee depends on level of experience, the part of the country where you live, and the type of firm. The hourly rate of a tax attorney is typically much higher than that of a CPA. As a business advisor, an attorney's fee may be prohibitive. On the high end, a partner in a law firm charges around $250 an hour or more.

Regardless of your choice, avoid going to either your accountant or your attorney for answers to questions you might be able to find on your own. It is a good idea to research your options and prepare a comprehensive list of specific questions before scheduling your consultation, so that you can maximize your investment.

If you choose not to seek legal help but want more information, the following suggestions should help get you started:

- Go to your local law library (located at the county court house or in a law school) and ask the law librarian to help you locate the state statute that governs the incorporation process.
- Call the general information number for your state government to determine which agency handles company formation. In many states, it is the Secretary of State. Clerks can tell you where to get blank forms and provide examples of completed documents.

- Access the Internet and go to your state department's website to find information on business and incorporation. You can also get the federal guidelines at www.irs.gov and see examples of finished documents.

Zoning, licenses and registrations

Local zoning laws: If you plan to operate your business out of your home, be sure that home-based businesses are sanctioned within your municipality's zoning ordinances. Contact your city's business license department to obtain a business license that grants you permission to operate a business in that city.

As more and more service-related businesses are formed, millions of Americans have found advantages to working from home. Many communities are working against this national trend. Your next-door neighbor might be opposed, too. The increase in home-based businesses has created a need for local governments to control them, and most cities and towns, and some counties now impose regulations on the use of a home for specific types of businesses. Some towns even disallow home-based businesses entirely.

Over the last several decades, zoning laws have seesawed back and forth between strict, prohibitive zoning laws and no guidelines at all. Some towns still have older zoning laws that were written in another era, when it was assumed that any business either manufactured or sold products. These older laws often prohibited business of any kind in residential districts because of concerns about hazardous waste, odors, or noisy machines. Many modern communities have structured their zoning laws around computer-based businesses. Some communities that have never had complaints simply have not addressed the issue of home-based businesses. Your situation may be something in between these scenarios, and the only way to find out is to visit your local municipal office.

> When I first started my business, there were no ordinances at all governing home-based businesses in my community. When I began to hire office assistance, I leased commercial office space, which required that I comply with the normal business licensing requirements. Seven years later when my children moved out and I moved my office back into my home; I was surprised to find that a whole list of zoning regulations had been adopted. Not only was I now required to apply for a business license and pay a fee, but also a physical inspection of the premises was conducted before my city would grant a business license.

Before you spend a dime on business cards or a telephone line, investigate the city and county regulations and ordinances that apply to you. Start at the lowest level, since local laws usually take into consideration and supersede the laws of a higher governing ordinance. If you rent your home, review your lease for restrictions that apply to operating a business out of your unit. If your home is part of a homeowner's association, check the covenant to make sure that there are no restrictions on operating a business out of your home.

Contact your town clerk's office to ensure that operating a home business in your community is permitted. Until you are familiar with local regulations, avoid disclosure of your identity and intentions. You might even consider posing as a potential homebuyer curious about regulations pertaining to a home occupation. Ask to see copies of the ordinances that apply to home occupations, and avoid using the word *business*. Check with your county board regarding home-based business regulations. The county is usually the highest level that gets involved; states do not regulate home occupations.

If you are tempted to skip this process, take your chances and ignore zoning, make sure that you know and trust all of your neighbors. The woman you do not even know that lives two doors away from you may be a busybody. She may have heard that you set up a business and may be wondering whether you are allowed to do that in this locality. She may call the local zoning board and inquire about the extra cars taking up precious few spaces on your street. She may complain that the UPS, FedEx, Airborne and USPS trucks are wearing away at the pavement her taxes help to pay for.

Local zoning laws restrict many different types of activities, from hiring employees that are not related to you, to displaying signs. Be careful that your business is not shut down before you even have a chance to turn a profit. Take the time to investigate zoning regulations in your region and take steps to work within those ordinances.

Licensing your business: Many new business owners wait until they run into problems before concerning themselves with permits, licenses and zoning. Make sure your business complies with federal, state and local requirements by researching, asking questions and resolving issues up front.

Business license requirements vary from state to state, municipality to municipality, and they are different from business to business. Many cities require you to get a general business license, even if you are a home-based business with a single owner and no employees. A business license is nothing more than recognition that you have paid a tax to the city for the privilege of doing business there. It is sometimes called (more appropriately) a tax registration certificate.

Your city or town clerk is your best source for determining the types of documents you are required to complete (if any) as a start-up business owner.

My suggestion is to take the time to go to your city, town, or village offices during off-peak hours and get to know the clerk, rather than make a phone call. He or she will usually be able to fill you in on county and state, as well as local ordinances, and will become as valuable a source of information as your librarian will.

Ask for information regarding the home-based business zoning and license application process. Typically, you will be required to pay a fee (usually around $25-$50) and complete a simple application that describes the type of business you plan to operate. Whether your clients are located in your municipality is usually irrelevant. Most local agencies are concerned with a few essential issues:

- That you pay a fee for the privilege of doing business within their jurisdiction
- That your business will not create traffic or parking problems
- That your business will not produce odors, noise, or anything hazardous
- That your business will not post signs or alter the character of the community in any way
- That your home will primarily be used as a residence, and that your business will not occupy more than a certain percentage of your dwelling

You may be asked to attend a meeting and explain your intentions, or you may be subjected to an inspection of your home if you are home-based. There might be additional requirements, such as personal property declarations and confidential information reports. Some municipalities levy special business taxes, such as asset-based taxes and property taxes on computers, desks and office equipment that your business owns. Practices vary from city to city.

Some organizers skip the business license and just try to keep a low profile. Business licenses are inexpensive, but penalties for operating without a license can be several hundred dollars. Operating without a business license is a misdemeanor in some cities.

Registering your business name: You must comply with government requirements for registration of business names. Conduct a name search before choosing a name for your business. Your attorney can perform a thorough search of business registry databases, or you can use phone books, city directories and professional organizer association directories to perform your own search and determine what names are already in use. If your plans are to operate beyond your immediate geographical area, conduct a broader name search using the federal register of trade and service marks. If your chosen name is available, you can enforce your rights to the name by registering the name as a business trademark or service mark.

If you are operating as a sole proprietorship or partnership, choosing a business name for your business is optional. Any business that does not use the full legal name of its owner, must officially and publicly register, as part of its business name, the name as a DBA (Doing Business As). A DBA is also known as Fictitious Business Names, Assumed Names and Trade Names. Even if your first name is part of your business name (Suzie's Organizing Services), you must register your business name as a fictitious business name. If you do include your full legal name in your business name (Suzie Smith Organizing Services), you can start using it without filing any paperwork.

Once you have secured approval from your town to operate your business, you will pay a small filing fee (usually around $10-$100) and register your business name with the appropriate agency. In most states, you will register your fictitious business name at the county level with your county clerk. In a few states, such as Florida, your fictitious name is registered with a state office. You might get away with not registering your business name, but keep in mind that many banks ask for proof that you have properly registered your business name prior to opening an account for you. In addition, any contracts that you sign under an unregistered name would not be enforceable.

Your city or town hall can assist you with registering your business name, and even notarize your trade name certificate, if required. You may simply be referred to the county government office to file a Fictitious Business Name, which allows you to conduct business under a name other than your personal legal name. This process typically involves paying a fee and publishing your intention to do business as (Suzie Smith d.b.a. SS Organizing Services) in a local newspaper for a set number of issues or weeks. In most cases, the newspaper where you publish your intention will file the necessary papers with the county. You can save money by inserting your notice in a weekly neighborhood publication instead of a major daily newspaper.

In most states, corporations and LLCs do not have to file fictitious business names unless they do business under trade names other than their own legal business name. Registering your business name with the Secretary of State is part of the process of incorporating, and the process will identify any conflicts with businesses using similar names. Incorporating may not give you the exclusive right to use a business name, since other businesses may already be using your business name as a trademark or service mark. Your registration does provide you with the exclusive right to use Your Business Name, Inc., or Your Business Name, LLC.

Tax issues

When you first start out in business, your primary concern is to make money. Owing and paying taxes might be one of the furthest things from your consciousness. If you are not informed, however, tax issues can sneak up on you and you might find yourself in a precarious situation. Here are a few things to know about business taxes.

Self-employment tax: Self-employment tax (SE tax) is a Social Security and Medicare tax primarily for individuals who work for themselves. Your payments of SE tax contribute to your coverage under the Social Security system. Social Security coverage provides you with retirement benefits, disability benefits, survivor benefits, and hospital insurance (Medicare) benefits.

You must pay SE tax and file Schedule SE, Self-Employment Tax, with your Form 1040 tax return if your net earnings from self-employment were $400 or more.

Income taxes and deductions: Observing tax laws is mandatory, but paying more taxes than demanded by law is voluntary. Yet many business owners spend so much time working on the business that they dedicate little time to reducing taxes and end up paying too much tax. There is nothing sinister in structuring and conducting your business to keep taxes as low as possible. It is well worth the fee to hire a strong tax professional with knowledge of the ever-changing tax laws to advise you about tax savings opportunities.

Federal laws are structured to allow you to apply strategies for saving on your federal income tax, legally. Because you intend to earn money from your work, the government considers you the owner of a privately owned business. You are entitled to tax benefits shared by all businesses, large and small.

The IRS offers these benefits to business owners for good reason. Tax incentives that help a business get started also produce extra revenue for the IRS once the business starts to earn a steady profit. Unemployment payments are reduced as the business begins to hire employees, and more taxes are collected from the people that have been put to work.

IRS codes are written so that the government has revenue to operate. They are also written to motivate us to put our money where it will benefit others, so that the government will not have to pay the cost of these services. Taking legal deductions from your taxable income is not tax evasion, which will land you in jail, but tax avoidance, which has the full knowledge and blessing of the IRS.

All businesses except partnerships must file an annual income tax return. Partnerships file an information return. The form you use depends on how your business is organized. It is important to structure your business entity in the most tax advantageous way.

It is advisable to hire a professional tax preparer to make sure you get all of the deductions to which you are entitled. A professional tax preparer will also be aware of any problems that might raise a flag at the IRS. Make sure that you understand everything on your tax return, since it is your name on the document.

How much you earn as a professional organizer is not nearly as important as how much you keep of what you earn. You may find that you have less to grumble about each year when April 15 – Income Tax Day – rolls around after you become a professional organizer, once you realize some of the tax benefits of being a business owner.

Consult with a tax accountant or the IRS about tax guidelines as they apply to your situation. Generally, you may deduct certain expenses from your taxable income, including your computer, paper and other office supplies, postage, and even part of your home. You can do this even if you keep your full-time job and only work as a professional organizer part time. The IRS recognizes you as a person who has a second job, and the tax deductions you earn because of your status as a business owner may be deducted from your total income, including the salary you earn from your full time occupation. Train yourself to always get a receipt for every business expense, and keep good records.

Check with your tax consultant to make sure you are entitled to each deduction, but according to the IRS publications as of this writing, you are entitled to the following deductions as a business owner, to which you may not have been entitled as an employee of another company:

Attorney fees	Meals while traveling on business
Educational expenses	Office furniture
Business cards	Travel expenses and mileage
Fax machines	Telephone calls
Computers	Office supplies
Postage and shipping	Contracted labor
Seminars	Business meals
Books, magazines, newspapers	Entertainment
Dues to professional organizations	Automobile expenses
Home office expenses	Printing

Notice that larger purchases have been omitted from this list. The IRS mandates that you capitalize larger purchases, such as computer equipment, furniture, and office equipment. You are allowed to depreciate (write-off as an expense) up to an annual percentage of the cost of major business purchases. By capitalizing major purchases, your deduction will take place over the useful life of the item as depreciation.

You do not have to spend your money in order to gain a tax advantage. Contributions to qualified retirement plans directly reduce your taxable income and help to provide for future cash needs upon retirement.

The IRS offers some nice tax relief for working from your home, and your home office space can be the source of a significant tax advantage. If you are a sole proprietor working out of your home, you are entitled to a deduction for business use of home. The IRS requires that your home office is either your principal place of business, or where you meet and deal with clients. It must also be used exclusively for business. If you use one-quarter of your home solely for business purposes, you can deduct 25% of most of your home expenses, including utilities, real estate taxes, mortgage interest, painting and repairs, and insurance. Home offices frequently come under IRS scrutiny, and the specifics sometimes become complicated. Your tax professional will know how the current IRS code affects you and your business, and can help you take full advantage of this deduction.

You may deduct the expenses of your home office only if they are less than the amount you earned that year in your business. The amount you can deduct depends on the portion of your home that is used for business. You can deduct both the direct and indirect expenses of your home office. Direct expenses include office furnishings and the cost of repairs. Indirect expenses are things like utilities, insurance, real estate taxes, mortgage interest and depreciation. If you rent, you cannot deduct depreciation or taxes, but you can deduct a portion of your rent and utilities.

If you declare a portion of your home as your principal place of business, the portion used for business must comply with IRS interpretations. The space must be designated exclusively for business. The IRS does allow you to block off an area of a larger room and designate that as your office space. However, the IRS frowns at using your office as a guest room or for personal storage.

Federal laws do not require you to incorporate and you do not have to obtain a business license (local laws may vary). According to IRS code, you must simply demonstrate that you are in business to earn a profit. It is generally accepted that people prefer to make a living doing something they like, but there is a limit on the deductions you can take if you do not carry on your business to make a profit. In determining whether you are carrying on an activity for profit, all the facts are taken into account. No one factor alone is decisive. Among the factors to consider are whether:

- You carry on the activity in a businesslike manner
- The time and effort you put into the activity indicate you intend to make it profitable
- You depend on income from the activity for your livelihood
- Your losses are due to circumstances beyond your control (or are normal in the start-up phase of your type of business)
- You change your methods of operation in an attempt to improve profitability
- You (or your advisors) have the knowledge needed to carry on the activity as a successful business
- You were successful in making a profit in similar activities in the past
- The activity makes a profit in some years and the amount of profit it makes
- You can expect to make a future profit from the appreciation of the assets used in the activity
- You can show you have made a valid attempt to earn a profit by saving copies of proposals and records of networking events attended and phone calls made. The IRS does limit the number of years that you are allowed to claim deductions as a non-profitable business to two out of five. In other words, you must make a profit at least three years out of five.

It is always wise to consult a tax expert before taking any deductions. Tax laws change from year to year, so what was deductible last year may not be deductible this year. Most organizers do not take advantage of all of the deductions available to them, either because they are not familiar with them, or because they fear an audit. A tax expert can help you learn what deductions are available to you so that you can declare all of them on your tax return.

There are a number of publications available from the IRS free of charge that will help you understand the items you can deduct. You can obtain these publications by calling 1-800-829-1040, or from the IRS website – www.irs.com.

Publication 15 – Employers Tax Guide
Publication 17 – Your Federal Income Tax
Publication 334 – Tax Guide for Small Business

Chapter Eight: Making It All Legal

Publication 463 – Travel, Entertainment, Gift and Car Expenses
Publication 505 – Tax Withholding and Estimated Tax
Publication 533 – Self-Employment Tax
Publication 534 – Depreciation
Publication 535 – Business Expenses
Publication 538 – Accounting Periods and Methods
Publication 541 – Partnerships
Publication 542 – Corporations
Publication 583 – Starting a Business and Keeping Records
Publication 587 – Business Use of Your Home
Publication 917 – Business Use of Your Car

You can also request the following tax packages:

Package 1040A Forms and Instructions
Package 1040 Forms and Instructions
Package 1120 U.S. Corporation Income Tax Forms and Instructions
Package 1120S S Corporation Income Tax Forms and Instructions
Package 1065 U.S. Partnership Return of Income Tax Forms and Instructions

Estimated taxes: Federal income tax is a pay-as-you-go tax. You must pay the tax as you earn or receive income during the year. If your business is profitable, the IRS requires you to pay estimated tax, which is paying your taxes in four installments during the year. Estimated tax is the method used to pay tax on income that is not subject to withholding, such as self-employment income. Estimated tax is used to pay income tax and self-employment tax, as well as other taxes and amounts reported on your tax return. If you do not pay enough through withholding or estimated tax payments, you may be charged a penalty. If you do not pay enough by the due date of each payment period, you may be charged a penalty even if you are due a refund when you file your tax return.

Pay estimated taxes on Form 1040-ES Estimated Tax for Individuals or Form 1120-W Estimated Tax for Corporation.

If you are an employee of another company, you can avoid making estimated tax payments by asking your employer to increase the amount withheld from your paycheck. By paying more tax through payroll withholding on your day job, you can offset the taxes that will be due on your business income.

Obtain Tax ID numbers: Generally, businesses need a Federal Employer Identification Number (EIN or FEIN), also known as a Federal Tax Identification Number. If you have employees or operate as a corporation or partnership, you must have an EIN. This number is used to identify a business entity. You may apply for an EIN in various ways, including online.

If you qualify as a self-employed business owner, and have determined that a sole proprietorship is the best form of organization for your business, you can file Schedule C along with your Federal Form 1040 tax return. Your Social Security number serves as your tax identification number. You would not be required to have an EIN unless you had a Keogh plan or hired employees.

You can apply for an Employer ID Number (EIN) using several methods:

- Phone – call the toll-free Business and Specialty Tax Line (800-829-4933). A representative takes the information, assigns the EIN, and provides the number to an authorized individual over the telephone.
- Fax – send the completed Form SS-4 application to your state fax number after ensuring that the Form SS-4 contains all of the required information. A fax will be sent back with the EIN within four (4) business days.
- Mail – The processing period for an EIN application received by mail is four weeks. Ensure that the Form SS-4 contains all of the required information.
- Online – The Internet EIN (I-EIN) application is another avenue for you to apply for and obtain an employer identification number. Once all the necessary fields are completed on the online form, preliminary validation is performed and you will be alerted to information the IRS needs that may not have been included. An EIN will be issued after the successful submission of the completed Form SS-4 online.

You must check with your state to make sure you need a state number or charter. In most states, you must collect state sales tax when you make retail sales. If your state requires that sales tax be collected on the type of services you plan to provide, investigate obtaining a registration number for sales and use tax. If you plan to sell products or anything that qualifies in your state for sales tax, you must apply for a resale number. The amount to charge and how and when to pay the appropriate agency will be fully explained when you obtain your resale number.

Sellers' permits and sales taxes: In most states, if you will be selling taxable goods and services, you must pay sales tax on what you sell. Sales tax can be challenging and somewhat confusing. States do not require that you charge sales tax. Whether or not you collect sales tax, you are liable to pay sales tax to the state in which you do business. The best practice is to become a reseller, so that you can be exempt from paying sales tax on items you will be selling to your clients. When you become a reseller, you will receive a seller's permit, a certificate of resale, or a certificate of authority.

The frequency of sales tax returns that you file, and the sales tax liability payments differ from state to state. You might have to pay sales taxes to different agencies, or pay city, county and state taxes separately. Some of your clients may be exempt from sales tax. You might have to tax clients at different rates depending on where they are located. Some items, like products, might be subject to sales tax, while others, like services, might not.

Writing client contracts and agreements

You can have your attorney write a basic contract for you, draft a contract for her review, or write the contract yourself. Whichever way you choose, a written contract with your clients is always a good practice. One of the main reasons for having a formal contract is to have a binding document that is legally enforceable. For a written contract to be an effective legal instrument, include the following:

- Identification of the parties of the contract by name and by contractual role (consultant and client)
- What you will give in value (your services), and when
- What your client promises to do (pay you), and when
- Terms and conditions (dates and jurisdiction)
- Confidentiality and non disclosure clauses
- Acceptance of the offer (signature)

In reality, it is highly unlikely that you will litigate in the event of a dispute. You will not want to spend your time, energy and emotions in small claims court chasing insignificant amounts of money and associated damages.

The second and more practical reason to have a written client contract is to protect your reputation. A written contract leaves no doubt in the client's mind about what to expect from you and your relationship. Two perceptions inevitably exist, your client's and yours. Each party naturally wants to give as little as possible and get as much as he can. Rather than leaving it to individual perception, a written agreement can be an effective way to clarify your intentions, avoid misunderstandings, and make sure each of you derives maximum benefit from the relationship.

It may be tempting to avoid formal contracts with your clients, especially if you are working with residential clients. A formal written agreement may seem unnecessary when all you plan to do is clean out a closet or organize a desk. Putting your intentions in writing before you begin a job enables you to define specifics clearly, such as:

- What services you will perform
- How much you will charge
- What sort of involvement you expect from your client
- The required notice to cancel an appointment
- What working conditions are unacceptable
- Who will pay for supplies

When the job is finished, you can collect your fee without wondering if you have met the client's expectations. It is all in writing. If the client does not seem satisfied, you can refer him back to the signed agreement and offer to extend your contract for an additional fee.

You can get beyond the contractual mind-set by calling it a Client Agreement or letter of agreement, rather than a contract. The agreement does not have to include legalese, or use words like whereas, henceforth, and heretofore. Simply write an agreement in plain English, make and sign two copies, have the client sign both, and keep one for your own files. It is that simple.

In the body of the agreement, you will want to include everything that you have already agreed on verbally. If your client lives in a different state, choose which state's laws will govern the contract. Your agreement with your client is a good opportunity to communicate your Code of Ethics and set your client's mind at ease about issues such as confidentiality. At a minimum, you will want to include the following in a Client Agreement:

- Date of agreement
- Date agreement good until
- Services to be provided
- Where services will be performed
- Who will be responsible for providing equipment and space
- Who will be responsible for purchasing supplies
- Desired outcome
- Date of first appointment
- End date, if applicable
- Cancellation policy
- Method for determining future appointments
- How much you will be paid
- How you will be paid, such as hourly, a set fee, etc.
- Amount of deposit, if required, and when it is due

- Payment schedule (what is paid up front, at completion, in installments, etc.)
- Who will be responsible for travel and other direct expenses
- Method of payment
- What circumstances would give you or the client the right to terminate
- Statement of confidentiality

To ensure that your client signs and returns a copy of the agreement, specify in the agreement that no work will begin until you have a signed agreement and any agreed upon advance payment.

If you are a sole proprietor, a written Client Agreement is a good way to establish that you are an independent contractor and not the client's employee. This can be very useful if the IRS or another government agency questions your status. You should include information in your Client Agreement relating to your independent contractor status, establishing that:

- You are an independent contractor
- You have any necessary licenses, if appropriate, to do the work
- You will pay your own state and federal taxes
- You have your own liability insurance
- If you are not a sole proprietor, include your Federal Tax ID (FEIN) in your Client Agreement.

For sample agreements and other helpful forms, see Organizing For A Living Workbook at http://www.organizingforaliving.com/docs.

Protecting your name and intellectual property

There are different kinds of protection for intellectual property, including trademarks, service marks, copyrights and patents. You will be mostly interested in trademarks and service marks for your business.

Trademarks and service marks: A trademark (™) is used to protect a word, name, symbol or device, which is used in trade with goods to indicate the source of the goods and to distinguish them from the goods of others. Trademark rights may be used to prevent others from using a confusingly similar mark, but not to prevent others from making the same goods or from selling the same goods or services under a clearly different mark. A service mark is the same as a trademark except that it identifies and distinguishes the source of a service rather than a product. The terms *trademark* and *mark* are commonly used to refer to both trademarks and service marks.

Registration of your mark is not required. You can establish rights in a mark based on legitimate usage of the mark. However, owning a federal trademark registration on the Principal Register provides several advantages, including a legal presumption of your ownership of the mark and exclusive rights to use the mark nationwide or in connection with the services listed in your registration.

If you are using a mark, be sure to indicate on all of your promotional materials that your company owns the mark. Any time you claim rights in a mark, you may use the TM (trademark) or SM (service mark) designation to alert the public to your claim, regardless of whether you have filed an application with the United States Patent & Trademark Office. You may use the federal registration symbol (®), however, only after the USPTO actually registers a mark.

You do not need a lawyer to get a trademark. You can apply for registration of a trademark over the Internet using the Trademark Electronic Application System (TEAS) at http://www.uspto.gov/teas/index.html. If you do not have access to the Internet, you can call the Trademark Assistance Center at 1-800-786-9199 to request a paper form. The process takes about 12-18 months, and costs under $400.

Find a way to date-stamp the first use of your mark, so that you can defend that you are the first to use it. Some people seal their trademark in an envelope and mail it to themselves. The postmark becomes evidence in the event of a conflict. Preventing others from infringing on your trademark takes constant vigilance. It is wise to retain an attorney to write a stern letter if you find that someone has imitated your mark.

Patents: A patent for an invention is the grant of a property right to the inventor, issued by the Patent and Trademark Office. The right conferred by the patent grant is not the right to make, use, offer for sale, sell or import, but the right to exclude others from making, using, offering for sale, selling or importing the invention.

An application for a patent is made to the Director of the United States Patent and Trademark Office and includes a written document that comprises a specification (description and claims), and an oath or declaration; a drawing in those cases in which a drawing is necessary; and filing, search, and examination fees.

Copyrights: A copyright (©) is a form of protection provided to the authors of original works of authorship including literary, dramatic, musical, artistic, and certain other intellectual works, both published and unpublished. The copyright protects the form of expression rather than the subject matter of the writing. In addition to helping to protect you, a copyright also carries prestige and validates your professionalism.

Chapter Eight: Making It All Legal

Copyright is secured automatically when the work is created, and work is created when it is fixed in a copy for the first time. Publication or registration is not a condition of copyright protection. Copyright registration is a legal formality intended to make a public record of the basic facts of a particular copyright. To encourage copyright owners to make registration, the copyright law provides several advantages. Registration establishes a public record of the copyright claim, and is necessary for works of U.S. origin before an infringement suit may be filed in court.

The copyright in the work of authorship immediately becomes the property of the author who created the work. Only the author, or those deriving their rights through the author, can rightfully claim copyrights. To register a copyright, send an application form, filing fee, and a non-refundable deposit of the work being registered to the Copyright Office of the Library of Congress.

Chapter Nine: Marketing and Public Relations

"Things may come to those who wait, but only those things that are left behind by those who hustle." - Abraham Lincoln

Marketing is about creating opportunities for building relationships with potential clients. In your personal life, you encounter many different people in many different scenarios. You relate well with some people and begin to build a relationship. With others, you simply will not connect. You will come to regard some with affection and trust, and others will remain mere acquaintances. With some, you will develop strong relationships and their friends will become your friends.

Marketing, just like making friends, is relationship building. The kind of relationship you want to build will plant the belief in the minds of your clients that you are their most trusted advisor. You are seen as their only viable solution. When your clients are under your care, there is constant hopefulness and trust. This chapter is about all the steps you will take to build the relationships that will nurture your business, from finding the best clients to building awareness and creating interest in you and what you have to offer.

Developing your marketing plan

Seizing opportunities to market your business is vital for your success. To be a winner, take advantage of every opportunity for developing new business, and stay alert to opportunities for expanding short-term projects into extended contracts. The methods that work best depend on your audience and your preferences. You may have to experiment a bit to find out what methods are most effective for you. After you try different methods, measure their effectiveness and focus your efforts on the best.

A marketing plan will get you started. It compliments your business plan and helps you to stay focused. You do not need an elaborate marketing plan, but you do need a foundation to ensure your marketing efforts pay off. In its simplest form, a marketing plan defines your commitment, your clients, your competition, your policies and your strategies. Your marketing plan should include your market research, your target client, your competition, your services and pricing, advertising and promotion, and your budget.

Market research: Effective marketing, planning and promotion begin with current information about your marketplace. Whenever you study the advertising of other businesses in your community, ask a prospect why she selected another professional over you, talk to your competition, or study your clients' buying habits; you are doing market research. Formal market research simply organizes the process of collecting market information, and helps you determine the right direction for your business.

To conduct market research you must gather facts and opinions in an orderly, objective way to find out exactly what people in your target market want and how you can appeal to them. Gather information about the type of people with whom you would like to work and the specific people who need your services, your target market. What kinds of buyers are out there for your services? Where do they live? What is their gender, race, or average age? What is their occupation? What is their industry? What is their income? What are their needs? What are their values? Now, narrow your list by eliminating the types of people who would not (or could not afford to) give you money for your services.

Find out what people need, not just what you want to sell them. Put yourself in your client's shoes. Ask yourself why a client should invest in your services. What would motivate him to hire you? What will your services do for him? What would your clients say about you to others? Why would they recommend your services? List all of the groups or types of clients that might use your services. With regard to these groups, here are some questions to answer:

- Which group has the greatest urgency to hire you?
- In which group do you have the least competition?
- What benefits can you offer that your competitors cannot?
- Which group does your expertise best serve?
- In which group are you already known?
- Do you need to build your expertise in order to work with any of these groups?

Design a short survey or send out a brief questionnaire to people who might be interested in your services and become clients. Include three or four simple open-ended questions. Indicate your interest in working with them, and give them the option to include their name in their reply. Explain why you want the information and what you plan to do with it. You can increase your response rate by offering a prize drawing or by offering a discount on your services. Even if people do not respond, it gets your name in front of them and gives you a reason to follow up.

Research publicity possibilities, and build a file of the contact information for newspapers, magazines, associations, and online newsletters. Very few of your competitors do much ongoing research, so you can be ahead of the game by being more informed and proactive. Try online searches in your field and scout out resources you can use in your public library.

Define your business: Defining your business involves determining the value that you are going to give those who invest in your services. You must be able to describe clearly what you will deliver and how you will meet the needs of your prospective clients. What specifically do you have to offer? What makes you irresistible? Sell something that people want to buy. Sell results that clients want. Be specific when describing what services you will offer in terms of expertise and result. Identify the unique attributes that distinguish your services: innovation, availability, high quality, convenience, afford-ability, reliability, etc. List not only the major services you will offer, but also additional services that enhance your clients' level of satisfaction.

Define your business location and delineate the geographic area where you will provide your services, whether it will be national, regional, or limited to a certain county, town or neighborhood. Define your competition and specify how you will differ from them. Include their promotional methods, and describe how yours will be different. Write about what makes you special.

Describe how you will package your services and how much you will charge. Include particulars such as your fee for the initial consultation and travel costs. Describe your policy regarding follow up calls. Specify whether you will provide written proposals.

Define your clients: To connect with the clients you want to reach, you need more than just a general idea of your potential clients' needs and preferences. The more clearly you define your potential clients, the better your chances of reaching them and encouraging them to hire you. Even though you cater to a variety of clients, becoming knowledgeable about your core target will help you to deliver the right marketing message.

Clarity on your target market is imperative, as it is the foundation of your business. The stronger the picture you paint of your target client, the greater your chance for success. Define your target audience by understanding the characteristics of the people who would pay for your services. As you think of each possibility, ask yourself:

- What makes your ideal client tick?
- Does this group need what I can provide?
- Would I enjoy working with this group?
- What would their vision be?
- What are their likes and dislikes?
- Would this group pay for my services?

You can define your clients using demographic information, like women in their 30s, or legal professionals who live in the suburbs. What are their habits or interests, what do they read, listen to or watch? Are they people who own yachts, football buffs, or people who like scrap booking? What do they value most? Describe how your clients will learn about you and your services: advertising, direct mail, Yellow Pages, word of mouth, etc. Questions to ask yourself to learn more about your potential clients can include:

- Are your potential clients primarily male or female?
- What is their age group?
- What is their occupation?
- What is their industry?
- What is their income range?
- Do they have children, and if so, what age group?
- Are they retired?
- Where do they live?
- What is their level of education?
- What are their hobbies or special interests?
- What do they do for recreation?
- What is their lifestyle?
- To what professional or fraternal organizations do they belong?
- What are some ways they can learn about my company and my services?

By combining these factors, you can get very specific in defining your target audience. For instance, you may find that your clients are students who enjoy music and collect audio CDs, upper-income families with preschool children who like to travel, or wealthy members of corporate Boards of Directors. You can then use this data to learn about your clients' needs and preferences as they relate to the services you provide and tailor your marketing objectives accordingly.

Marketing budget: It is essential that you give your marketing some serious attention. You must lead your marketing activities and determine how much you will devote to your marketing efforts. Put in writing what you will do for marketing and estimate what it will cost you, not just in money, but in

Chapter Nine: Marketing and Public Relations

time as well. Make a list of where your clients will come from, and what you are willing to do to make connections with potential clients (visit a business group, attend a chamber of commerce meeting, join a networking group, etc.). Make lists of specific things you are willing to do to get clients (write an article for a local newspaper, buy a Yellow Pages ad, give a free talk, etc.), and how much time and money you will dedicate to each activity.

Outline both the marketing methods you can implement immediately, as well as possible future marketing methods to attract new clients. Determine a percentage of profits you plan to allocate to each marketing effort. Define which specific marketing tools you can afford to implement: newspapers, Yellow Pages advertising, direct mail, public relations activities such as community involvement, or press releases. Develop methods for measuring results of your marketing efforts.

You will have to spend some money to get the word out about your business so that clients can find you. Many professional organizing businesses have marketed themselves on limited budgets, and you can, too. By being creative, you can attract clients without investing a lot of money. There are many easy and affordable ways to find new clients and promote your services. Some of the ideas in this chapter will spark your creativity.

Commit to a certain amount of time to develop skills and implement your marketing strategies. Teach yourself how to establish name recognition, build your reputation, and gain exposure. Allow time to read books, brainstorm marketing ideas, and take action. Determine how many hours per day or week you will devote and build these activities into a schedule. Considering times that will not interfere with client work or other distractions, make a list of times and day of the week that you will work on your marketing.

If your time more limited than your budget, you can hire marketing expertise. You can employ a variety of specialists to help you gain exposure. Public relations experts can put your company in the public eye by writing press releases and contacting the media for you. Graphic artists can help you create a company image to make you look professional. Advertising specialists can help you develop a positioning scheme. website developers can help draw attention to your site and arouse interest in your services. Determine where expert help could give your business the biggest boost, and then hire appropriate professionals in those areas to help you achieve your objectives.

Marketing objectives: The final component in your marketing plan should be your overall marketing objectives. Here you will set specific goals for the type of clients you want to reach and how many new clients you want to gain each month; how you plan to communicate your message and create an awareness of your services; how you will move clients to hire you. Once you have defined your objectives, it will be easier to choose the most effective method and stay on track.

As you learn more about your target audiences and write specific descriptions of them, decide what your primary objectives are with each. Your primary objective might be to have your most profitable clients refer you to other similar clients, or to have your most frequent clients spend more time on each appointment. Using the information you have gathered, you can decide whether you can best achieve your objectives by producing one marketing program to accommodate various audiences, or creating separate programs for each audience.

Finding potential clients

For every person who has hired a professional organizer, probably seven or eight people need to hire one but have not. It is up to you to tap that audience. If you are just getting started or looking for additional clients, ask people you know for suggestions for people or companies you might contact. Start thinking of ways to help you locate the types of people who would be your ideal clients.

Visit places your target client might frequent. For example, if wealthy homemakers are the type of individual you would like to work with, you might start getting a monthly facial in the ritziest spa in the area. Make a day of it and hang out in the lounge or the juice bar, so that you can get to know people who can afford luxury and value the free time you will help them achieve. If a 65-year-old male interested in woodworking is your target client, see if there is a woodworking class available at your local community college.

Getting community exposure: There are many ways to reach your target market by getting exposure in your community. Offering to give a talk is a great way to display your knowledge and services. Community organizations and civic groups such as Chambers of Commerce, PTA's, Rotary Clubs, libraries and church groups will welcome your offer to give a talk about how to get better organized. Know your audience and tailor your presentation to meet its needs. Use visuals and bring handouts with pertinent information, along with plenty of brochures and business cards.

If families are your target market, giving a talk at a school may be a great place to practice, get over your stage fright, and learn good speaking techniques. Many high school and junior high school teachers will welcome a guest speaker to share his expertise in the classroom. This age group can certainly benefit from learning to be better organized, and you can benefit from getting professional feedback from teachers about ways you can improve your speaking. If you provide a handout, there is a good chance it will find its way back to the parents who need your services. Do not overlook any opportunity to get exposure.

Another way to help get exposure is to donate your services to community or church auctions and raffle drawings. Prepare a gift certificate describing fully the service you will provide. To protect yourself, provide details about the limits of the gift certificate, including the maximum number of hours you will work and the expiration date of the certificate. If you are well known in the church or community, your services will likely be offered in a live, rather than a silent auction. If the auctioneer reads a detailed description of you and your services at the auction, everyone in the room will know about your business! If you expect your donation to be offered at a silent auction, put your gift certificate in a gift basket surrounded by clever organizing gadgets. Although you will not be paid for your services, the money goes to a worthy cause, you will gain valuable experience, and the work may lead to repeat business or referrals.

Contests are another clever way to promote your business. Contact local stores and radio stations that conduct contests and offer your services as prizes. Again, you will not be paid for your services, but you will get some powerful exposure.

Combing the classified ads and business registers: Being proactive pays off, and classified ads and business registers provide a wealth of information. Houses being sold by owner can be approached about staging or relocation assistance. Classified ads reveal companies that are expanding, relocating, or otherwise in need of organizing solutions. Business registers publish fictitious name filings and new corporate business listings in your area. Use your creativity and look for ways that you can fill their needs.

Not long after I took the plunge and started my business, my husband lost his job. He jumped right into job-search mode, and so did I! Every day when he was finished looking through the want ads, I circled all of the jobs that listed organizing skills as job requirements. The next day, I called those employers and talked to them about how I could fill their interim needs. The extra cash generated through those efforts not only got us through some rough days, but created contacts that are still cycling referrals for me today.

Advertising

The first thing that usually comes to mind to get business is advertising. Advertising means paid marketing. It may be an easy way to take action, but it is not always cost-effective. Investing money in advertisements is not a sure thing today, since technology has opened up new ways to get the word out. There are endless opportunities to advertise, and unlimited potential to reach many people, but keep in mind that advertising can be expensive.

Be careful not to overspend on advertising, and do not even think about paying for advertising until you have a small, precisely focused niche. Shortly after registering your company and acquiring a business phone line, advertising salespeople will undoubtedly approach you and try to pressure you into signing up for their method of advertising. My advice to most new organizers is to just say "no," and skip advertising, at least in the beginning. Before you sign up for paid advertising, make certain that it is a good fit for your business.

Since advertising is impersonal, it is not particularly effective for marketing professional services. If your services are simple to understand and referrals for the type of service you offer are unlikely, you may have some success with ads. For instance, if you provide bookkeeping services, computer consulting, or run personal errands, you may be able to structure an ad in such a way that your prospective clients can clearly perceive the benefits of what you offer. Here are a few of the ways to advertise your business.

Direct mail: Never underestimate the power of traditional direct mail for building interest and arousing awareness in your services. Direct mail has been an effective tool for many professional organizers. With direct mail, you do not have to worry about spam or do-not-call restrictions. Low-tech mail marketing can be effective, especially if you are announcing a special event or promotion.

There is a fine line between desired and junk mail, so be creative if you plan to send mailers to your potential clients. According to the U.S. Postal Service, Americans receive more than 65 million pieces of direct mail each year. You do not want to be responsible for more clutter. The most effective mailers are the ones that get recipients to interact with the piece, so if you can come up with a reader response card or a game to make it fun, you have a better chance of getting your reader involved with the message.

If you have a tri-fold brochure with a space for a mailing label, and simply want to send the prospective client information, you can seal it and send it without an envelope. The quickest, easiest mailer is the post card, though room for content may be limited. With a postcard, there is no folding, stuffing or sealing. Most word processing software includes predefined templates for postcard printing. You can print postcards directly from your printer, add address labels, add postage, deliver to the post office, and you are done. In addition, the postcard postage is less costly than regular first class mail.

Be careful about where you get your mailing lists. Purchasing a list from a membership-based organization, like the Chamber of Commerce, is a good bet, since it is updated regularly. Avoid renting or buying expensive lists from mailing list companies. Their lists are often outdated and contain inaccurate or inactive addresses

Imprinted promotional products: Paying to put your name and phone number on specialty items like pens, envelope openers or calendars may be effective if your item is the type people will hold onto. Once you register your business name, vendors will probably solicit you by mail for advertising specialties, or you can request catalogues from providers that can be found through the Yellow Pages or on the Internet.

Make sure that whatever you spend your money on is truly useful to your potential clients. The best specialty items are those that generate conversations about what you do, or put your name and phone number in a place where people will see it when they need your services. For instance, a magnetic document holder might be effective if you specialize in organizing filing systems. Be very careful when giving out advertising specialties. You can sabotage your own efforts to help your clients reduce their clutter if you encourage them to collect novelties and trinkets.

Internet promotion: The Internet is a powerful marketing tool, and the best way to spend your advertising dollars. Since people are now in the habit of looking for information on the Internet, you might be surprised how many clients find you through the Web. If you can figure out ways to promote your services and products in other countries, you can even reach clients around the world through the Internet.

In addition to marketing through your own website, you can pay to post your information and receive consulting referrals from a number of professional organizer websites. There are websites and electronic magazines that take advertising and articles from organizers. Submit articles in the places you are considering advertising, to see what generates interest. Consider experimenting with free online listings like craigslist.org, before shelling out money for online advertising.

Magazines: Magazines allow you to target very specific demographics, such as age, gender and interests to ensure the right people read your message. With regard to layout, colors, and options for displaying your image, the sky is the limit with magazine advertising.

It is very expensive to advertise in major magazines; however, you can reach tightly targeted audiences through magazines with smaller circulation. It is practically impossible to measure the results with any accuracy. Before contacting a magazine and spending your advertising dollars, find out audience size and a description of the magazine's readers. Get several issues of the magazine and study the ads. Call a few people in your area of specialization and ask them their opinion of the magazine.

Costs for placing magazine ads vary from publication to publication, and depend on size and position. Magazine ads are significantly more expensive than newspaper ads. Most magazines offer space ranging from a full-page ad down to a quarter-page ad or smaller.

To place an ad, magazines require a lead-time anywhere from 1-6 months. Once you place an ad in a magazine, it will appear once a month. You can cut the cost in half and still get repeated impressions over time by choosing to run your ads every-other-month instead of every month.

Magnetic vehicle signs: If it is in good condition, clean and rust-free, your car can be a traveling billboard with your identity displayed on magnetic door signs. For less than $50, you can have a customized magnetic sign made for your car to call attention to your business everywhere you go. Car signs are made of magnetized vinyl and apply easily to your vehicle. Some car doors are not made of metal (like Saturn), so do make sure that magnets adhere to your car doors.

Be sure to keep business cards and brochures with you. Be prepared when people inquire about the signage on your car. Be aware that some of your clients may be very private about whom they hire, and they may not want your signs displayed in their driveway.

Newsletters: Because of the Internet and the ability to send newsletters electronically, the organizations that publish printed newsletters are dwindling. Those that still do, offer great opportunities for inexpensive advertising. Putting an ad in a targeted newsletter can generate good results, so it might be worth your while to investigate and advertise in newsletters that will reach your target audience. Try to find a newsletter that targets your audience. Examples might be groups and social clubs like mom's newsletters and mothers of twins.

Newspapers: Because of their wide distribution and affordable options, newspapers are the most common form of advertising for small businesses. The author of *Taming the Paper Tiger*, Barbara Hemphill started her business by placing an ad in the local newspaper. Barbara was a pioneer, and professional organizers were unheard of back then, so it may be tough to gauge whether that would be a comparable investment today.

People are more likely to remember and recognize you if they have recurring impressions from a regularly appearing ad. Your ad should appear frequently, consistently, and deliver one simple message. Ad space in newspapers can be purchased by the column inch. The lead-time to place an ad in your local newspaper is usually no more than a few days. Once you place the ad, it will appear daily for the length of time you purchased. If you do advertise in newspapers, avoid large-circulation publications. You will get more for your money with small, tightly focused publications.

Radio and television: If you want to get on radio or television, your best bet is to try to be interviewed, or to be included in an organizing program. It is safe to say that radio and television advertising is cost-prohibitive for your business. Radio advertising costs vary by region. A radio ad can cost anywhere from $100 to $5,000. Radio stations usually sell sponsorships for specific segments of their programming. If you sponsor an event such as a traffic report or weather forecast, your company will be mentioned at the same time every day.

The cost to produce a 30-second national television commercial is anywhere from $1,000 to $500,000. That does not include airtime. The cost to air your 30-second commercial varies according to the expected number of viewers. A 30-second spot during the Super Bowl could cost $2-3 million. A 30-second time slot in a medium-sized market can be purchased for as little as $5 per 1,000 viewers.

In radio and television advertising, frequency is the big factor. If the listening or viewing habits of your target demographic are such that they will be tuned in for hours at a time, once a day might be enough. If your demographic tends to tune in for a few minutes at a time, you will miss them if you do not run your ad multiple times each day. The good news is that the National Association of Professional Organizers has implemented initiatives that gain media exposure for our industry, benefiting all professional organizers.

Trade shows: Business expos, trade shows, and vendor fairs can be a valuable part of your marketing plan. They are designed to allow you to meet potential clients face-to-face in a brief period. In addition to establishing a presence in the marketplace and enhancing your image and visibility, they are a great place to network and prospect for new clients. Many associations and Chambers of Commerce have yearly exhibits that are affordable for small businesses. They provide you with a small booth or tabletop to exhibit your services. At many trade shows, there is more business transacted between exhibitors than with attendees. For those who provide services for businesses, this can produce a good deal of business for a professional organizer.

Booth space is generally inexpensive, costing anywhere from $2 to $13 per square foot. The typical small booth covers 100 square feet. Sharing a booth with other complementary service providers can save expenses and give you some occasional relief from the trade show floor while you take a break.

The fact that most business-to-business shows do not allow selling on the show floor is not an issue for the professional organizer. The main objective for your participation is to introduce yourself and your services, make an impression, and generate leads. You may also have an opportunity to generate PR for your company at a trade show. Editors and journalists attend trade shows looking for stories, and it is very possible you can capture their attention and get your company or services featured in their publication.

A little planning and effort will make your trade show booth effective. Although you initially may not be able to afford a professional trade show display, you can design a good trade show booth with materials purchased at your local office supply store and a little ingenuity. Create an attention-getting sign that announces a benefit of your services. Have a drawing for a prize in order to capture names and give people a reason to come by your booth and talk to you. Provide something of value for the attendees, like a handout with a list of organizing tips.

The most important part of your exhibit is you. Do not just sit back or give out business cards. Greet people as they come by your table and introduce yourself to exhibitors at nearby booths. Rather than giving away brochures at the show, offer to mail information and get the person's name and address. Follow up the very next day with anyone you agreed to contact or mail information.

Yellow Pages: The Yellow Pages can be an important advertising medium for you. A business phone line will automatically get you a free basic listing in the main Yellow Pages, which is what most people use. Although you are not directly paying for advertising, a business phone line does cost more than a residential phone line. It may be worth your money to get a business line, if for no other reason than the business the Yellow Pages may attract for you.

A relatively new heading can be found in most Yellow Pages publications for organizing businesses. Category names such as Organizing Products and Services – Household and Business, or Organizing Services and Systems are commonplace. Depending on your specialty, you may want additional listings so that potential clients can find you, and not your competition, when they need your services. Other possible category headings might be Home Design and Planning, Office Services, Personal Services and Assistants, or Relocation Services.

Be careful about spending money on a large Yellow Pages ad, as additional or more enhanced listings are quite costly. For a three-line listing, you might pay from $150 to $300 every month. A full year commitment (the life of the directory) is required, and you will not be able to change the design, so plan carefully and do not let anyone talk you into more than you can afford.

Measuring the effectiveness of advertising can be difficult. If you pay to advertise, be sure to code your ads or put other tracking mechanisms in place to keep track of the results from each source and ensure your advertising dollars are paying off.

Window decals: Like a magnetic sign, a window decal can function as a traveling billboard with your identity displayed on the windows. For less than $50, you can buy custom decals that apply to your car windows. You can display your company name, phone number and website, and even your company logo.

Developing promotional tools

Business cards: Business cards are one of the smallest, cheapest and most convenient ways to promote your business. Send your business card with every piece of correspondence, and carry them with you everywhere you go, even social events, your kid's soccer games and the local carnival. I am always amazed by the places where I meet people who are interested in what I do, even on vacation. Having my business card available makes it easy to share my contact information and set up the opportunity for a business connection.

If the back of your business card is blank, write a personal handwritten note on the back each time you distribute your card to help people remember who you are, how you met, and why they should call you.

Coupons: You can create coupons on your desktop printer and display them in your local area to generate interest in your services. If you have a good relationship with other professional colleagues, you might ask them to put your coupons on the counters of their offices or waiting rooms, and offer to give out their coupon in exchange. When clients see your coupons displayed by someone they trust, it is an implied referral from the person giving them out.

> Liz gets a manicure every week and a haircut every six weeks at the same professional salon. Since she has gotten to know her nail technician and other stylists at the salon quite well, Liz has arranged a reciprocal agreement to exchange coupons. She created coupons the size of business cards that sit in a container on the nail technician's table. When the topic of getting organized comes up in the salon, the stylists give their clients one of Liz's coupons. In exchange, Liz has a supply of coupons that she hands out every time she gets a compliment on her nails or hair.

It may also be appropriate for your business to post coupons on the bulletin boards of your local convenience store, grocery store, or other local merchant.

> Tracy is a professional organizer who specializes in children's rooms. She belongs to an exercise gym for women. The gym allows its members to post advertising on its bulletin board. Tracy posts coupons on the bulletin board offering a free twenty-minute consultation. Between the coupons and using her exercise time as an opportunity to network with local moms, 75% of Tracy's business is generated from contacts she makes at her exercise gym.

Flyers and brochures: Although they are becoming somewhat outdated because of websites, flyers and brochures still have a place in marketing. Written sales material does not really sell, but it does tell. Even if you have a great website to which you can refer potential clients, it is a good idea to have some brochures that people can read at their leisure. Some of your prospective clients will expect to see a printed brochure.

Unlike phone conversations or face-to-face meetings, you can take your time writing and editing brochures to make sure they communicate the message you want to convey. If you include a picture of yourself, your brochure can help to identify you to your client before you meet her, alleviating some of the anxiety of that first meeting.

Be careful not to overload your materials with information. Concentrate on one or two key messages and do not try to jam too much information into one piece, or you may risk losing your audience entirely. The most effective brochure includes a listing of services, pictures, graphics, benefits of your services, and testimonials. Be sure to include your member logo if you belong to a professional association.

Include your brochure in press kits and information packages you send to the media. Take plenty of brochures to trade shows and offer one to every visitor to your booth. Take a handful of brochures to Chamber of Commerce meetings and any other events where a networking table is provided. If you are at a networking event and collect business cards from potential clients, mail them brochures as soon as you get back to your office.

If you plan to post your flyer on public bulletin boards, use brightly colored paper and promote a discount or special offer to get people's attention. Post fliers on grocery store bulletin boards, malls, libraries, post offices, banks, churches, and any place that allows the posting of literature.

Postcards: Postcards are a quick and simple way to keep in touch with your prospects and clients. Unlike other literature, postcards are usually read. They are inexpensive to buy, easy to personalize, and cheap to send via first-class mail. You can buy postcards two or four to a page and print a message on your laser printer, such as "Maria Smith announces the opening of Maria's Concierge Services," or you can use postcards to send a personal note like, "Hi, I have not seen you for a while." It is even appropriate to send a client a postcard while on vacation.

Besides being a great marketing tool, postcards can be used as tools for cleaning up your mailing list. Simply add, *Address service requested* below the return address, and you will receive notification of forwarded mail.

Signature line: When you send a letter via electronic mail, you can attach a signature that is actually like a business card or an ad for what you do. A signature is a block of text that is added automatically when you compose a new message or a reply to an email. Your electronic signature can include your name, company name, tag line, address, phone, email address and website URL. The signature line can be a very effective method of getting people to your website.

If you have an event or special promotion to announce, your signature line is a great way to do it. It costs you nothing to add a line in your signature mentioning the upcoming event. Even better, add a link to the page on your website promoting your event.

Newsletters: Keeping in touch with your clients and prospects can be challenging, and a periodic newsletter can be the solution. A newsletter is a powerful means of displaying your knowledge and help build brand awareness. Newsletters are also a great way to keep your mailing lists up to date.

Make it easy for your readers by giving only informative content that is relevant to the services you provide. For instance, if you help clients eliminate clutter, you might include articles about new ways to recycle, resources for donating goods, tax advantages of donating unwanted possessions, etc. Another idea is to include case studies of ways your services helped your clients become more productive. If you deliver your newsletter through the mail, be sure to use good quality paper.

Distributing your newsletter via mass electronic mail is cost effective, but you must be knowledgeable about current anti-spam laws. The best way to stay within the anti-spam guidelines is to allow people to sign up for your newsletter through your website. HTML newsletters, though slower to download, produce greater response rates than plain text, and graphics and colors tend to make the publications appear more professional.

Voicemail greeting: If you do not have staff to answer your phone, have an answering machine or contract with your phone service for voicemail. The way callers are greeted when you are away can be a very effective marketing tool. The tone of your greeting should be friendly and sincere. If you find that you get many calls with a specific question, you might answer that question within the context of your greeting. Refer your callers to your website for more information.

Networking

The essence of a thriving business is the ability to build and maintain successful long-term relationships. Networking is fundamental to building those relationships. Networking is not necessarily about encounters that lead to relationships with potential clients. Networking is about making connections that take your business where you want it to go. No prosperous businessperson ever stands alone, and by networking, you create a team — a network —to help you succeed in business. The people you surround yourself with become your team. Your network of knowledgeable people can increase your expertise and save you time, energy and money.

Definition of networking: Networking means different things, from the opportunity to meet someone new, to the ability of professionals to meet and exchange ideas, to opportunities to market, to opportunities for support and personal growth. Networking can put the power of what others know to work for your business. Good contacts will nourish your business, and networking is critical to building your list of contacts.

How long does your contact list need to be? The power of networking is not in the people you know. It is in the people your contacts know. *Six Degrees of Separation* was a 1993 film based on the premise that anyone in the world can be connected to any other person through a chain of only six acquaintances. Based on that theory, you are only a few links away from people who may help you. Networking helps to build the chain.

Networking allows you to interact with others and gives you the opportunity to spread the word about your services in the circles in which you are involved every day. You will have a chance to network and get business referrals just about anywhere you meet people. You already belong to networks, even if they are not within the framework of organized business networking. From friends and neighbors to recreational and other leisure activities, you are involved in networks that are a source of social fulfillment, encouragement and support. Sometimes these groups are the best for business networking, since friends are the best business and referral contacts. Sharpen your networking skills and show up on the professional scenes as the face of your company. You are!

Your introduction: Who are you? What is it that you do? Why do you do it? What is in it for the client? Before you attempt to introduce yourself or your company to prospects, be clear about who you are and what the benefits are in working with you. Be prepared to describe what you do, emphasizing the strengths and uniqueness of your business.

Marketing services is quite different from marketing products, which can be seen and touched. The only way a potential client can comprehend your services is by your personal description. To sell your services, you must sell yourself and communicate the benefits of hiring you. In order to gain the trust of your prospective clients, you must convey your personality, your uniqueness, and your technical skills in a precise manner.

People will not enter into a relationship unless they have a clear idea with whom they are dealing. Why do they buy from one service provider and not another? Their reasons may include reputation, availability, credentials, background, personality, price, or convenience. What, about you and your services, will make a client choose you over another organizer?

People need to see the advantages, or benefits of using your services. "I'm a professional organizer" or "I organize home and offices" will not differentiate you. Rather than focusing on your features, think about the client's goals. You might organize financial records. That would be a feature of your services, but in order for clients to see the advantage of hiring you, they need to see how your service will help them meet their goals. An example of a benefit would be, "hiring me to organize your financial records puts information at your fingertips", or "hiring me to organize your financial records makes it easier for you to complete your tax return." Your service gives clients the peace of mind of not having to worry about the IRS auditing their returns.

Based on the premise that you usually have about 10-20 seconds to make an impression, marketing advisors recommend preparing and memorizing an elevator speech. In this short introduction, you have an opportunity to begin a meaningful conversation with a potential client or someone who can refer a client to you. Position yourself and your business within the first few seconds in terms of benefits and outcome. Concentrate on what happens when your clients use your services. Use simple, conversational language that focuses on what types of clients you serve best and how you help them achieve their ambitions.

Prepare a statement that describes how your clients are better after having hired you. Once you have developed and perfected your elevator speech, work on a one-minute commercial to use on those occasions when you have at least 60 seconds to make your introduction. Then, develop a statement that articulates what you do in five seconds, and you will be prepared the next time someone asks," What do you do?" It may take some time to develop a great statement of introduction. Try using this simple structure:

"Hi, I'm _____. I work with _____ who want to _____. I enjoy being a professional organizer because my clients tell me that I _____."

A great introduction conveys who you are and what you do, feels natural to you, gets people interested in talking to you, and helps them to remember you. Compose several self-introductions, and then combine several of them. Practice giving your elevator speech to close friends or family and ask for feedback. While you are practicing, work on your handshake. Use a firm grip, focus on the face of the person you are meeting, make eye contact, and smile.

When you believe you have a great introduction, use it repeatedly not just in your face-to-face introductions, but also in your brochure, on your website, in your press releases, in your voicemail greeting, and anywhere there is an opportunity to introduce yourself and your business.

Where to network: Every time you have lunch with a colleague, serve on a board for an organization, recommend a resource, or lend a helping hand, you are networking. Networking can happen just about anywhere and here is a list for starters:

Social mixers	Your church
Charity events	Your fitness center
Sporting events	Trade shows
Seminars	City Council meetings
The Country Club	Professional organization meetings
Arts events	Networking groups
Chamber of Commerce meetings	Conferences and conventions

If you are involved in your community, you already have an excellent resource for building a word-of-mouth referral base. If you are not already active, research groups in your community that you can join, or at least attend the general membership meetings of your local chamber of commerce to get to know other business people in your community. Investigate clubs that are designed to help members generate leads and referrals. Find out about trade shows and fund raisers in your area. Read the business calendar section in your local papers and look for upcoming meetings. Choosing the groups that have the kinds of people who are good prospects for you is the key. Some community groups might even list you in their directory or allow you to speak to their organization about what you do.

An alternative form of networking, the latest trend is to connect in cyberspace. Online networking is efficient and allows you to increase your audience beyond your local region. You can hold discussions 24/7, from the privacy of your home in chat rooms, message boards and websites dedicated to your specialty. If you are not able to attend local chapter meeting of NAPO, you may be able to participate in their message boards. Although online networking is not a match for a handshake and a smile, it may be worth your while to investigate groups that match your interests to supplement face time.

Effective networking: Being a casual visitor is not enough if you want to build business. You will only benefit from networking if you are active. Just signing up for membership and having your name on a roster will be of little use. Attend meetings, get involved with committees and events, and actively seek out ways that you can contribute. If you find a group that fits for you, volunteer to do something, even if it is just standing at the door to welcome attendees. People usually have to see you several times before they feel comfortable with you. Without effort and commitment on your part, you will not be able to build any lasting relationships.

Networking is not about meeting people to sell your services. The true benefit of networking is that it allows you to build relationships and make friends. We can all recognize the person in a group who is there just to see how much business she can get. Networking is a process of building a trusting relationship with another individual, learning about mutual needs, and exploring ways of working together to help each other. As you build trust, you will eventually establish a desire to assist each other and work together for each other's success.

You will benefit from networking if you are always thinking of how you can help other people and solve their problems. Some of the most effective networkers have a reputation for what they do for others in the business community rather than for the services they sell. Others are likely to want to do things for you if they appreciate you as a person, rather than a professional organizer. Establishing yourself as a lead generator, a matchmaker, a resource center, a mentor, or a trusted advisor will tend to bring about a spirit of reciprocation among your business contacts.

Generating interest: Showing interest in other people often generates interest in you and your services. Ask questions of the people you meet. Focus on them and hear what they have to say. Do not start a conversation by introducing yourself, like "Hi! I'm Suzie. I'm a professional organizer. Blah. Blah. Blah." Instead, start a conversation based on what you see, hear, smell, taste or feel. If you are in the locker room at the health club, you might say, "Wow! That was really torture today." If you are at a formal networking event, you might say, "Tell me what made you decide to come to this event." You might also ask, "What other organizations do you belong to?"

After the conversation goes on for a few minutes, people will naturally want to know about you. Speak with your heart and tell people what you love to do. Cast a positive light on your business and everyone with whom you associate, and avoid matters of confidentiality. Everyone likes success stories, and speaking with passion inspires others.

If you meet someone at a business function that you think might be a suitable prospect for you, ask for his business card. Tell him you would like to have his contact information to distribute to your clients or other people you know. Jot a note on the back of his card (date, event, topic discussed, etc.) to help you remember him and to show you are genuinely interested in him. Chances are he will become curious about you as well and will ask for your card, so always carry a supply of business cards in your pocket. Write down the results of your networking after every event, whether you made a new friend, got a good business lead, or heard a great story. You do not want to pull out that pile of business cards the next day and forget why you kept a particular card or what you agreed to do for someone.

People can become defensive and clam up if you directly ask for business. Learn to ask for ideas and referrals, instead. Even if you suspect the person you are talking to has a need for your services, ask if he knows anyone who could use your services. Better yet, ask the question in terms of your specialty, like, "Do you have any ideas about how I might find someone who has a need for someone to help him organize his garage?" People will not always respond favorably. It depends on the person, place and time. Do not get turned off. Some days you win.

Other benefits of networking: Getting new business and referrals is only one aspect of organized business networking. I have found that the friendships I have made in those circles have become much more than just acquaintances. Some have become my business confidantes. I have learned that no matter what fields they are in, other small business owners understand my frustrations better than anyone else does. They give me the best free, candid advice without sparing my feelings. I like to network with other small business owners to bounce around ideas and sometimes just to vent. The short time I spend with them boosts my spirits and sometimes saves my sanity.

As much as I advocate a helpful and giving spirit in business relationships, I must caution you to stay aware. Unfortunately, there are selfish people out there who will never appreciate your generosity. If you do not see any indication of reciprocation, stop giving

Getting referrals

Every business owner and service professional knows that referrals are by far the best way to generate business. People prefer to have referrals for services because someone they know and trust referred them. Referrals are the most valuable means of marketing your services, and bring about the greatest return over other methods. Getting the word out about what type of client you help is very important. Building your referral base takes time and nurturing.

Referral arrangements: You can get referrals by paying a fee to a referral service. These arrangements may be geared towards consultants, small business people, or even specifically towards professional organizers. With these types of referral arrangements, companies maintain Web portals offering to match prospects with organizers. If the prospect's needs match your services, you will be contacted. Another means of referral arrangements are your professional memberships. Become a member of every association suited to your specialty, and make sure to be listed in their referral system.

Do not expect high-quality, pre-qualified referrals from these arrangements. Many of the names you get from these services are actually tire-kickers who are unlikely to become customers or clients. They might even be amateur or rookie organizers posing as potential clients. Be cautious before investing a lot of time in pursuing these leads.

Commercial referral groups: Some groups (often called leads groups or tips clubs) have been created for the sole purpose of generating referrals. Some leads groups are affiliated with Chambers of Commerce, and others are franchises like BNI (Business Networking International) and LeTip Clubs. The primary purpose of these groups is to exchange qualified business tips and leads with fellow members. These referral groups are administered in different ways and rules vary. Some have strict attendance policies and permit very few absences from meetings. Most allow one person per professional classification, and prospective members must be approved via an application process. This means that the business type you represent must be exclusive to the group, so that you are not competing for business with another individual in the group. They generally meet once a week or every other week.

There is usually a requirement that you contribute a minimum number of leads or referrals. If sharing leads is mandatory, the quality of leads may be questionable. When you receive a lead from another member, you will need more than a name. It is critical that you qualify the lead and find out all the circumstances behind the referral. It can be quite awkward to contact a cold lead, since your call implies that someone thinks he is disorganized. Calling a prospect and saying that someone suggested he needs help getting organized, can be similar to saying someone said he needs therapy.

Although these types of groups are often more effective for those selling product than service, they can be a great way to build business relationships. Many organizers benefit from membership, and some have built businesses on the referrals gained from membership.

Word of mouth referrals: Market surveys show that word-of-mouth is the most influential factor in a client's decision to choose a consultant. As your business becomes a part of your daily life, more and more people will be curious about what you do. Try to find an unobtrusive way to bring the subject of your business up during every conversation you have with friends, at social gatherings and at business events. Each time you help others understand what you do, you start a trickle effect that leads to a perpetual source of referrals. When those people are in a conversation and the subject of getting organized comes up, your name will come to mind.

> I once got a call from a woman who wanted to hire me immediately, which made me a bit skeptical. She asked no questions, except to find out when was my next available appointment. When I asked who referred her to me, she said that she overheard a conversation in a restaurant (about 35 miles from where I live, incidentally). Some executives at the next table were talking about a professional organizer, and describing how she redesigns office space, sets up new filing systems, and teaches people how to manage their time effectively. This woman interrupted their conversation long enough to ask them for the name of this professional organizer. The executive pulled my phone number from his PDA. I never did find out who these men were, that were talking about me. She did not get their names, but she made sure to get mine.

Chapter Nine: Marketing and Public Relations

Let your friends and family know that you make it a practice to work only with ideal clients. Well-meaning friends and family sometimes refer prospects that turn out to be lousy clients who pay late and do not appreciate you. The best way to avoid this scenario is to create an Ideal Client Profile and do your best to communicate your ideal client to everyone you know. The process of client referral and the client evaluation should weed out most deadbeat clients and projects, alleviating your need to collect payment.

Vendor referrals: Taking the time to develop a close relationship with a vendor or service provider often means referrals. Professional organizers develop relationships with vendors for various reasons, including product discounts and commissions. Strategic alliances with vendors and suppliers can help to solidify your specialty, so that people see you as an expert. Probably the greatest benefit of vendor relationships, however, is that when the need arises for professional assistance in the area of organizing, you are the person who gets the call.

Client referrals and testimonials: Once you start working with clients, they will become one of your best sources of future referrals. Having your existing clients do the work for you saves you time and money in finding new clients. Referrals are your reward for providing high quality service. Client referrals are your easiest source of advertising and cost you nothing.

So, how do you get referrals? You get referrals by asking for them! Enthusiastic clients are usually so happy with your work that they want to tell the world, so encourage them to spread the word about your services. Pay attention to your clients to get insights on potential clients. Clients who are mothers of soccer players may know other soccer moms who could use your services. You might even offer your clients a discount or some sort of reward for bringing you new clients. Direct word-of-mouth referrals are the best referrals, because your existing clients have testified about the quality of service you provide. Your reputation will eventually grow your business.

If your clients have great things to say about you, take advantage of the opportunity to build your reputation. When a client calls to tell you how great it is to feel in control of his life and elaborates about the positive changes you have brought about, ask, "Would you be so kind as to put that in writing?" Each time you complete a job; ask the client for permission to list him as a reference. Ask whether he would agree to being contacted by prospective clients. When you get electronic mail from a client full of praise for your work, email him back and ask for permission to post his testimonial in your brochure or on your website.

Ask clients to put their thoughts down on paper. Even clients who comment to you about how pleased they are with your services are not likely to take the time to write a letter, unless you specifically ask for their written feedback or testimonial. Alternatively, you can get testimonials from your clients to help you improve your services by sending out a client satisfaction form or having them complete a client survey. Ask them why they believe you deliver more value than your competition. Send them a form to complete, or simply send them a letter welcoming their suggestions or criticism and asking them to give you their opinion of your services. Be sure to include a permission statement ("You have my permission to use my comments in your website and other promotional materials") at the bottom of the survey and a place for your client's signature and date.

If your clients are members of Angie's List, they can help you gain new clients by sharing the experience they have had working with you. Angie's List is a website that lists unbiased reports and reviews about service companies in specific geographic areas. Angie's List is a growing collection of homeowners' real-life experiences with local service companies. Angie Hicks founded the List in 1995 with 1000 members in Columbus, Ohio. The people who join Angie's List are looking for a way to find trustworthy companies that perform high-quality work. Companies cannot pay to be on Angie's List. A service company gets on the List only after a member submits a report about her experience with that company.

You may receive some great testimonials, or you may find new opportunities to improve your services as you gain your client's perspective of the quality of your services. When you get a client testimonial, ask his permission to reprint it and use his name in your printed brochures and on your website. If you have a client who is a raving fan, ask if you can occasionally give his phone number to a qualified prospect who is looking for a recommendation about you.

Referrals from colleagues: Sometimes colleagues will refer their own clients to you when they reach a point where they can no longer serve them effectively. If your colleague knows you and your specialty, she understands the nature of your services. She understands her client's needs. She has earned her client's trust. If a colleague recommends you as a way to serve a client when she is unable to do so, you have received a precious gem. When you receive a qualified referral from a colleague, you have no marketing costs. You do not have to spend your time, money, or energy to gain this client.

If you do not know the colleague who made the referral, though you belong to the same professional organization, be sure to follow your normal pre-qualification process. Colleagues will occasionally pass along your name when they do not have time or have no interest in serving a particular client. Because a colleague referred a client, does not necessarily mean he is the type or quality of client you desire.

Referral fees: Organizers often act as intermediaries, helping their clients find services that they themselves do not provide. You may help your clients in this way and refer clients to other organizers when they are outside of your specialty or geographic region. When you identify a potential client, interest him in organizing services, and actually arrange a meeting between the client and another organizer that involves work, a referral fee may seem appropriate.

A referral fee, sometimes called a finders fee, is a monetary reward for introducing new business. When it involves professional services, it is usually called a referral fee. You may be offered a referral fee for referring work to an organizer who is better located geographically, or who you believe is better qualified to assist your clients. Paying a referral fee is a time-proven business practice. A referral fee shows an organizer's gratitude to you for accepting responsibility for his work, and for saving him from having to market and sell his services.

If your intention is to earn a referral fee for introducing a client to another organizer, the manner in which you make the introduction is important. If you casually suggest that a client call so-and-so to inquire about her services, it is unlikely that you will ever receive a referral fee, let alone acknowledgment of your role in the introduction. It will be more valuable for you to call the organizer, suggest that he get in touch with the client, and ask him to follow up with you when he has done so. From my experience, unless you ask for a referral fee, you are not likely to get one. If you are thinking about making an introduction and believe it merits a referral fee, you may consider agreeing on the details of the fee beforehand.

Referral fees are usually a percentage of revenues. Referral fee percentages in the organizing industry range from 10% – 20%. You are not obligated to pay a referral fee, but you may establish good will and a better chance of continued referrals if you do reward your colleague with a referral fee. Not paying a referral fee when one might be expected could bring about resentment and misunderstanding.

Referral fees can play a role in tutoring new organizers or building trust with an experienced organizer. You may be reluctant to accept a client because you perceive yourself inadequate to serve the client effectively. On the other hand, you may be reluctant to refer the business to another organizer because you will lose the fee. If you accept a job for which you are not qualified though, not only do you risk having an unsatisfied client, you also deprive the client of a qualified organizer. When you refer the client to a more qualified organizer, you can benefit in several ways. If you request to shadow the experienced organizer, you can observe and learn, while the experienced organizer best serves the client. You receive training, experience, and your client's respect and appreciation, while being compensated with a referral fee.

Laws in some states restrict the sharing of fees or division of fees, and the referral of work between professionals. The circumstances vary, so you should know the rules in your state. If you do not think it is appropriate to accept a referral fee, you might ask your colleague to reduce the client's proposal accordingly.

Referral tracking: Keep track of where your clients come from and be aware of your most effective centers of influence. Where are your centers of influence? You may be surprised to discover that a large percentage of your work is due to your relationship with a single person or group. Referrals are treasures, and it will benefit you to cherish and nurture the relationships with those who transfer their enthusiasm for your services and refer business to you!

> My husband and I are members of a vacation ownership program (timeshare) called the Disney Vacation Club. Every year, we host a party for a growing number of friends and family who are members. Last year we sent out invitations to 16 families. We've never really kept track of how many people we have directly referred, but when we sat down to figure out how our party got to be so large, we realized that almost all of those invited to our party could be traced back to us. Our enthusiasm transferred to three families who became members, who in turn passed on their enthusiasm to others. We discovered that we are a valuable center of influence for the Disney Vacation Club.

Cross-promoting: Your specialty may be a perfect fit to gain visibility by sharing promotional expense and effort with others who share your market. For instance, if your niche is Feng Shui, your target market may be the same as an interior designer, a massage therapist, and a furniture distributor in your area. By combining resources, you can create a joint advertising campaign.

Another idea for cross-promotion is to approach a compatible supplier and offer a 10% referral fee plus a 10% discount to his clients. The cost to you would be 20% of the fee paid by a client you might otherwise never have met.

Getting free publicity

Promoting yourself through publicity, commonly referred to as PR (public relations), is about getting the media to generate coverage of you and your business. Imagine a full-page spread featuring you as a professional organizer with photos displaying your best work. That is free publicity. Publicity is cost-effective, and gets word-of-mouth going. It can play a key role in marketing your services and building your credibility. Good reviews about you and your business can generate many more inquiries than paid advertisements. Publicizing and creating a positive image of your company can easily translate into paying clients.

Make it your PR objective to get calendar listings, news briefs, or even feature stories about you printed or broadcast. Get to know editors and reporters in your area and at the trade publications that cover your clients. When building your media contact list, include local newspapers, radio stations, network and cable television stations, magazines, online media, and trade publications. Set up a regular schedule for sending out press releases.

Writing and submitting a press release: The usual first step to gaining publicity is to submit a press release to newspapers, radio stations, television stations, and magazines. A press release should be brief and contain the same basic information as an advertisement.

A press release should be typed double-spaced on a single sheet of company letterhead. At the top of the sheet, type NEWS RELEASE or FOR IMMEDIATE RELEASE (use capital letters and left-justify the text). Insert the release date on the next line. A separate header should be included titled FOR MORE INFORMATION (use capital letters and right-justify the text) Type your name, phone number, and email address on the lines below.

The first paragraph of your press release should be an attention-getting headline (use capital letters and align text in the center of the page). The headline grabs the reader's attention and gets her interested enough to keep reading. In the next paragraphs, give detailed information, in descending order of importance and briefly stress the benefits (convenience, cost, quality, etc.) of your service. Be sure to answer the who, what, where, when, and why questions. The last paragraph should describe your company and what it offers, and include your website. After the final paragraph, insert two line spaces and three number signs (###) centered in the page to indicate the end of the press release.

Send your press release via mail or email to the appropriate editor of the publication where you want to have it printed. You will find editors' names and addresses in the front pages of most publications and on the websites of larger publications.

Make your own news: Never pass up an opportunity to generate publicity. Many small newspapers have a business section and welcome information about new businesses in the area. Send your press release with a cover letter to the business editor of your local newspaper. If you market to businesses, send a news release to the managing editors of business trade publications. Be sure to specify in your cover letter why your services would be of interest to their audience.

You must take a proactive approach to getting free publicity by identifying interesting story ideas. You can make a press release newsworthy by emphasizing how your business relates to something currently happening in the news. Look for something the media might find interesting, or a hook. You could create your own news by sponsoring a contest or giving an award. A popular contest among organizers is the messiest office or messiest desk contest. You could assume sponsorship of this contest if it does not already exist in your area, or get a charity or trade group to sponsor the contest with you. Some other possible news ideas for press releases

- Attendance at a national organizing conference
- Speaking engagements
- A new service you are offering
- A new certification you have earned
- A seminar or workshop you are giving
- Election to a board or appointment to a committee
- An office move
- Service projects for charities, non-profits or community events
- An interesting alliance you have formed with another business
- An unusual service you offer
- Upcoming speaking or training events
- Membership in an association
- The anniversary of your company
- Professional achievements, awards or accomplishments
- A client success story (with the client's permission)
- Your contribution to the community

You might be able to tie into a season, a holiday or even a relatively unknown national observance. Christmas might be an opportunity for publicity if your service involves helping people be more productive during the holidays. There are a number of calendars available, such as Chase's Calendar

Chapter Nine: Marketing and Public Relations

of Events, which list national days, weeks and months that are dedicated to events or occupations. The following table lists some examples of annual holidays and observances that should generate some ideas for publicity opportunities for your business (observance dates are subject to change, so check Chase's Calendar of Events for accuracy).

Chase's Calendar of Events Annual Event	Date Observed
National Clean Out Your Desk Month	January
National Get Organized Month	January
New Year's Day	January 1st
National Clean Off Your Desk Day	2nd Monday in January
National Archive Your Files Month	February
National Clean Out Your Computer Day	2nd Tuesday in February
National Pay Your Bills Week	3rd Week in February
National Procrastination Week	1st Full Week in March
National Clutter Awareness Week	4th Week in March
National Organize Your Home Office Day	2nd Tuesday in March
Stress Awareness Month	April
Organize Your Files Week	3rd Full Week in April
Income Tax Deadline	April 15th
National Moving Month	May
Revise Your Work Schedule Month	May
National Scrapbook Day	1st Saturday in May
Small Business Week	2nd Week in June
Financial Freedom Day	July 1st
Simplify Your Life Week	1st Week in August
National Self-Improvement Month	September
Fight Procrastination Day	1st Wednesday in September
National Clean Out Your files Month	October
America Recycles Day	November 15th
National Stress-Free Family Holiday Month	December

The National Association of Professional Organizers declared the month of January Get Organized Month. Many professional organizers tie into this annual event by putting on workshops or coordinating projects to increase public awareness of organizing and their businesses.

Other ways to get noticed: Writing articles for magazines, newsletters and other publications will get you exposure and help to build your reputation as an expert. If your article is interesting enough to attract people to your business, it can be a powerful method of advertising. Submit your articles to publications that reach your potential clients. Most publications welcome free content and are happy to publish your interesting and well-written article. You can make yourself known by writing articles and then reprinting them as handouts (as long as you have retained the rights) to build your credibility. Here are just a few ideas for some *how to* articles you might write:

- How to encourage children to stay organized
- How to prepare for or avoid a tax audit by keeping your records in order
- How to organize a desk or work space
- How to save money by having an organized kitchen and planning meals
- How to prepare a house for quick sale
- How to save time running errands
- How to make space in a crowded office
- How to prepare for the hectic holiday season
- How to manage multiple priorities
- How to plan a party

Regular articles written by you will gain visibility for your name, establish your credibility, and build a steady flow of business. Offer free advice and let reporters know they can call on you when writing stories about your area of expertise. Be sure to insist that your name and business information is printed in the byline

Giving a talk at your local Rotary, Chamber of Commerce, library or similar group is a great opportunity to gain free publicity. Most local papers have calendars of monthly meetings and seminars. There are always groups and organizations looking for presenters, and getting organized is a very popular topic. You can be included by submitting a simple news release with just a few lines giving the facts about your talk and letting people know how they can attend.

Once you create a presentation, you can tailor it to your particular audience. Use flip charts and props to help demonstrate your topic and make your presentation more interesting. Prepare a handout or some other way for your audience to get your contact information. Make sure you get their contact information, too.

You can actually be paid to market your business through presentations, once you have enough experience. Offer to teach a class at your community center, park district, high school or community college. When you are paid to speak, your knowledge and expertise must do the work of promoting your business. You will generally not be allowed to talk about your services or distribute brochures and business cards. Always check with the venue about limitations with regard to promoting your business.

A simple method of getting free publicity that is often overlooked is to write a letter to the editor. Take a strong stand on an issue that will draw attention to your expertise. Sometimes just adding your two cents or some additional tips to an article already published can get you some visibility. Your odds of being published are very high if you write a pertinent letter to your local paper, association newsletter, or a trade magazine read by your potential clients. The odds of your letter making it to the editor's desk ranges from 2-5%, for major publications like Newsweek or USA Today to 50% or greater, for local newspapers.

If one method is not working for you, try another. Keep track of your publicity results. If you do not know where your clients are coming from, you will not be able to tell what is working and you will be spending a lot of effort on dead-end activities. As you track the effectiveness of your marketing programs, be sure to periodically refresh and refocus your research on your target audience. The most successful business owners are those who adapt their businesses to the constant shifts and perpetual changes in the market. You will get 80 percent of your results from 20 percent of your efforts (or clients). Determine what is working in your marketing and focus on pursuing the most profitable 20 percent.

Chapter Ten: Setting Your Fees

> *"What they pay for, they'll value. What they get for free, they'll take for granted, and then demand as a right. Hold them up for all the market will bear."* - Lois McMaster Bujold

It has been said that if you put the right service in front of the right person at the right time for the right price, your business will be successful. What is the right price? How much should you charge? Of all the questions that bother professional organizers, this one seems to be the most vexing. There is no right or wrong answer. What are the effects if you charge too much? Will your clients laugh at you? What are the consequences if you do not charge enough? Will you go broke?

Even those of us who have been in business for a long time occasionally wonder why we won a high-priced contract or lost a job to a lower bidder. When I started out, I knew nothing about pricing my services so I charged by the hour – $35 per hour. I did not take into consideration the time to get to and from my client's location, the time I invested in marketing, or the time to take care of bill paying and other administrative tasks. After paying my expenses, I was actually making a little better than $12 per hour. When I considered self-employment taxes and loss of benefits, I was making far less than my corporate wage.

Fee setting is a marketing function. You do not want to price yourself out of the market, but at the same time, you want to generate a sufficient margin to cover overhead and generate a profit. There are dozens of factors to consider when determining an acceptable and affordable fee. Every situation is unique and only you can decide what is right for you. But the cost of running the business, expected net gains, what the market will bear, the experience and skills you bring, and competition are just a few of the elements to consider when pricing. This chapter explores the various options for pricing and selling your services to attract business and make a profit.

Understanding antitrust laws

Many professional organizers who are indecisive about what to charge for their services seek advice about fee setting from other professional organizers. At NAPO Chapter meetings, new organizers often ask the question, "What is the going rate for a professional organizer?" That topic is forbidden at NAPO meetings. To discuss our rates at a chapter meeting could be construed as price fixing, or trying to reach an agreement on fees. Practices such as price fixing are in violation of antitrust laws and are subject to criminal prosecution.

The FTC has enacted laws that promote competition in the marketplace, called antitrust laws. The Federal Trade Commission (FTC) is a consumer protection agency with two mandates: to guard the marketplace from unfair methods of competition, and to prevent unfair or deceptive acts or practices that harm consumers. Antitrust laws benefit consumers by keeping prices low and the quality of goods and services high, while at the same time fostering opportunity for businesses by ensuring a level playing field among competitors.

Antitrust laws exist to promote competition in our industry, which is encouraged both by professional organizers vying for business and clients seeking the best deal. These laws prohibit competitors from making agreements on rates or fees. Since professional organizers can be in a competing relationship, discussing rates amongst ourselves could be interpreted as an attempt on our part to lessen competition, and could raise antitrust suspicions. Any mention of fees in conversations or correspondence with other professional organizers could be construed as price fixing. In order to keep from being involved in sticky situations with regard to fee setting, the best practice is to avoid discussing your fees except in negotiations with potential clients.

The psychology of fee setting

Developing a profitable mind-set: A profitable mind-set is essential to your existence as a business owner, and goes beyond survival and covering costs. It focuses on providing value, increasing clients and building the business. A profitable business will go beyond making a living by providing a service that benefits your clients. A thriving business will allow you to accumulate and reinvest profits gained from your business endeavors.

When setting fees, you may need to examine your attitudes about materialism and capitalism. If you cling to the notion that wealth must occur at the expense of everyone else, you will have a conflict with setting fees. A self-limiting belief is that profit is synonymous with greed and excess. The world is indeed full of people who desire wealth with little interest in ethical matters. Gaining money by engaging in fraudulent and deceptive tactics is not profit – it is taking advantage.

Profit is not a dirty word. Profit is nothing more than the surplus left to a business owner after deducting expenses. Your profit is not your client's loss. Your success does not mean another's failure. If you have a sense of scarcity or lack belief in the abundance of opportunity and wealth, your options and alternatives will be limited.

Making a profit is not necessarily synonymous with cash, and this distinction is important to understand as you develop a profitable mind-set. You can lose money for several years in a row as a new business, and yet be extremely profitable. Acquiring new clients and other business contacts, increasing knowledge and experience, and learning how to develop your strengths and compensate for your weaknesses can all pay off big in future years. Being profitable can also be described as new computer equipment, growing investment accounts, or new employees. Simply put, being profitable means you gain more than you lose.

If you want to generate a profit, you must be able to be competitive while balancing business volume with optimal pricing that is affordable for your clients. You must consider several factors in order to judge what price is reasonable for your services. Your rate will depend on:

- The type of services you provide
- The type of client you serve
- Your geographical area
- Your local market
- Your experience
- Your level of specialization
- Your knowledge of your clients and their issues
- The competition

Some well-meaning books and websites suggest that professional organizers should charge between $30 and $50 per hour. That may be a fair range if you have limited skills and experience, live in a region with a low cost of living, or plan to work for someone else. However, if you intend to build a business and spend your time, energy, money and creativity to market your services, you must establish a profitable price structure. Structure your fees so that you can replenish your capital and proceed toward your business goals.

A profitable mind-set opens up possibilities for creativity and discovery. It says, "There are plenty of opportunities in my market that I can identify and take advantage of productively. The more I need to know, the more I will learn. The more I produce, give, and sell, the more there is to produce, give, and sell. I am prepared to receive all that is available to me." If you develop this attitude, you will feel confident in setting reasonable fees for your services.

To be profitable, you must understand that as a business owner, your time will be split between attending to the tasks of developing your skills and knowledge (non-billable time), running your business (non-billable time), and attending to the needs of your clients (billable time). You must market and administer your business, and deliver your services. You will not be able to earn money for the time you spend looking for new business, investigating and preparing proposals, and pitching your services.

If you become so involved in delivery that you do not allow time to market, you will suffer, having intense periods of work, with periods of no work in between. If you do not work, you are not paid. Therefore, you must set your consulting rates high enough to allow for time off and time for marketing. A rule-of-thumb is to allow half of your time for marketing and administration, and half for the actual delivery of your service. When pricing your services, account for all of your non-billable activities and achieve a delicate balance.

Market conditions can influence a business, as many organizers who were in business on 09/11/2001 or during the September 2005 hurricane season can attest. Scarcity can drive up prices, just as supply and availability can drive down prices. Along with the economy, the endurance of a professional organizing business depends on many other factors, and incorrect pricing can have the most devastating effects. You must offer your clients good economic value, and you must ensure a healthy profit for yourself.

Acknowledging your value: One of the main reasons many professional organizers struggle is that they routinely undercharge. When trying to calculate what your services are worth and what the market will bear, you may find yourself in a dilemma. Money may be an uncomfortable conversation for you and it may be difficult for you to talk about your fees. You may have been providing organizing services for family and friends for free, and now have difficulty putting a price on your talent, time and effort. Your beliefs and attitudes will drive your fee setting. If you lack self-esteem or believe that it is fraudulent to charge for doing what you enjoy, you will have difficulty building a profitable business.

Chapter Ten: Setting Your Fees

It is common and natural to feel as if you are not really a professional organizer – that you are just playing the part. This feeling may be especially significant if you are new to the field. Just as when you first entered high school, became a spouse, became a parent, or when you changed jobs, there is a period during which you build experience and confidence. Your confidence will grow along with your abilities as you attend seminars and classes, read books, join entrepreneur organizations and work with clients.

Surprisingly, even experienced organizers are often unsure about their value or the viability of their fee structure. Some veteran organizers admit to having guilt feelings about how much they charge, even though they have many satisfied clients and get tons of referrals. My question for those who doubt their worth is, "if a client felt regret about writing you a check, why would he influence others to hire you?" Referrals are evidence that your clients want to share the joy and positive change you have brought into their lives. Referrals are testimonies that you are worth every penny you are paid.

Although you may be new to this phase in your career, you have other life experiences that make you capable. Whenever you are feeling insecure, remind yourself of your skills and talents and give yourself credit for your accomplishments.

The most certain way to avoid feeling like a fraud is never to be one. Be honest when potential clients ask about your experience, and do not ever misrepresent yourself. Try to overcome the feeling of uncertainty as fast as you can by concentrating on the value of your services. Value what you provide and make sure it is outstanding. Never be embarrassed to charge a fair fee for your services.

Avoiding the empathy trap: An attendee told me, at a recent seminar I taught, that she could not quit her day job because she could not make a living as a professional organizer. She said that people in her region could not afford to pay a hefty fee for organizing services. I asked if the going rate in her area for a pedicure was more or less than her hourly rate. She responded that it is higher – 60% higher than what she was charging for her services.

It is not a good practice to charge what you perceive your clients are willing to pay. If you leave it to your clients to determine your market worth, you are likely to sell yourself short. Do not forget that your clients are sitting on the other side of the negotiating table. No one will offer to pay more for your services than what you ask. If you do not charge enough, your business will fail and you will not be there for them at all. Do not undersell your services by attempting to predict or outguess the market.

Many consultants set their fee structure through trial and error, rather than evaluating what they will need to maintain a successful business. They make an educated guess at what people will pay for their services and at what volume business will drop off if they raise or lower their price by a few dollars. They start at what they believe their service is worth (or lower) and when business picks up, they experiment at raising their fees. If their clientele starts to drop off, they lower their rate in hopes of attracting more business. Although this method is quite a common practice among many types of businesses, it is ineffective.

Other consultants assume that clients will be willing to pay a fair wage, and they base their fee on the hourly rate of the corporate job they left. Basing your rate on the amount you earned as an employee may gain you instant acceptance with your clients, but it is small thinking and will not secure your business for the future. The money will be gone and the game will be over. No business owner is immune to this reality. Get out of the job and hourly pay mentality, and learn to help your clients do the same.

The most common mistake new organizers make when setting their fees is assuming that a low price will attract more clients. In truth, low prices often attract a lower scale of clientele. Low-balling your fees may get you clients, but not necessarily, the business you want. People expect to pay a professional what he is worth. Imagine an attorney quoting $30 per hour. Would you be suspicious? Would you question the value of his services? The vice president of a large corporation will not hire you for $25 per hour, no matter what service you provide. Do not discount your prices for fear of not getting enough business. A low rate devalues your service in the eyes of the client. Do not sell yourself short.

You must always remember that although clients pay for hours, days, or projects, what they really want is your expert opinion. You are competent. You have devoted your earnest time and effort to this career, and you are a professional. You are not a wage earner like the clerk who takes a part time job at Christmas time, trading her available time for money, collecting a wage from the beginning of the shift until she punches out at the end of the day. Although job security and advancement are dependent on competency, the only requirement for being paid is the clerk's time commitment.

This is not the case with a professional organizer. Your client, the person who pays you, does not have a store that needs to be watched over. Your client needs a combination of your talent, experience, education, skills and your available time. Your value and worth are not defined by the hours in your day. Your clients pay for your expertise. The hours you put in are not nearly as important as the progress the client makes because of your consulting. Convince your clients that you provide great value for their dollars. Your clients probably will not care how long a project takes as long as they get their money's worth

Calculating your hourly rate

It is hard to charge by the hour and make a decent profit. However, you cannot determine how much your fixed fee should be unless you know roughly how many hours the job will take and what you need to earn per hour to make it worth your while. No matter how you bill your clients, first figure out how much to charge per hour – even if you charge a fixed fee for the whole project.

Many organizers transition from salaried employment, so their basis of comparison, or frame of reference is a salary. In setting their fees, they simply want to be able to match their previous salary. When calculating your hourly rate, do not forget to cover indirect costs for overhead and benefits, and add on a reasonable profit for your business. Professional organizers usually use one of the following five methods to determine an hourly rate (dollar amounts shown are arbitrary):

Method One: Guess. When you guess what to charge, you may find that your fees are not high enough for you to survive. You may find that your fees are too high and clients cannot afford them. On the other hand, you could be right on target. In any event, guessing at what to charge is risky.

Method Two: Divide your employment salary by 1,000 hours (the number of hours you can bill if you work 20 billable hours per week, 50 weeks per year), and that is your hourly rate. If your salary as an employee is $50,000, you need to bill $50 an hour to make it as an independent.

Method Three:

Take a desired annual salary figure:	$50,000
Add the cost of benefits (vacation, insurance, retirement plans)	$12,000
Add expenses such as utilities, supplies, equipment, and rent.	$ 5,000
Subtotal	$67,000

Divide this total by the number of hours you can realistically expect to work in a year. Allowing for two weeks of vacation, and taking into consideration the amount of time needed for marketing and administrative activities, the typical full-time professional bills about 20 hours per week (allowing for marketing, networking and administrative tasks) x 50 weeks per year (allowing for two weeks of vacation), or 1,000 hours a year. The result will be the amount you should charge per hour.

$67,000 ÷ 1000 hours = $67.00, rounded to $70.00 per hour

Method Four: Business schools teach this standard formula for determining an hourly rate:

(Labor + Overhead + Profit) Hours Worked = Hourly Rate
($50,000 + $25,000 + $20,000 = $95,000) ÷ 1000 = $95.00 per hour

To determine labor, pick a figure for your annual salary. This can be what you earned for doing similar work when you were an employee, or how much you would like to earn. In this example, $95.00 per hour is the minimum you must charge to pay yourself a salary, pay your expenses, and earn a profit.

Method Five: Take the salary plus benefits that you would earn when working for someone else and then double or triple it. Doubling it will allow you to make a living. Tripling your hourly wage is the wisest move when using this method, since one third can go to your wage, one third to expenses (including employees), and one third to administration, low utilization, and profit.

($50,000 salary + $12,000 benefits) / (50 weeks * 40 hours) = $62,000 / 2000 = $31.00
Double: $31.00 * 2 = $62.00, rounded to $65.00 per hour
Triple: $31.00 * 3 = $93.00, rounded to $95.00 per hour.

So, is it this easy to figure your hourly rate? These methods for determining your optimum hourly rate may be insufficient. There are variables that must be further analyzed in order to arrive at a more realistic analysis. In addition, these examples do not address the issue of whether clients in your area will pay $50, $70, or $95, or more per hour.

You must calculate the actual cost of overhead, including medical plan, employer's portion of Social Security, down time, other benefits and business expenses. Time off to recharge your energy and save your sanity will reduce your billable hours. Include in your budget time off for vacations, holidays, sick and personal days, and parental leave if you have children. You may be willing and able to bill a great deal more than 20 hours per week, although any self-employed person will tell you it is a rare occasion when you are able to take on 40 billable hours in a week.

If your goal is to replace your regular job with freelancing rather than to build a business, these formulas may be sufficient for your purposes. Before you settle on these simple formulas, though, consider the cost of working for yourself.

To get a better idea of the difference between working for an employer and working for yourself, let's look at the example of Patty and Cindy. Patty and Cindy each earn $50,000 per year. Patty works for a company who issues a paycheck twice a month. Patty's employer provides usual benefits and withholds income tax, payroll tax, and Patty's share of health insurance. Here is how her income breaks down:

Patty's Compensation	Monthly $	Annual $
Annual salary	$ 4,167	$ 50,000
Two week's paid vacation + holidays	$ 417	$ 5,000
Employer's share of health insurance, disability, worker's compensation, and unemployment coverage	$ 250	$ 3,000
Office, space & equipment, computer, phone, Internet	$ 167	$ 2,000
Supplies	$ 42	$ 500
401k Matching	$ 125	$ 1,500
Other benefits and perks	$ 83	$ 1,000
Total cash and benefits	$ 5,250	$ 63,000

Cindy has her own business and is a sole proprietor. Here is how her income breaks down:

Cindy's Compensation	Monthly $	Annual $
Gross income	$ 4,167	$ 50,000
Employer's share of self-employment tax	$ (250)	$ (3,000)
Health insurance	$ (167)	$ (2,000)
Office equipment, computer, phone, Internet	$ (125)	$ (1,500)
Supplies	$ (42)	$ (500)
Total compensation less expenses	$ 3,583	$ 43,000

The compensation difference between Patty and Cindy is $20,000. Although some of Cindy's expenses are tax deductible, it will not be enough to make up the $20,000 difference. If Cindy wants to make as much as Patty, her hourly rate must be increased by roughly $15 per hour to make up the $1667 monthly shortfall. If she wants to make a profit, the increase will have to be even more. I hope this illustration helps you to understand the actual cost of overhead, and the difference between employee wages and being an independent contractor.

Preparing a break-even analysis: Business experts advise that you prepare a *break-even analysis* as the first step in determining your fee. A break-even analysis is a technique for calculating the amount of revenue you will need to bring in to cover the costs of running your business. Preparing a break-even analysis can help you determine whether you will make enough money to build a profitable business. If you can surpass your break-even point, your business stands a good chance of making money.

A break-even analysis is a part of every formal business plan, so if you put in the effort here, you will already have completed part of your business plan.

As with many other economic formulas, the break-even formula requires research, deep thought and analysis. For the non-mathematically minded individual, the process can be perplexing. Although this is not the fun part (for most of us), think twice before taking a short cut in this area. Incorrect pricing can have devastating effects. Once you master this tool, you will have a better understanding of how to make a profit in your business, and you will be able to make better decisions with regard to the pricing of your services.

So, what is a break-even analysis? At the break-even point, a business does not lose any money, but it also does not make any money. Since you want to make a profit, you must know your break-even point and surpass it. To determine your break-even point, you need to estimate your expected sales and expenses. In addition to out-of-pocket expenses, you must include overhead like advertising and office expenses, and benefits such as health insurance, vacation and retirement benefits. Once you have determined a price that covers your overhead and expenses, you can begin adjusting it up or down to maximize profits. Decide on a percentage of profit over cost that you want and then price accordingly.

Visit http://www.organizingforaliving.com/docs to download The Professional Organizer's Fee Setting Planning Guide. This supplemental workbook includes formulas, examples and worksheets to help you calculate your break-even point. If you are the type of person who avoids formulas and analysis, you may want to consult with an accountant, financial planner or SCORE (Service Corps of Retired Executives) counselor who specializes in helping small businesses. Let your advisor crunch the numbers and come up with an hourly rate that you should charge, based on your estimate of billable hours per year.

Packaging your services

When you are starting out, you will probably use just one system for charging your clients, such as an hourly rate. When you are more experienced, you may find yourself charging different clients different rates or different pricing structures, and an open-ended contract may be the exception. For example, you may have one or two clients who form a stable core for you that you charge an hourly fee, but you may charge new clients a fixed fee. You may have a tiered approach with one fee for individuals, another for business owners and another for large corporations.

Whether you decide to charge by the project, by the hour, or charge a daily rate, your value to the client involves your knowledge, skills and experience, not just the amount of time you spend. The primary goal is to

Chapter Ten: Setting Your Fees

establish long-term relationships with clients and to get referrals from them. Satisfied clients will come back for more, so you want to make sure every client is a happy one. If your client believes she has not received value for her money, she will not refer you to others.

Projects frequently need to address long-term solutions that clients may not have even considered. You must be able to determine how the project fits into your client's life or business and how it affects the client in the long-term. You will need to find a balance between a client's budget and the feasibility of meeting her long-term needs.

Make it easy for clients to keep working with you by having a range of services so clients can choose the level of investment that makes them feel comfortable. For instance, you might have a package that includes a series of 10 organizing sessions. If the client frowns on signing on for that package, have an alterative to suggest right away: "Let's schedule one month of sessions and see how it goes?" Alternatively, "I have a 3-session starter package that might work for you."

Determining how you will package your services is a creative process. There are two primary goals in fee setting. The first is that both you and the client agree. The second is that the fee allows you to profit from the work. Packaging your services in different ways gives you more bargaining power. The method you use to package and price your services is determined by several factors, from the size of the project and the travel distance to the client, to the involvement of the client and other factors that are out of your control.

Clients can sense an organizer's discomfort around fee negotiation. The manner in which your fees are established and presented to clients can set a professional tone and boost your confidence around this discussion. Because services are intangible, it helps to form a package that seems to clients like a product that gives them more free time, maximizes their space, lowers their stress, or provides other distinct benefits. Think about how you might organize your services into packages that can be sold for a flat fee based on what they can accomplish for your client. There is a variety of ways to package your services, starting with the initial consultation.

Initial consultation fee: Whether to charge for the initial consultation really depends on how much value you will be able to provide during that initial meeting. Charging for the initial consultation is not recommended if the purpose of the meeting is nothing more than a discussion to determine your interest in working together. In that case, the initial consultation is nothing more than a sales call. However, if you had thoroughly pre-qualified a client and performed a preliminary needs assessment by phone, your first meeting may be much more than that.

The initial consultation is your opportunity to establish your competency and gain the client's confidence by giving quality advice. You may be able to jump right in and start organizing the minute you arrive at the client's location. If you are still gathering facts about the client and assessing the situation, you may not actually accomplish anything during the first meeting, but the quality advice you provide and the recommendation you offer at the conclusion of the initial consultation should be valuable enough to be worth buying.

Think twice before giving your first client session away free. As a business owner, you must take into consideration two important realities:

- Advice is the most valuable service you can offer.
- Every hour you give away is money your business is losing

During the start-up years when you have more time than money, you may be tempted to test your closing rate on converting prospects to clients by offering free consultations. A free initial consultation is nothing more than a sales call. It is an opportunity to learn about your client and talk about what you can provide. Clients walk away with nothing more than a general idea about the available services and possibly a price list. With a free consultation, the prospective clients do not get any relevant advice. If you proceed to provide the advice, you have given them a meal, not a free sample.

Some professions (like physicians) commonly inflate their fee for a first time visit, while others (like accountants) offer free initial consultations. Professional organizers have varying opinions about how initial consultations should be handled. Many offer free initial consultations. Some offer a free half-hour consultation for clients within 10 miles. Some do initial consultations only by phone, and begin charging their hourly rate the moment they first arrive at the client's location. Some charge a fee that can optionally be applied toward a future arrangement if the client decides to use their services. Other organizers simply charge a set fee for a two-hour initial consultation.

To help you decide whether to charge for the initial consultation, ask yourself, "Am I certain that I can help this person?" If the answer is "no," and you have not been able to pre-qualify them, the person is still a prospect. It would be premature to schedule a consultation, since you are not yet in a position to give advice. It may be appropriate to schedule a one-half to one hour meeting to evaluate the client's environment, get more information and determine whether you can help her. Make it clear to the prospect that the

Chapter Ten: Setting Your Fees

purpose of the meeting is to gather more information so that you can make a recommendation. Spend your time asking questions, collecting information, and taking notes. Then offer to get back to her with a proposal. No matter what you decide to call it, this type of meeting is a sales call.

When the answer is "Yes, I am certain I can help this person," you have pre-qualified the person. When he schedules the first session, he is no longer a prospect, but a client who will benefit from your knowledge and advice during the initial consultation. Just as your doctor performs an examination and makes a diagnosis during the initial visit, you will conduct a needs assessment during the initial consultation to identify the nature of your client's issues. You will take stock of the current situation, determine a course of action and make a recommendation about how to proceed. For this valuable advice, you will charge the client a consultation fee.

Are your competitors giving away free consultations? If prospective clients are using the initial consultation to compare you with other professionals and you give your knowledge and expertise away in the form of free advice, the clients will walk away with your ideas, whether they hire you or not. Keep in mind that whatever information and ideas you share with a client during an initial consultation can be implemented by the client in ways other than by hiring you. He can do the work himself or hire someone else to implement your ideas and suggestions.

What makes you different from your competition is your level of expertise and knowledge of your specialty. As the old saying goes, do not expect to sell your milk if you give away the cow. If you want to make the initial consultation free for your clients, charge them up front and offer to credit the first invoice for the amount paid once they contract for additional consulting.

Develop a consistent policy about your fee for an initial consultation, and let prospective clients know beforehand if you will be charging a fee for your sales call or initial consultation. If you do plan to charge clients an initial consultation fee, always give something of value. Make sure your initial consultation fee is reflective of your regular rates, set a time limit (usually one to two hours) and quote it as a flat fee. Require payment to be made before or at the beginning of the initial consultation. Do not delude the prospect into thinking your rates are cheap by charging a token consultation fee. Spend your time wisely by setting policies regarding your fees and initial consultations before investing unpaid hours on initial consultations that lead nowhere.

Charging by the hour: Although it is difficult to make a decent profit when charging by the hour, hourly fees may be appropriate when projects are especially small or open-ended, or tasks are undefined. With time-based pricing, you can be sure of being paid for every hour you work. As long as you are paid, there is no risk on your part; however, you may not make a great deal of money.

You may charge a large corporation a higher rate than you would a small company; a for-profit organization more than you charge a not-for-profit (although not necessarily). You may charge different rates for different kinds of work. When I am hiring an office helper, for example, I may hire a full time employee who wants to earn extra money on the side. That person may charge me a certain hourly rate for the brainy work, such as bookkeeping, and a lower hourly rate for the mindless work, such as stuffing envelopes.

Hourly rates scare some people. Some clients are just not comfortable working with professionals who charge by the hour. Many people are afraid of runaway consulting costs and skeptical of hiring consultants in general. Unfortunately, many consultants have a reputation of extending their time (and hence, their fee) beyond what is necessary. Quoting an hourly rate may turn away some clients who may be more accepting of a flat-rate estimate or a daily rate. When charging an hourly fee, you should give your client an estimate of the time required. Notify the client when the estimated time is close to running over, and get her approval to continue.

An individual that is going to be spending her own money, whether she is a homeowner, a student, or a business owner, will naturally be more cautious. If you are charging by the hour, she may feel more comfortable if you put a cap on the project.

Daily or half-day rate: Many professional organizers work out an hourly rate, but actually charge by the half-day, day, project or another arrangement. The daily rate is the simplest form of packaging your services. To set a daily rate, simply multiply the hours you work in a day by your hourly rate. To give your clients incentive to hire you for an entire day, apply a discount (such as 10 percent). For your half-day rate, apply a discount that is less than the discount you offer for your daily rate (such as 5 percent).

Fixed or flat fee: When projects are predictable or routine, you can charge one comprehensive fee. The advantage of a fixed amount for an entire project is that it adds predictability to the budget, both yours, and your client's. Another benefit of pricing per project, rather than charging a time-based rate, is that normally you could make much more money that way. You could also lose money if you price incorrectly or if you do not control your costs while delivering the service. When providing services for a fixed fee, you must commit to the project and price as quoted. Do calculate all costs and profit in your fixed fee that you quote. It is important to be very specific in defining the characteristics and scope of the project when charging a fixed fee, so that you do not spend more time than expected in the project. If you foresee additional cost increases developing, discuss them with your clients and obtain their authorization before proceeding.

Bundle: You can bundle consulting services with product sales or training and educational offerings. You can build a portfolio of structured packages or create packages to meet the unique requirements of each client. Another example of bundling is to package a set number of consulting hours with a certain number of follow-up calls. The number of ways you can bundle your services is limited only by your creativity.

Project: Some organizers set their rates by the project. They estimate the number of hours they expect to spend on a project, and then multiply by their hourly rate. Project fees can be adjusted up or down considering the value the client derives from the professional organizer's advice.

Per person: A per person rate structure might apply if you were the speaker at a community event or if you were presenting a program for a group of employees. Corporations often do not like having to worry about the clock, and relate to a cost per head structure. To establish a per person rate, figure out how much you want to earn during the allotted time. Then, get an estimate of how many people will attend. No matter what per person rate is agreed upon, insist on a minimum guarantee to ensure that you get a fair fee.

Trade or barter: If a client has a product or service from which you could benefit, you might consider trade or barter. You might also consider trading services with associates that you contract or with whom you subcontract. Trade may also come into play when a project is modified and the client may opt to trade for services on another project. Bartering is not a common pricing scheme with large companies whose policies or accounting systems may not be compatible. Keep in mind that bartered contracts are taxable, the same as any other service, and income must be tracked in your accounting system and reported to the IRS accordingly.

Retainer fee: You may be paid a set fee as a down payment against future services. A retainer fee is an advance payment on your hourly rate for services to be performed in the future. It is intended to insure that you will block out certain specific blocks of time for the client (every Tuesday morning, for instance). Usually, a retainer fee arrangement comes into play when a client comes to you with a project requiring extensive work. You may arrange a retainer agreement with a client when you want to assure the client that you will reserve your calendar and stick with him until the project is completed, but at the same time, you do not want to be left with large unpaid fees. Retainer fees for professional organizers are usually paid monthly and are non-refundable.

Combination: You may want to mix pricing schemes for different tasks of a project, especially if some elements of the project are abstract. For example, you may charge a fixed fee for installing a closet organizer, and then an hourly rate for sorting clothes, if that task involves working with a client who has undeveloped decision-making skills.

Travel and other expenses: It is acceptable to charge for travel expenses. If you will be spending an hour or more in transit, you will be spending a considerable amount of time that is not available to you for billing other clients. Consider your travel time when setting your fees, and make sure to communicate your policy with the client up front. If you charge by the hour, you might include the time you leave your office (or that of the prior client's location) until the moment you are finished with your current client for the day in the total number of hours that you bill that client. If your travel is long distance, you are justified in billing your regular daily rate for travel time, as long as you are losing billable time.

If you are charging by the hour, be careful not to charge your clients for items that may seem petty. The time you invest in research and reviewing client materials is certainly valuable, and you may be able to squeeze more profit out of a job by charging for these extras. Keep in mind, though, that you may discourage a client from hiring you for additional work and larger projects. Small jobs often hold the promise of continued work and long-term profits, so give a little extra so that your client feels that she has gotten her money's worth. Rather than trying to get as much as you can out of a job, think of every job as possible repeat business.

Direct costs, like supplies, can be billed to the client at your cost; however, insignificant amounts are usually covered in your fee. Consider the perception your client will have when she sees your invoice. Any staff, support, and overhead that you hire should be covered in your fee, as well. It is reasonable to charge mileage, as long as your client agrees to the charge in advance. It is wise to have a policy and stick to it. For instance, your policy might be to charge mileage at X cents per mile for any client more than 25 miles.

Estimating and project planning

Among the first questions prospective clients may ask you are "What will it cost . . ." or "How long would it take . . . , (to organize a closet/office/garage, etc.)?" I usually beat them to the punch by asking two questions up front, "How long do you think this project will take?", and "What would you expect to pay for a project of this size?". Most prospective clients reply that they have no idea. Others have a clear, but unrealistic budget in mind.

The most interesting responses relate to time estimations, which usually fall into the range of 25%-50% of the amount of time actually required. Reality TV shows about space organization help to distort people's perception about our ability to rapidly, and economically turn chaos into order. Getting clients to understand the actual time and effort involved in organizing their lives can be a challenge.

Estimating organizing projects is more art than science. I wish I could give you a simple formula or fixed rule for estimating and negotiating client projects, but there seems to be no two clients or situations that are alike in the field of organizing. Ideally, we should be able to estimate a job the same way that a contractor estimates a remodeling project, as follows.

A construction customer indicates her desire, which the contractor sketches. The customer then gets out of the way while the contractor completes the project. There are two major differences between this scenario and working with organizing clients. First, a rare organizing client has a good understanding of what she wants. You will not be able to provide a sketch. You do not know how much stuff your client has or how concerned she is about trivial details. Rather than a description of the ideal environment, your clients will usually describe what they do not want (years of accumulated clutter, piles of papers everywhere, chaos, feeling of overwhelm).

The other difference is that your client will probably not get out of your way while you build order, and the variable you have to deal with is how fast she can make a decision. Professional organizers must spend whatever time is necessary working with clients to assist them in weeding out their unwanted items, clearing out clutter, storing items out of the line of vision, learning their productivity challenges, teaching organizing skills, etc. Consulting work requires that you address individual, unique problems, and work as long as the client wishes you to work to achieve her organizing goals.

Of course, it is easier and less risky for you to charge an hourly rate, but clients understandably prefer to know in advance, what a completed project is going to cost them in terms of time and money. Even when a client is willing to pay your hourly fee, she is not going to hand you a blank check. At the very least, she will want a *not-to-exceed* figure.

With practice, you can learn to estimate projects. From experience with organizing a space of similar size and condition, you can approximate what a job will cost in terms of time and resources. Estimates are not guarantees, and you can turn the *not-to-exceed* concept into a condition that benefits you. By specifying time limitations, you can provide your clients a fixed fee contract that makes them feel more in control and gives them a sense that their problem will be solved.

Base your estimates on experience, considering the amount of effort and duration to perform each task. Develop a project plan to make sure you do not overlook anything or underestimate the time needed to complete the project. Divide the proposed project into components and continue to subdivide the project until each task can be estimated in terms of time and resources. For each task, ask, "How long will it take me (or my associate) to finish this task?" If you cannot answer the question, break it down even further. Be sure to include supplemental tasks, such as shopping for supplies, removal of trash, and delivery of donations.

You can predict how much time the project will take and how much it will cost you, but many factors cannot be anticipated. While charging by the project is optimal, you will never eliminate the risk. You will have to negotiate your contract based on your best estimate. Since your clients are usually involved in the process of getting organized, the amount of time you devote varies depending on their readiness, willingness and trustfulness.

A client's involvement can provide the greatest assistance or present the greatest obstacle to the completion of a project. Some clients are completely absorbed and committed to the project, while others allow interruptions and distractions to slow the process. Variables are what make estimating organizing projects difficult. Make sure your client understands and is willing to abide by the assumptions built in to the contract, and be prepared to renegotiate before your project falls too far behind.

It is of ultimate importance to understand your client's needs fully to help you accurately appraise a project. In order to give an accurate and realistic time and cost estimate, it is imperative that an initial consultation with the client is scheduled in order to assess the situation. During your initial assessment, evaluate your client's willingness to help and to bring the project to completion. Ask pertinent questions to determine potential obstacles you should consider when estimating the project. You may be able to organize a closet in three hours on your own, but once you involve a client in the process, that time could easily be doubled. The client might debate for ten minutes about getting rid of a two-size-too-small jacket that you might have tossed into the donation bin without a second thought.

Find out in advance what emotional roadblocks you will have to overcome and consider them in your estimate. Take into account also the time involved in instructing the client in the principals of organizing as you are helping her restore order to her space.

If you are a new organizer, consider in your fee that projects will take longer than they would with an experienced professional organizer. With experience, you, too, can complete a project in less time, and be better equipped to evaluate the client's needs and estimate the amount of time a project will take. Review the following two cases from the perspective of the client. Put yourself in the client's shoes and ask yourself if these professional organizers have been fair and reasonable in their billing.

> Kevin is a new professional organizer. He is confident, but a bit hesitant about rearranging his first client closet. He fumbles a bit with the supplies, since he has not yet figured out the tricks of installing closet organizing supplies. He is patient with the client while she makes decisions about what to keep, what to donate, and what to toss. Kevin quoted $65 per hour and completed the project in eight hours. He billed $520.00 for his services.

> Steve, a veteran professional organizer, has organized hundreds of closets. He has found ways to streamline the closet organizing process, uses proven supplies that he can install proficiently, and has perfected ways to move a client through the decision making process with ease. An average closet takes Steve five hours to organize, and his average billing for a closet-organizing project is $500.00. Steve charges the client $500.00 for his services.

Before you discuss a fixed fee with a prospective client, make sure you are mentally prepared. Unless you are quoting an hourly or daily rate, make it a practice to get back to her later. Do not act under pressure, even if you feel like you are being backed into a corner. Give yourself time to evaluate the time involved so that you can quote a price that is fair to both you and the client.

Getting paid

The best way to avoid having problems in being paid is to openly and clearly quote your fees upfront, and get your agreements in writing before starting to work. Once you agree to perform services for a client, you are entering into a legal contract. You agree to do the work, and the client agrees to pay you for it.

Many organizers start out by relying on handshake agreements with their clients until they start running into problems completing projects, gaining client satisfaction, and ultimately collecting payment. Using written contracts will help you prevent misunderstandings about what you agreed to charge or what work you agreed to perform. As long as you clearly define the expectations you and the clients have about the project in writing, you will be able to prove your case if there is a disagreement.

When possible, get payment up front. If you are working on a project, get a 50% retainer up front before beginning work on the project. Establish your billing and collection policies before you accept your first client. Consider the following issues:

- Will the client receive an invoice before payment is expected?
- Will a deposit be collected to compensate you in case of cancellation?
- When will payment be due? (For example, payment is due within 30 days of project completion.)
- What are the consequences for nonpayment?
- Will there be a late fee?
- Will you charge interest on outstanding balances?

Put your billing and collection policies in writing and communicate them in the written agreement you provide to your clients. Always invoice your clients promptly and clearly state the details of the transaction and the due date on the invoice. Unless you collect at the time you render your services, when you invoice a client, you are actually extending credit. Be sure to include your contact information on your invoice, and invite the client to call you if she has any questions.

The best way to create an invoice is by computer, as this method allows you to retain a digital copy. You can create an invoice from within your accounting system, where the information will be automatically retained and posted to the client's accounts receivable record and electronic audit trail. Forms are also available in word processor and spreadsheet programs that allow you to print a professional looking invoice. If you feel more at ease with a paper trail, print two copies of the invoice – one for the client and one for your files.

If you want to collect from the client at the time of service and you do not have a predetermined fee arrangement, you will not be able to preprint an invoice. You will need to handwrite an invoice form, or fill out a partially completed form at the client's location. Invoice forms can be purchased at office supply stores. Once a week, enter the invoice information into your accounting system to update your Accounts Receivable and Sales records.

Asking a client for a non-refundable deposit in advance is not only reasonable, but a good practice. A deposit is the only means of protection from the client canceling at the last minute. You have reserved a slot of time for your client that will not generate revenue for you if your client cancels. If she is serious about the organizing project and your services, she will have no problem paying a deposit. You can charge a flat fee, like $200, or a percentage, like 25%-50%. If you have a merchant account, you can take a deposit over the telephone via credit card. Before collecting a deposit, draft a cancellation policy and put it in writing for your client so that your client has no confusion about your expectations.

Large projects will likely be paid in installments, so stipulate in advance when the payments are due. If you are working on a project that will take six months, for instance, specify that an installment is due on the first of each month.

Bartering is a great way to conserve cash and expand your referral base. It also could be a way to gain a client who is reluctant to part with cash for your services. For instance, you could exchange consulting services with a Marketing Consultant and get some help promoting your business. Your accountant, who works from home, may be willing to trade his services for an organized closet. You can barter with contractors, plumbers, photographers, and window cleaners. There are endless possibilities for bartering. Not only can you receive great services in return for consulting, you can get great referrals, too. Do keep in mind that bartering revenue is subject to income tax.

Nonpayment has nothing to do with you or the work; so do not take it personally. The first step in any collection process is to find out why you have not been paid. You may find that it is the result of an error, or you may get a promise of payment. It is important not to wait until the payment is seriously overdue to make the first contact. Whether you place a phone call, send electronic mail or mail a letter, use a neutral tone. You might call and ask, "How is your reorganized closet working out for you? By the way, we have not received your check yet, is there a problem?" Be sure to keep a record of all communication with your clients, because a collection agency will want to see the history of your collection attempts. Remember that you did the work and deserve to be paid. You have bills to pay, too.

If the invoice goes beyond 30 days, send a letter informing your client that the invoice is 30 days overdue, and ask when you might expect payment (QuickBooks® includes an option to generate these letters automatically for you). If you do not hear from her at all for another thirty days, give her a phone call. If she has financial troubles, offer to work with her to collect the balance in installments. At 60 days, take more stern action, with an overdue notice demanding payment by a certain date, with consequences specified. The consequences (attorney, collection agency, etc.) will depend upon how important the relationship is to you. Send the letter by certified mail and require a signature.

If you still do not receive payment, you will have to decide whether you are interested in working with the client any longer. If not, you can invoke a collection agency. Expect to pay 10-15% of the collection amount to the collection agency. I hope that you will never have to go to this extreme.

Raising rates

Many professional organizers are afraid to raise their rates for fear they will lose clients. That is a natural fear, and everyone wants happy clients who feel as if their money is well spent. As part of your standards, your fees will need to be raised periodically. Raising your rates is a smart decision that ensures the well-being of your business. You create value for your clients and deserve to be fittingly compensated for your time and skills. If your clients like you and are happy with the service you provide, they will accept periodic increases with few objections.

If all of your clients are your ideal clients then you have an indication that it may be time to raise fees. You can justify a rate increase if you are filling your available work hours or have a reputation as an expert in your specialty. Gauge your fee to your clients' view of your worth and their ability to pay. If you have reached a point where your clients pay your rates without the slightest hesitation, you are probably charging too little.

Keep your fees in the upper range of your market. You do not want to give the impression that you lack the skill and experience to command higher fees, or that the quality of your work is substandard. If you are very busy and your business has expanded so much that you cannot handle much more work, it may be a good opportunity to raise your rates.

Revisit your fee structure at least annually. Ideally, fees should be raised at least once per year and more frequently if you have added new skills or learned something that increases the value you extend to your clients. Raising rates slowly is less disturbing to clients than larger increases every few years.

Do not raise your rates too often, and keep each fee increase reasonable so that your clients will be able to absorb the increase.

When you raise rates, it is advisable to apply the new rates to both new clients and existing clients. You may be reluctant to raise rates on older, loyal clients. Of course, you can choose to continue working with them at the old rate. Be careful, though, that you do not get to the point where you are resentful of the work because the rate is so much lower than you are now worth.

Just as your local dairy or gas station raises rates without consulting you or your neighbors, you do not need to ask for permission, or justify raising your rates. Simply advise your clients that you will be raising your rates. Warning your clients ahead of time will make it much easier to raise your rates when the time comes. If you quote jobs based on a flat fee, advising your clients of an increase is not required.

Chapter Eleven: Running a Small Business

"In the midst of difficulty lies opportunity" Albert Einstein

Going into business for yourself means that you will be responsible for a great deal more than just providing your services. All of the marketing, administrative and managerial duties will fall on you. You will be responsible for the entire business; therefore, you must lay the groundwork for managing every aspect of your business. In The Small Business Survival Guide, Robert Fleury said "…if you want to run a business successfully, you must run it like successful businesses are run. You must do the things that 'businesses' do."

Managing your business

Statistics from the U.S. Small Business Administration and Dun and Bradstreet confirms that one in five businesses fails within the first year and between 55 and 60 percent of all businesses will not see their fifth anniversary. Poor management is blamed for about 95 percent of those failures. Professional organizers are brilliant technicians, but unfortunately, many acknowledge themselves lousy business owners. Being prepared to handle all of the business challenges you will encounter will prevent you from being part of the statistics. Remember in the discussion on fee setting, we estimated that you would be able to bill 20 hours a week. In the remaining hours, you will be participating in every aspect of running your business.

Until you can afford to hire staff, you will depend on technology and outsourcing for assistance. Many of your office chores can be outsourced, as well as talent to help you accomplish marketing, legal and accounting objectives. Used effectively, computer technology will improve your efficiency, provide quick and reliable data, save time, cut costs, increase profits and enable you to provide better service to your clients. You can expect to use your computer for the following:

- Business planning – you will create your business plan on your computer and keep it up to date with ease using business planning software or a simple word processor. Your computer will help you to perform complicated calculations to help you determine your fees and analyze your profitability.
- Keeping in touch with your clients – your contact management software will store your client records and profiles and help you to keep in touch with clients and prospects. You will use your computer to track and follow up on leads, handle appointments and callback schedules, generate personalized letters, mailing labels, and postcards. Your basic brochure, flyer and newsletter can be created using desktop publishing software with professional-looking results.
- Tracking income – your accounting software will help you to keep track of every detail about your income, including who has paid you, how much, for what service, the client's check number and date of deposit into your bank account, and a complete history of every transaction. Your computer will assist you in keeping track of who owes you money, and you can even generate reminder notices with ease.
- Controlling expense – using accounting software on your computer helps monitor expenses and automates the tedious job of check writing. It will also reduce the amount of time your accountant spends figuring out your profit and calculating your taxes.
- Day-to-day administration – coordinating your calendar and task list on your computer will ensure that you never miss an appointment, remember to pay your estimated taxes or payroll taxes on time and keep up with the daily tasks that keep your business running smoothly.
- Internet access – the Internet is one of the most valuable tools available to you through your computer. Besides keeping in touch and informed through email, the Internet facilitates online research, and helps you to locate supplies for your clients from online merchants.

Here are some of the roles and responsibilities you will have to assume or hire out as a business owner (i.e., your Job Description). Where applicable, hints for using technology to assist you with your workload are included. To download a free document about selecting computer hardware and software for your business, see http://www.organizingforaliving.com/docs.

Administrative clerk: You will have to handle your own paperwork and correspondence, and handle other daily tasks. As the administrative clerk for your business, you will open and sort mail, maintain a filing system, maintain

Chapter Eleven: Running a Small Business

a calendar, maintain a tickler file, make travel arrangements, order supplies, process mailings, manage email and manage faxes.

You can use database software to store everything from names and addresses to a CD collection. Database software is like an electronic filing cabinet, which you can use to store just about any type of information you want to organize. With database software, you can keep records in a format you design yourself.

Although it is not an absolute necessity, a photocopy machine can be a blessing, especially if you use it to produce sales literature or duplicate invoices. It can save many trips to the copy shop, not to mention the fact that every time you go out to make a copy, you lose time you could have invested in something more important. Use a basic copy machine for those one or two copies a day you need, and take the larger copy jobs to the copy shop. Alternatively, you may find that a copy machine/laser printer/scanner combination is right for you, especially if space is limited.

Go to your local post office and obtain a post office box to use for your business mail. While a bit more expensive, renting a private mailbox (UPS Store, etc.) will give you the added benefit of freeing you from having to be in your office when anticipating express mail or packages.

Bookkeeper: You will need a basic knowledge of accounting, and be able to understand your financial statements. As the bookkeeper for your business, you will pay bills, enter transactions into the general ledger, file tax returns and pay taxes, process payroll and submit payroll taxes, reconcile bank and credit card statements, prepare invoices and statements and collect and submit sales taxes.

You will be able to keep up with all of these chores with the help of accounting software. Accounting software provides a graphic representation of your business. It keeps track of revenue and expenses, and performs accounting functions such as accounts receivable, accounts payable, asset management, payroll, and general ledger. It will help you know whom you owe and who owes you.

Bill collector: You will have to keep track of who owes you and how much. If your clients owe you money, it will be up to you to collect from them. For assistance, use an accounting program that keeps track of receivables and enables you to enter date-stamped notes about client conversations and follow-up.

Business strategist: It will be your responsibility to evaluate your business and plan and implement any needed changes. Whether you decide to add services, sell products, or otherwise expand your business, you will have to weigh all of the pros and cons and monitor the effect of each of these decisions.

Computer technician: More than just a valuable tool, a computer has become a necessity for running a business. The ability to wear a dozen different business hats will probably depend on whether you can effectively leverage computer technology. Maintaining an efficiently running system is essential, and can be challenging and frustrating.

You will not have an IT Department, so unless you have a reliable source for computer assistance, you will need to keep current with technology. You may have to install upgrades and load software, and you may be the one to troubleshoot and fix your own computer when it fails.

Utility programs can help improve system performance and perform maintenance functions. They can help repair or speed up your hard disk, recover files that have been erased, backup and manage your files, and keep your PC running smoothly. Be sure to install anti-virus software to detect and remove programs that can cause damage to your computer. To be properly protected by anti-virus software, you must download frequent updates. If you do not plan to upgrade your anti-virus software annually, you must purchase a subscription to continue to receive anti-virus definitions.

Financial analyst: You will be responsible for all budgeting, risk assessment and investing activities for your business.

Legal council: You will have to hire an attorney, or know the basics of business law (and employment laws, if you have employees). You will be responsible for all of your contracts and other legal documents.

Marketing manager: You will have to conduct market research to determine whom your clients are and where they are located. As the marketing manager for your business, you will develop a marketing plan and update it regularly, coordinate printing and desktop publishing, write promotional copy for brochures and advertising, coordinate website design and hosting, and design marketing materials.

Your word processor can produce basic flyers, business cards, and postcards, but to produce the highest quality publications, like newsletters, books or brochures, you will need desktop publishing software. If you buy a digital camera, a graphics program will probably be included. You can also buy photo-editing software that is easy to use and allows you to do basic editing of graphics, like clipart and logos.

You can design basic Web pages without spending a lot of time learning software with a variety of WYSIWYG (what you see is what you get) Web page programs. Another alternative is to choose a Web hosting company that

Chapter Eleven: Running a Small Business

offers a website building tool. These tools allow you to create a website by using a series of wizards.

Messenger: You will have to run errands, like going to the bank, the post office, the supply store, and the recycling center.

Receptionist: Even though you will not have to greet walk-in clients, you will have to answer your own telephone, check and respond to voicemail messages and book your own appointments. The sound of a ringing phone in your office can be exhilarating. That sound may represent a potential client or follow-up business from a previous client. Initially, you may find yourself spending a great deal of time in your office, and the interruption of a phone ringing is a welcome sound. Nothing can be more frustrating for a business owner than to wonder how much business you might be losing because potential clients do not reach you, and that becomes a real frustration as your calendar starts to fill with client activities and you spend less time in your office.

One of the most challenging aspects of working on your own is being available to prospects and clients when they call. Until you can hire someone to handle your incoming calls, you will have to depend on technology to fill the gap. Use either a high quality answering machine or the voicemail service available through your phone company.

Call waiting works well for the residential line, but placing clients on hold to respond to the call-waiting signal may not be an acceptable solution for business. While more expensive than using a digital voicemail system, the phone company's voicemail option is preferred. Besides presenting a more professional image than call waiting, it allows you to access your messages when on the road. If you do not answer, or are on the line, callers will have the option of leaving a message in your voicemail system, an option they would not have with an answering machine. This option usually includes Caller ID.

You will need a minimum of two phone lines in your home to operate your business. You probably already have one phone line coming into your home, your residential phone line. Invest in another phone line or two for your office. One can be your main business number, and the second can be a dedicated fax line. You can get by with a single phone line, but invest in a telephone splitter that allows your fax to work on the same line as your phone.

If you do decide to use a single landline for business and personal calls, check to make sure that you are not violating local telephone company regulations by answering your residential phone number with your business name, or by advertising your home number for your business.

Sales executive: As the sales person for your business, you will manage a contact database, call potential clients, negotiate with clients and prepare agreements, conduct needs assessments and prepare proposals, follow up with existing clients and make sure they are satisfied. To build your circle of influence, join business groups and attend breakfasts, luncheons and after-hours events.

Contact management (client tracking) programs centralize information about your business contacts and automate the way you track sales opportunities. A good contact management program helps you to grow business relationships by enabling you to access key contact and client information, manage and prioritize activities, and handle communications. It reminds you of appointments and tasks and puts your most critical client information at your fingertips.

Whatever contact management software you choose, make sure that it is compatible with your PDA, your accounting software, and your word processing software, so that you do not end up having to perform duplicate data entry of your contact information.

Supervisor: If you have employees, you will be responsible for recruiting, hiring, training, firing, and benefits administration. You will oversee your employee and subcontractor's work and ensure your clients are happy. You will need to spell out your employees' responsibilities, the limits of their authority, their job objectives, and provide feedback as to how they are doing and what is expected of them.

Do not underestimate the amount of time required to manage your business. Plan to dedicate even more time to these activities during the initial startup period. You may end up spending much more time than you anticipated attending to the details of running your business, and less time on the activities you really enjoy. Do not make the mistake of devoting all of your time to providing services to your clients, and neglecting the crucial business management activities that will make your business a success. The personal satisfaction of creating and running a successful business will be your reward.

Hiring employees and subcontractors

Starting your own business means that you get to be your own boss and do what you love to do. Unless you work for someone else, though, you will not be able to do what you love all the time. If it is your own business, you are not just the chief cook; you are also the chief bottle washer. You will have to wear many hats, like the bookkeeper's hat, the marketer's hat, the collector's hat and the janitor's hat. Not all of those hats will fit as well as the organizer's hat and that may mean hiring additional assistance (i.e., bookkeepers {including tax/accounting personnel} marketing, collecting, etc.).

You may not have extraordinary skills in everything required of a business owner. Juggling multiple priorities and responsibilities goes beyond your business, and another professional organizer might be able to assist in organizing business functions, as well as personal issues such as young children or aging parents.

Exchanging services or bartering with a professional organizer whose specialty is opposite yours might be a great partnership. Perhaps you specialize in organizing closets, but do not have a clue about financial matters. You might hear at a meeting that a colleague who specializes in financial systems needs to get his closets organized. Offer to barter with him, and ask him to set up your accounting system.

Once you have built a reputation and established a strong client base, you may also choose to hire other organizers to assist you with client projects. You may even hire other organizers to assume full responsibility for client projects that you have contracted.

It is critical to determine correctly whether the individuals you hire are employees or independent contractors. Generally, you must withhold income taxes, withhold and pay Social Security and Medicare taxes, and pay unemployment tax on wages paid to an employee. You do not generally have to withhold or pay any taxes on payments to independent contractors.

In determining whether the person providing service is an employee or an independent contractor, all information that provides evidence of the degree of control and independence must be considered. Before you can determine how to treat payments for services, you must first evaluate the business relationship that exists between you and the person performing the services.

Independent Contractor: As the client, you have the right to control or direct only the result of the work done by an independent contractor, and not the means and methods of accomplishing the result.

> Judy, a professional organizer, submitted a job estimate to ABC Organizing Services for organizing services at $50 per hour for 100 hours. She is to receive $1,250 every two weeks for the next eight weeks. This is considered a contract and not payment by the hour. Judy determines when she will work and how she will perform her services. Even if she works more or less than 100 hours to complete the work, Judy will receive $5,000. She also provides additional organizing services under contracts

> with other companies that she obtained through referrals and advertisements. Judy is an independent contractor.

These are the major checkpoints for classifying an independent contractor:

- They make their services available to the general public
- They work for more than one employer at a time
- They cannot be fired at will
- They are liable for failure to complete a job
- They obtain their own training
- They determine the hours worked to complete a job
- They are paid for the results of their work, not for the time worked
- They are responsible for their own business expenses
- They provide their own tools and equipment
- They control and pay their own assistants
- They have a significant investment in their own business
- They assume risk and can realize profits and incur losses
- You can only control them with respect to the specific contracted result
- You cannot tell them how to do a job or control how they produce the end result
- It is your sole option to terminate them at the end of their contract

You may be required to file information returns to report certain types of payments made to independent contractors during the year. For example, you must file Form 1099-MISC, Miscellaneous Income, to report payments of $600 or more to persons not treated as employees (e.g., independent contractors) for services performed for your business.

Employee: A general rule is that anyone who performs services for you is your employee if you can control what will be done and how it will be done. This is so even when you give the employee freedom of action. What matters is that you have the right to control the details of how the services are performed. All evidence of control and independence must be considered. Facts that provide evidence of the degree of control and independence fall into three categories: behavioral control, financial control, and the type of relationship of the parties.

> Jim is a professional organizer employed on a part-time basis by Mary of XYZ Organizing Services. Jim is paid by the hour. Jim usually works two days a week and Mary determines which days and times he will work. Lists of prospective clients belong to XYZ Organizing Services. Jim evaluates client needs and appraises orga-

nizing jobs, but his appraisals are subject to Mary's approval. Because of his experience, Jim requires only minimal assistance in most phases of his work. Jim is an employee of Mary.

When hiring employees, you are required to get each employee's name and Social Security Number (SSN) and to enter them on Form W-2. You must verify that each new employee is legally eligible to work in the United States. Have the employees you hire fill out Form I-9, Employment Eligibility Verification and Form W-4, Employee's Withholding Allowance Certificate. If your employees qualify for and want to receive advanced earned income credit payments, they must give you a completed Form W-5, Earned Income Credit Advanced Payment Certificate.

You generally must withhold federal income tax from your employees' wages. To figure how much to withhold from each wage payment, use the employee's Form W-4 and the methods described your Employer's Tax Guide.

Social security and Medicare taxes pay for benefits that workers and families receive under the Federal Insurance Contributions Act (FICA). You withhold part of these taxes from your employee's wages and you pay a matching amount yourself. You will report federal income taxes, Social security and Medicare taxes on Form 941 – Employer's Quarterly Federal Tax Return.

In general, you must deposit income tax withheld and both the employer and employee social security and Medicare taxes. You can make your deposits electronically, using the Electronic Federal Tax Payment System (EFTPS), or by taking your deposit and Form 8109-B, Federal Tax Deposit Coupon to an authorized financial institution or a Federal Reserve bank serving your area.

Keep all records of employment taxes for at least four years.

Federal Unemployment (FUTA) Tax: Federal unemployment tax is part of the federal and state program under the Federal Unemployment Tax Act (FUTA) that pays unemployment compensation to workers who lose their jobs. You report and pay FUTA tax separately from social security and Medicare taxes and withheld income tax. You pay FUTA tax only from your own funds. Employees do not pay this tax or have it withheld from their pay. You will report FUTA taxes on Form 940 – Employer's Annual Federal Unemployment (FUTA) Tax return.

This program is a state-federal partnership, financed by two different employer taxes. State employment-security agencies collect quarterly employer contributions (taxes) in order to pay unemployment benefits to eligible, unemployed workers. The federal government funds the administrative costs of the employment security programs in each state through a quarterly federal unemployment tax (FUTA). Consult the department of employment security in your state about filing wage reports and paying monthly contributions.

Employee status versus Contractor status: Many factors must be considered when classifying people who work for you, and there are consequences when treating an employee as an independent contractor. If you have employees, you are responsible for Federal Income Tax Withholding, Social Security and Medicare taxes and Federal Unemployment Tax Act (FUTA). If you incorrectly classify an employee as an independent contractor, and you have no reasonable basis for doing so, you can be held liable for employment taxes for that worker, and a penalty.

If you want to treat your workers as independent contractors and avoid Federal Income Tax Withholding, Social Security and Medicare taxes and Federal Unemployment Tax, you will not be able to insist on having things done your way. If you behave like a boss and insist that your subcontractors do it your way, you run the risk of having the IRS classify your subcontractors as employees. As an employer, you must determine employee status based on these factors:

- Instructions: You may tell an employee when, where, and how to do a job. Contractors set their own hours and determine how to perform the work.
- Training: You will train employees to perform services in a particular way, and you may require them to attend meetings or take courses. Contractors use their own methods and receive no training from you.
- Integration: Services of an employee are merged into the business coordinated with the work of others. You will not hire a contractor to perform a service that is an essential part of your business. Success and continuation of the business depend upon the services of an employee, but not of a contractor.
- Personal Services: Services must be rendered personally by an employee, but contractors are able to hire other workers to do the job.
- Assistants: An employee acts as your representative – hiring, supervising and paying at your discretion. Contractors hire, supervise and pay workers as the result of a contract.
- Continuous Relationship: An employee continues to work for the same person year after year. Contractors are hired to do one job, and will not continue the relationship with you unless there are multiple contracts.

- Work Hours: You will set the hours and days an employee will work. Contractors control their own time and determine the hours worked to complete a job.
- Amount of Work Time: An employee may work full time for you. You may not prevent a contractor from doing other work. Contractors are free to work when and for whom they choose.
- Location: Employees work at a location designated by you. Contractors use their own offices and choose where to work, unless the services can only be performed in one location.
- Sequence of Work: You may set the order an employee performs services. Services are performed at a contractor's own pace and sequence.
- Reports: You may require an employee to submit regular oral or written progress reports. Contractors are not required to produce interim reports.
- Payment: You will pay employees in regular amounts at stated intervals. A contractor is paid for the results of his work, not for the time worked.
- Business and/or Travel Expenses: You will pay employees' business and/or travel expenses. Contractors are responsible for their own expenses.
- Tools and Materials: You will furnish tools, equipment, materials, etc. for your employees. A contractor agrees to provide materials and labor and is responsible for the results.
- Investment: An employee has no significant investment in the business. A contractor has a real, essential and significant investment in the business, such as a home office.
- Profit or Loss: Employees cannot realize a profit or loss from their services. Contractors are responsible for the results of their decisions and work and can realize a profit or suffer a loss.
- Multiple Jobs: An employee usually works for one employer at a time. A contractor works for a number of persons or firms at the same time.
- Availability: An employee does not make services available to the public. Contractors have their own offices and assistants, are listed in business directories, maintain business telephones, and otherwise generally make their services available to the public.
- Termination: An employee can be discharged at any time. Contractors cannot be fired so long as product results meet contract specifications.
- Liability: Employees have the right to quit their jobs at any time without incurring liability. Contractors agree to complete a specific job and are

responsible for satisfactory completion; or they are legally obligated to make good for any failure.

Recruiting employees: You can create a strong team of professional organizers by being clear about what you are looking for and by providing incentives that will attract skilled candidates. The professional organizing field enables most employers to provide the incentive of flextime, which lets employees work part-time or complete a full workweek in four days. This is one of the most attractive features of becoming a professional organizer, and can be attractive to potential employees, as well.

You can attract high school and college students by offering internship programs. This type of program has several benefits. It gives you an extra set of hands for those extra large projects, enables students to learn organizing skills, and helps you to find talented future employees among the interns you hire.

Offering training opportunities may be another way to attract potential employees. You may be able to interest other owners of professional organizing businesses in your area in collaborating on a training workshop to attract potential employees. To those who are re-entering the workforce, the opportunity for on-the-job learning may be an enticing prospect. They may be willing to accept a lower salary during the training period.

Employees and subcontractors who are satisfied will stay with you longer and enhance your reputation with your clients. The following tips will help to ensure their satisfaction.

- Provide clear expectations about what you want them to do.
- Provide opportunities for their input, so that they are continually challenged.
- Make sure that they have the proper tools, materials and equipment to do the job.
- Whether or not you agree with them, acknowledge the importance of their opinions and spend the time with them to discuss alternatives.
- Recognize and praise their good work; acknowledge their value to your business.
- Be sincere; treat them as partners, not just as an extra pair of hands.

To come up with a reasonable salary for employees, do some research. Salary surveys are not yet available for this industry, so you will need to talk to professional organizers in other areas to find out what typical salaries are for assistants. Since salaries in general vary from city to city, factor in your geographical region to arrive at a fair salary.

Chapter Eleven: Running a Small Business

Most potential employees are looking for three main benefits in a company. First, they look for a comprehensive health plan. Offering medical insurance, as well as dental and optical coverage, could make your company very attractive to potential employees. Employees want to build their nest eggs, so offering a retirement plan such as a 401(k) would be an attractive benefit. Finally, paid vacation time has become a standard benefit that you will want to offer employees, if your goal is to attract talented people who will stay with you.

Part-time employees will not expect to receive employee benefits, and may be the best option while building your business. While it is important to offer a competitive salary and incentives in the compensation packages you create, always make sure that your company remains profitable.

Collaborating with subcontractors: Once you have enough work to make it economically feasible, you can move in the direction of becoming a marketing hub. Generating business to other professional organizers will enable you to bid on larger contracts, serve more clients in the same amount of time and increase your income. You can quadruple the work you currently handle without increasing the hours you work, provided you have the management skills to keep it all functioning. Consider the numbers:

Case Number 1: Shirley currently bills 150 hours of client work per month. At $50 per hour, her income is $7500 a month.

Case Number 2: Nancy puts in 100 hours of client work per month. Nancy's subcontractors work 200 hours a month. Nancy bills 300 hours a month at $50 per hour, grossing $15,000 a month. She pays her subcontractors $30 per hour. After paying her subcontractors $6,000, Nancy's income for the month is $9,000.

Subcontracting is a great way to extend the services that you offer. You can widen your range while keeping costs in check by delegating certain portions of a project that require a lesser skill set. You can maintain your independence while broadening your services and offering a skill set that is different from yours.

Since you cannot control the means or way that a subcontractor works, you are actually the client when you hire a subcontractor. Even if you are working with a subcontractor who previously hired you for a project, be sure to know your role in each project and stay in character. You assume the liability for all aspects of the subcontractor's work, including quality, cost and timeliness; you should maintain the client-subcontractor relationship throughout the project. Keep it professional; the more personal and informal the relationship between you and the subcontractor, the more risk you assume.

Long before you decide to hire subcontractors, you will build a network of trusted associates that you can turn to when you need help. Before hiring a new subcontractor, take the time to get references and follow up on them, just as you would for an employee. Prepare and sign a written agreement between you and first-time subcontractors. Include your expense policies, client-subcontractor protocol, production schedules and payment terms in your subcontractor agreements. Since you, and not the subcontractor, are responsible for fulfilling your obligation to the client, you must always be the custodian of the documents.

As the business owner, you are responsible for the quality of your subcontractor's work. Your client may have agreed to allow your subcontractor to do the work, but she hired you. Regular inspections will be necessary in order to maintain the trust that you have built with the client. Just as you would review and assess the performance of an employee, you must inspect and rate the performance of your subcontractors and ensure that your clients are satisfied with their work. Be subtle about inspections and do not make the client think that you are checking up on your subcontractor.

To avoid confusing the client, you and your subcontractors should convey the idea that you are one entity. Be clear with your subcontractor that she is not to deal directly with your client without your approval. These protocols should be specified in your subcontractor agreement. Be involved with her work and help her when possible. Develop methods of communication, to be sure production stays on course.

On the other side, since you represent the subcontractor to the client, you must defend her work to the client as if it were your own. Build respect, loyalty and trust and never pit the subcontractor against the client. Express confidence in your subcontractor, and be sure to let her know when her work is exceptional.

Occasionally, when favors are owed or when small tasks or parts of a project do not justify the work to establish a formal agreement, you may decide to trade services with a subcontractor. Be cautious and always get a commitment for the trade. There are risks involved in the exchange of services without money, including issues with the IRS and the potential to ruin a relationship with a colleague.

When hiring a subcontractor, provide a detailed description in writing for the work that she will be doing and that you will be marking up. People who work for you certainly have the right to leave you and start their own business. They do not have the right, however, to take your clients or your trade secrets. Have the subcontractor sign a non-compete agreement, and be clear with her that she does not have the right to take your clients as her own. Insist on a written agreement of the project specifications prior to the start of any work, to avoid misunderstandings. Agree on terms of payment prior to any project work, and always insist on an invoice from the subcontractor. Pay her as she completes the work, and always pay promptly.

Alternatives for increasing revenue

If you are not a skilled manager, skip the previous option. You have been successful because your work is good and you get recommendations for more work. Employees and subcontractors are not as dedicated as you are to the business. If they do not show up or their work gets sloppy, you will have to deal with the complaints.

Moving into a manager's role will create certain failure, if you are not adept at managing. Managing people brings on a completely new level of stress and responsibility, so make sure you have the ability and fortitude to handle it. You must consider not just your subcontractors, but also your clients. You will have people relying on your expertise and you will have to manage their expectations and any problems that might arise. Unless your subcontractors have E&O (errors and omissions) insurance (unlikely), you will also incur all of the risk. In addition to marketing, you will need to be available full time to manage your subcontractors as long as they are working.

Consider these alternatives to increase your revenue if you have reached your professional capacity:

- Hire an office assistant to help you with administrative tasks, so that you can handle more client work.
- Hire a virtual assistant for help with a variety of tasks: general administrative tasks; sending out brochures, thank-you notes and follow-up letters; updating your website; contacting clients; setting up and maintaining databases; handling billing and bookkeeping.
- Reduce the number of new clients you accept.
- Fill your practice with ideal clients. Terminate clients that do not fit your ideal client profile to make room in your schedule for those who do. Let them know that you are reassessing your practice and no longer feel that they are a good fit for you. Help them find a professional organizer who is a better fit.
- Narrow your niche, raising your fees as you increase your level of expertise.

- Teach or speak about organizing.
- Write articles and books about organizing.
- Create an organizing product.
- Sell or promote organizing products or services.

Having a larger company with greater earnings may entice you. When considering your options, remember your reasons for starting your business in the first place. If freedom and schedule flexibility were important to you, be sure to evaluate how much time and effort you want to devote before expanding your business. If you started your business because you have a passion for organizing, consider the greater responsibility of expanding your business and make sure your choices fit your life goals. What is your definition of success?

Developing your policies and procedures manual

Earlier, we addressed goals and objectives in the section on Business Plans. Now, we will address the tactical side of our business strategy – identifying the *how to* of running a business – developing a Policies and Procedures Manual for your business.

Even for a one-person business, making a habit of documenting everything that you do in your Policies and Procedures Manual is a sound business practice. Documenting policies and procedures comes naturally to some professional organizers; in fact, some offer this as a service. However, if documenting business processes is not your area of expertise, you may appreciate some assistance.

I have worked with many organizers who are on the verge of failing in their business because they are wandering aimlessly from client to client without written goals, plans, or procedures. Other organizers handled their business just fine until they needed to hire help. When they had to figure out what, when and how to delegate tasks to their part-time workers, they realized they could have saved themselves lots of effort had they built this habit early on. To make matters worse, by the time they decided to hire help, they were so busy that the idea of documenting procedures was overwhelming. The time to write job descriptions is before you are ready to hire help.

Your company Policies and Procedures Manual is your guidebook, and it is constantly evolving and changing. Just about everything you do can be delegated, if properly explained, so take the opportunity now to set yourself up for success in your business by creating a Policies and Procedures Manual. Document all of the routine and repetitive tasks that you dislike but are necessary to run your business, so you can offload them to others when the opportunity presents itself.

To build your Policies and Procedures Manual, you can start out with a basic word processing document. Do not worry about format; just get the information in writing. At the front of your Manual will be the Code of Ethics for your business. Next, build sections for marketing, fee structure, accounting and office procedures, as well as a section for dealing with clients (more on this topic later). Administrative tasks can be broken down into sections for annual, quarterly, monthly, weekly, and daily tasks. For instance, you file your income taxes annually; you check your voicemail daily. The schedule section will eventually evolve into a timetable that an assistant can manage for you.

Every section in your Manual answers the question "How do we handle this area?" For every topic, first think about what your policy is with regard to that area, and then document the actual procedures that are followed. Examples of entries into the Manual with regard to policies are:

- It is our policy to charge our regular hourly rate for the initial consultation.
- Bank statements are reconciled within 48 hours of receipt.
- Handwritten thank-you-notes are sent to every client after the first appointment.

Communicate policies with your clients as appropriate, as well as your Code of Ethics. You may find that paying attention to this detail will avoid misunderstandings.

You will be developing procedures for everything you do, and assembling a detailed schedule of when everything must be done. Each time you encounter a new circumstance or do a repetitive task, you will learn the best way to handle the situation. Write whatever you learn in the Manual. When you encounter that same circumstance or task again, review what you have written and ascertain whether you can improve upon the way you handled it. If so, revise what you have written in the Manual.

Document what you do and how you do it. Do you prepare a list of mailing labels every quarter to send a postcard to your clients? How do you do this? Do you use Avery software or a word processor? What are the specific steps for printing out those labels? Do you have a standard label size that you use? Approximately, how long does it take to complete this task? How do you load the labels in the printer? And so on.

Review the steps, as you do the same tasks repeatedly, to ensure that they are efficient and that the written explanation is workable. Revise your schedules and make necessary adjustments and revisions to the written processes. Eventually, you will be comfortable and confident that your Policies and Procedures are the most advantageous and efficient for you and your clients.

Document everything you do in your business and update it every time there is a change. Each minute you spend on documenting Policies and Procedures may save you hours later on in your business and will help you determine what functions can be assigned to staff, outside suppliers or a virtual assistant

Managing your money

If some struggling professional organizer asks to borrow your book just so that she can read the section about managing your money, say "No", because the time to learn about money management and cash flow is before you start your business, not when the money is nearly gone. "But I have no money to manage yet", you may say. Waiting to set up money management systems until you have a substantial amount of money is futile. I cannot emphasize this point enough. If you cannot manage what you have, you will not get any more. The habit of managing money is more important than the amount. It is critical that you set up a system for money management and get in the habit of following it, no matter how small your current income.

Make a commitment right up front to learn how to manage your cash flow and establish an accounting system to monitor your performance. Positive cash flow is essential to the survival of your business. Cash flow is the steady flow of money coming into and going out of your business. Not knowing how much cash you have, how much you owe, and how much you are owed at any given moment is one of the deadliest mistakes an entrepreneur can make.

One of the assumptions we established in the beginning of the book was that you are not wealthy, and that you need this business to make money. If you are among those who will not be depending on this business for your livelihood and are pursuing this profession just to satisfy an inner urge, you can skip this section.

Since you are still with us, you are among those who will need to manage your business finances carefully, to avoid depleting your savings, damaging your credit rating and cutting off the basic services that are the lifeblood of your business. The number one reason that businesses fail is lack of working capital. I personally have never known a professional organizing business to fail for any reason other than being unable to get paying clients fast enough. They ran out of money, plain and simple. (We are talking failure here, not professional organizers who chose to close their business for other reasons, like having a family or changing professions).

Getting started right away on accounting software is the best way to be on top of your financial situation and manage your cash flow. Accounting software can give you insight into your financial situation, helping you identify opportunities and anticipate potential problems. With accounting software, you can pay bills, create invoices, track credit card charges, and organize all of your finances in one place. Keeping entries up-to-date simplifies the month-end process and helps you to manage your business and keep on course with your business plan.

Accounting software makes it easier to track your income and expenses, and saves a lot of aggravation when it comes time to prepare tax returns. Keeping your accounting records on your computer enables you to pull reports regularly to learn what percentage of your income is generated from what type of business or client. You will be able to tell how your business changes from one year to the next. This will help you determine where to focus your marketing attention.

Many new business owners wait to implement accounting software until months or years after they start their business, only to find themselves stressed out when they have to find a way to input all the back data. Unless you have an accounting background, you will have a learning curve, and there is no better time to get through it than when you first start your business. You have more time available, and you can learn the process systematically as you build your business and your activities become increasingly more complicated.

Although it is unlikely that you will need financial statements to apply for a business loan, the balance sheet, income statement and cash flow reports available in your accounting software are invaluable tools for helping you stay within budget and identify profitable activities.

Pay yourself first: Your business can provide the means for you to retire some day, and enjoy the fruits of your labor. Do not kill the goose that lays the golden egg by consuming your profits. "Pay yourself first" is a common phrase heard from business consultants advising new business owners. That does not mean to write yourself a check and spend your profits. Paying yourself first means putting money away for your future. Small businesses have a variety of options for retirement plans. You can choose from a

Simplified Employee Pension (SEP), a Savings Incentive Match Plan for Employees (SIMPLE), a Keogh Plan, defined benefit plans, defined contribution plans, profit-sharing plans, and salary reduction plans, such as a 401(k).

Some plans require a plan administrator because of the record keeping and reporting requirements. Be careful if you have employees. The rules of some plans specify that you must provide comparable benefits to anyone qualified to participate, meaning that if you contribute 10% of your salary to the plan, you must contribute 10% for every employee covered by the plan. Talk to an investment professional or a financial planner to help you narrow down your choices and pick the best plan that suits your style.

Watch spending and conserve cash: Conserve your operating money by analyzing every expense. Before investing in office space, equipment, software or furniture, ask if it is necessary. A good rule-of-thumb is to test each purchase to see how it will boost growth.

Just as your parents might have told you to turn lights out when leaving a room, or not to leave the faucet running while brushing your teeth, there are practices you can employ to conserve cash for your business.

You can save 80 to 90 percent of list price by buying re-manufactured equipment, furniture and supplies. Laser print cartridges can usually be refilled three times before needing to be replaced. Re-manufactured ink cartridges can save between 30-60%. Used office furniture in almost new condition can be purchased for a fraction of the cost of new.

An effective way to conserve cash is to lease equipment instead of buying it. Although leasing office furniture, computers and copiers can be more expensive in the end, leasing will help you avoid spending your capital all at once.

Buy enough supplies to last you a couple of months, at the maximum. Keep lists of needed supplies and make it a practice to buy only what is on the list. It is not a bargain if you do not need it, so do not buy supplies just because they are on sale and you might need them. Do not buy large quantities of supplies, even if there is a quantity discount. Storing office supplies can be cumbersome, especially if your storage space is limited. Paper quality degrades with humidity, pens dry out, batteries give out, and toner cartridge warranties expire while sitting on the shelf.

When shopping for supplies, you will get attention that is a lot more personal if you go with an independent supplier, and you may be able to negotiate a discount. While you are devoting so much energy attending to your clients and building your business, you do not want to be spending your time wandering around discount office-supply stores, especially if one supplier can offer you the best price with free shipping.

To get good quality printing without spending a fortune, get printing quotes in person, where you can show them what you want to produce and view actual samples. The quotes you end up with will be more realistic. Proposals vary when shopping around by phone, because your order is subject to interpretation (unless you know printing terms and jargon). Your printing company knows what costs extra and what produces about the same result at a lower cost, so ask for advice. Ask about cost-effective ways to produce your desired result.

Laser business checks can be printed on your own printer, resulting in substantial cost savings. I do not recommend this option, however. Identity theft and check fraud have reached epidemic levels. Purchase your business checks from a reputable check printing company who produces business checks with watermarks to ensure security. Just as your grandmother taught you, do not be wasteful. Reuse anything you can, if you need to conserve cash. You may not save a lot on any single item, but the savings can add up over time, so recycle and reuse whenever you can. Get in the habit so that you can be a model for your clients.

Get paid faster: If you collect from your client at the time of service, use your accounting software to document cash received. If you bill your clients, use your accounting software to generate an invoice right away. Processing these tasks in your accounting software automates the process of setting up accounts receivable records, enabling you to produce statements and reminders that you can send to your clients. If you bill your clients, be sure that you communicate your billing terms in your Client Agreement, so that it is clear to your client when payments are expected.

As your business grows, you can be paid even faster by upgrading to Web-based accounting software to invoice your clients via electronic mail, accept credit card or direct transfer payments online, and automatically record the payment transaction in your books.

Know who owes you and how much: One of the keys to financial survival in the professional organizing business is to keep your money collected. When you finish a job, get the check immediately if at all possible. Talk to commercial clients up front and find out their accounts payable aging policy. Some commercial clients can pay within 15 days of receiving an invoice. Even if your cash flow is in great shape, remember that you are not a bank! Be tough, and ask for your money.

> I lost $3000 on a corporate account several years ago by trying to be Ms. Nice Guy too long. Since they had already paid most of their balance, I was patient. This was a big mistake! They stalled every month and became more and more difficult to reach until we had to put collection pressure on them. It was too late and they went out of business owing us money.

Use your accounting software to run aging reports every month to see which clients owe you money. Identify past-due accounts and take immediate action to notify your clients. This information may help you to avoid further cash flow problems by postponing further work with a client until his balance is paid. You can also use this information to help you determine whether you should consider changing your billing terms or offering a discount for early payment.

Track expenses and react to potential problems: In certain organizing specialties, cash flow fluctuates, depending on the time of year. Professional organizers who specialize in record keeping find a surge of activity in the first quarter, just before income tax time. If you use your accounting software to compare your budgeted expenses to your actual expenses, or to compare your current expenses to your historical expenses, you will be able to react to such fluctuations by making sure you keep enough cash on hand for times when business is slower.

If you have recurring clients, talk to them to try to understand their future needs. Check to see that your planned expenses are in alignment with your sales. Project sales based upon trend and last year's sales for the same period and be careful not to overstate your forecast. As the actual sales numbers come in, adjust expenses as necessary.

Small business accounting software not only helps you to organize your financial information in one place, but it can also give you better insight into your company's financial position. Having the information you need at your fingertips may help you to be more proactive and make better business decisions.

Record keeping: Whether or not you have bookkeeping experience, as a business owner, you will need to keep accurate records for your business to help you monitor the progress of your business, prepare your financial statements, identify sources of receipts, keep track of deductible expenses, prepare your tax returns, and support items reported on tax returns. You may choose any record keeping system suited to your business that clearly shows your income and a summary of your business transactions. For most small businesses, the business checkbook is the main source for entries in the business books. Your books must show your gross income, as well as your deductions and credits.

Many business owners are needlessly terrified of an IRS audit. There is no reason to fear the IRS unless you are being less than truthful. Granted, those who do not report all of their income may risk serving time in jail. According to the IRS Office of Public Affairs, most changes made to audited returns are the result of mathematical errors or the lack of proof for claimed deductions, rather than the result of a taxpayer deliberately trying to cheat.

Keep accurate records and avoid excessive mistakes and you will be able to avoid a dispute with the IRS. As unwelcome as an audit may be, taxpayers have nothing to fear as long as they have been honest and have kept adequate, accurate records. This includes all expenditures, both personal and for business. Maintain clear, accurate records of all transactions and develop a system of tracking your expenses as they occur, noting what was purchased along with the date and the cost.

The key to a smooth audit is proof of deductions. You must not only prove that you spent money, you must prove for what it was spent, and so a cancelled check is insufficient proof. With the IRS, you are not innocent until proven guilty. The burden of proof lies with the taxpayer. You may be able to prove that your deductions are legal and appropriate, but that will be of no help to you in the event of an IRS audit if you cannot prove you made the expenditures. You must be able to substantiate them to the satisfaction of the IRS. You must have a paper trail, and a valid receipt is the most solid proof of your claim. If you have worked in the corporate world, you may already be in the habit of saving receipts, since you needed them to submit with your expense reports. If this concept is new to you, get in the habit of obtaining receipts for every business expense.

Organize every single receipt for both personal and business expenditures and categorize them. It is very common for business and personal funds to cross, especially if you are deducting expenses for a home office or vehicle. It is critical to separate your business and personal accounts. Sure, it is all your money, but opening a separate checking account for your business is smart and will save you headaches at the end of the year.

The cost of a business checking account is minimal compared to the cost of unscrambling the bookkeeping mess, or the risk involved in co-mingling funds. In addition, the fees and interest are deductible. Pay all of your business bills and deposit all earnings from your business into your business account, and balance your bank statement as soon as it arrives.

It is also advisable to have a separate credit card to use for all items associated with your business. If you pay for business expenses out of your personal cash, save the receipt and write on it the purpose of the expenditure. Recap your cash receipts periodically (this summary is called an expense report). Write yourself a check out of your business checking account to record the business expenses. Never use your business credit card or checkbook to pay for groceries, personal gifts, etc.

Generate an invoice for each consulting job and keep a copy of each invoice. Make photocopies of all checks and endorse them immediately. Make frequent deposits, itemizing fully the source of each check (or cash) received. You may receive 1099 reported income statements from your clients, and you will want to check the amounts against the checks written. A discrepancy between the amounts of income you report and the amount your clients report may flag you for an audit.

If you plan to accept credit card payments from your clients, open up a merchant account. Include payment gateway and shopping cart capability if you plan to accept charge cards over the Internet. The transaction fees and monthly statement fees can be significant for merchant accounts. Ask your banker to explain the most cost-efficient way to accept charge cards, and take the time to shop around and research the best solution for your business.

Maintain supporting business documents: Purchases, sales, payroll, and other transactions you have in your business will generate supporting documents such as invoices and receipts. Supporting documents include sales slips, paid bills, invoices, receipts, deposit slips, and canceled checks. These documents contain the information you need to record in your books. It is important to keep these documents because they support the entries in your books and on your tax return. You should keep them in an orderly fashion and in a safe place. For instance, organize them by year and type of income or expense.

The following are some of the types of records you should keep:

- Gross receipts: Gross receipts are the income you receive from your business before expenses and taxes. You should keep supporting documents that show the amounts and sources of your gross receipts. Documentation for gross receipts includes invoices, copies of client checks, bank deposit slips, and 1099 forms.
- Purchases: Purchases are the items you buy and resell to clients. Your supporting documents should show the amount paid and that the amount was for purchases. Documents for purchases include canceled checks, cash register tape receipts, credit card sales slips and invoices.

- Expenses: Expenses are the costs you incur (other than purchases) to carry on your business. Your supporting documents should show the amount paid and that the amount was for a business expense. Documents for expenses include canceled checks, cash register tapes, account statements, credit card sales slips, invoices and petty cash slips for small cash payments.
- Travel, transportation, entertainment, and gift expenses: If you deduct travel, entertainment, gift or transportation expenses, you must be able to prove (substantiate) certain elements of expenses.
- Assets: Assets are the property, such as furniture, equipment and computers that you own and use in your business. You must keep records to verify certain information about your business assets. You need records to compute the annual depreciation and the gain or loss when you sell the assets.
- Employment taxes: There are specific employment tax records you must keep. Keep all records of employment for at least four years. Records retention guidelines can be found by ordering IRS Publication 552 or obtaining the PDF version from the IRS website at www.irs.gov/pub/irs-pdf/p552.pdf .

Protecting your assets

It is impossible to prepare for all possible situations, but time spent early on planning for your security and that of your assets will give you peace of mind. Being protected by an insurance policy does not mean that you will want to use it. Be prepared and take commonsense measures to protect yourself from disasters.

Protect your computer system. Unlike large businesses, you will not have a specialized computer department to maintain your computers, and protect them from electronic intrusions like viruses, spam, and spy-ware. A good source of information to help you protect your computer can be found in a PDF booklet produced by the U.S. Chamber of Commerce and Microsoft, Inc. entitled Security Guide for Small Business. This PDF booklet is available for free download by clicking on Computer Security from www.microsoft.com/smallbusiness.

If you have ever suffered from a computer crash or failed hard drive, you know how crucial it is to back up your computer. It is not a question of whether it will happen, but *when* it will happen. Take the time to back up your data. Keep regular backups of your system settings, My Documents folder, and any other folder where you store data. Use a secondary method of storage, such as tapes, CDs, external hard drives, or use an Internet backup service. Make sure you have your backup stored in a location away from your computer where it will be protected from heat, dust and contamination.

Develop a disaster recovery plan. There are special considerations for the home-based business owner. The security of your home is at stake, in addition to you and your assets. The following action list will help you be prepared, and will help you when organizing client's offices.

- Keep important documents in a fireproof vault or bank safe deposit box
- Install protective equipment, such as smoke detectors and deadbolts
- Keep your computers and office equipment out of view of windows
- Do not overload electrical circuits
- Keep walkways free of clutter
- Install surge protectors and/or uninterruptible power supplies
- Back up data according to a regular schedule
- Back up your data to multiple forms of media
- Store clearly labeled backups offsite
- Practice preventive maintenance on your equipment
- Use a post office box and make it a practice to avoid revealing your street address in promotional literature

Insuring your business: Your homeowner's or rental insurance policy may cover certain aspects of running your home-based business, but it may need to be augmented to provide adequate coverage for your business. Purchasing a business rider on your homeowner policy or renter's insurance policy will protect your equipment and supplies against loss or damage.

Shop around and get bids from several agents to get the best possible premiums. For that matter, just register your business name and get a business phone number and insurance agents are likely to come crawling out of the woodwork. Most insurance professionals are paid out of the premiums collected from their clients, so it typically costs you nothing to have a professional guide you through your insurance choices. When choosing an insurance agent or broker, remember that his primary goal is to sell you insurance.

The basic difference between an agent and a broker is that an agent represents one company, and a broker has a wider range of options. Check on the agent's experience and make sure the insurance department for your state licenses the agent. If you already know what kinds of insurance you will need, try to choose an agent who specializes in that type of insurance.

Most people will be honest about their insurance experiences, so get referrals from business colleagues, friends and family. Choose an agent you can trust. If you choose an agent for a cheap premium, you may have to become an insurance expert yourself just to make sure you are adequately covered. Find someone with whom you feel comfortable, and who will be accessible when you have insurance questions.

Public liability and property damage insurance: Contact your personal insurance agent and tell him that you are operating a business from your home. Your homeowner's or rental insurance policy may cover certain aspects of running your home-based business. At the very minimum, you will need an endorsement to your homeowner's policy for business pursuits. A home office policy or a business owner's policy will probably be more appropriate to cover your professional organizing business. Whichever policy you select, liability and property damage insurance are the most important coverage.

A home office policy combines homeowners and business insurance to eliminate gaps or duplicate coverage. It covers hazards like fire, theft, lost income and loss of data. It also covers business liability like accidents and injuries. If you or an employee injures someone or damages property and she makes a claim against you, this insurance will pay the damages. This insurance will also defend you if you are sued, and cover any legal costs. Liability insurance does not cover your workmanship. If your work is sloppy, or if you damage a client's property through carelessness or inexperience, you are responsible. You should be prepared to make it right.

A business owner's policy is a step up from a home office policy. If you work from home, you might not need a business owner's policy since the structure housing your business is covered under your homeowner's policy. Review your policy yearly to make sure you have adequate coverage for your business.

Errors and omissions insurance: Errors and omissions insurance protects you in the event a client claims that something you did on his behalf was done incorrectly, and that this error cost him money or caused him harm in some way. The litigious world we live in today may demand that you protect yourself with errors and omissions insurance (E&O).

E&O insurance is appropriate for professional organizing consultants who give advice, make recommendations, design solutions, or represent the needs of others. It can help to protect you and limit your liability if you formalize a contract with your clients. The biggest expense in an errors and omissions claim, however, is the legal defense needed to prove liability or innocence. E&O insurance will cover the defense costs. If you do not win the case, E&O insurance will cover the final judgment, as well.

Worker's compensation insurance: If you have employees, you are bound by law to carry this insurance, which compensates your workers for on-the-job injuries. Check with your agent, because you can usually buy this insurance as part of a business package. Some states require you to buy your worker's compensation insurance from the state.

Vehicle insurance: If you have a business vehicle, carry insurance just as you would for your own personal vehicle. The same principles apply as for insuring personal vehicles. You can lessen your cost if you tie your vehicle liability insurance in with your other business liability insurance.

Health insurance: Health insurance is practically a necessity. Without it, a major illness or surgery could completely wipe you out financially. If you are not already covered under another plan, you will have to shoulder the cost of your own health insurance premiums.

Group health insurance for employees is optional. It is common practice for employers to include health insurance as part of a compensation package, so you may be expected to offer health insurance as a benefit if you have employees. The cost of your own insurance through a group policy will be less than an individual policy and the savings increase when more people join the plan. If paying your employees premiums is cost prohibitive, you can make a health plan available, but have your employees pay part or all of the premiums themselves. Part-time employees may have health insurance through their main job or through their spouse's employer.

There are a several alternatives for healthcare plans. There are two main types of managed care health insurance programs: Health Maintenance Organizations (HMO), and Preferred Provider Organizations (PPO).

Generally, the more extensive the plan's options for medical providers, the more you will end up paying for the plan. An HMO is usually considered the most economical type of plan. With an HMO, your options are limited. You pick a medical provider from the HMO's list, and you typically have to get prior approval from a gatekeeper doctor to see a specialist.

A PPO is similar to an HMO with a preferred provider list from which to choose medical providers. You pay less if you choose a doctor from the list, but the PPO will allow you to choose any doctor, including a specialist. With a PPO, you usually pay a co-payment for each visit.

If having the flexibility to choose any doctor or specialist is important, a fee-for-service plan would be the best choice. You will pay the full medical costs up to a predetermined amount, called a deductible. Once the deductible has been met, the insurance company pays a percentage of your healthcare. The insurance company negotiates the rates, so they are typically less than actual cost. The costs to you will be higher with this type of plan, and the premiums will increase as the deductible decreases.

Small businesses can save money on health insurance by joining a coalition. For more information, contact The National Business Coalition on Health at www.ngch.org or National Federation of Independent Business at www.nfib.com.

Disability insurance: You have worked hard to establish your business and survived the pressure of irregular income. You are able to pay your expenses without a regular salary. While breathing a sigh of relief can be tempting, be vigilant and do not let a drastic change blind-side you.

Financial stability can be rocked by unexpected storms. You will want to prepare for the unexpected and protect your financial security. Disability insurance is a good way to insure that you will not be at financial risk if you are disabled. With disability insurance, you can replace a part of your salary and make ends meet while you are unable to work due to a disability.

Most insurance companies will pay only a percentage of your basic monthly salary, but if you have not established an average monthly income, you can calculate your monthly spending to come up with a reasonable figure. Use that information to choose a disability plan that will allow you to support yourself in the event you are unable to work.

When choosing a disability plan, make sure it is renewable and has provisions for cost-of-living adjustments. It is also a good idea to choose a policy that allows you to stop paying premium payments while you are collecting benefits.

Bonding: Some clients may request or even require you to be bonded before you start a job for them. Before you are bonded, question those who want the bonds and make sure they understand what they are asking for. There are several types of bonds.

A Bid Bond guarantees that you will sign a contract and complete the work according to your bid if it is accepted. Performance Bonds essentially promise that you will do the job right and finish it according to the contract. Larger companies and government jobs might require this type of bond. If you go out of business or do not finish the job, the bonding company arranges to have the job finished. Then the bonding company comes after you for reimbursement. Neither of these types of bonds has much application in the organizing industry.

The bond that you might be required to have is a Fidelity Bond, which insures your client against employee thievery. If you have a bank as a client, you would need this type of bond. If you have a dishonest employee who is found guilty of stealing, the bonding company will cover your client's loss and then go after the employee for reimbursement. The catch is that the bonding company will not pay without a criminal conviction. Make sure that your client understands that he must sue you and you must be convicted before the bond will pay. You can get bonding from your insurance agent if it is required. You might want to question the clients who requested the bonds to make sure they know why they are asking for the bonds. Make sure that they understand what the bond will and will not do for them.

Taking care of the boss

Entrepreneurship is a roller coaster. Your motivation and drive to succeed alone will not give you the high energy level you need to run your business. It is a big mistake to spend all of your time and energy on your business and allow the most precious asset – YOU – to suffer from abuse and neglect. Spend your time and talents not just taking care of business, but also taking good care of you. You cannot expect your business to thrive if you do not feel great in body, mind and spirit.

There will undoubtedly be times when you are not at your peak because of unforeseen situations. Your clients will understand that you have to reschedule an appointment because of the occasional flu or minor injury. However, do not wait until something goes wrong to seek medical care. Establish healthy eating habits, a physical fitness routine, get plenty of sleep and visit your doctor and dentist regularly to prevent the long-term health conditions that may be lethal to your business.

You deserve to be able to take a break when you are sick, need to take care of your family, or have a personal crisis. Create a policy regarding how you will handle those occasional urgent matters. Communicate up-front how you will deal with urgent personal matters that keep you from focusing on your busy clients. When something does come up, change your voicemail greeting and send an email (use BCC, or whatever means necessary to protect your client's privacy) explaining your situation. Simply letting your clients know you will be unavailable that day shows your respect for your clients, and allows you to focus on what really matters right then in your life.

Leave time in your day for reflection and self-care. Set some boundaries around your business activities. If you have let your clients know, you are flexible and willing to structure your time to meet their needs, be careful that your business does not spill over into your personal or family time. In order to sustain both your business and your personal life, balance is as important for you as it is for your clients. Set a good example for your clients by implementing stress reduction strategies in your own life. Allow yourself plenty of personal time to rest, rejuvenate, pray, and meditate.

Structure time off for you and your family and turn off professional work every now and then. Be sure to make time for doctor's appointments, hair care, massage therapy, exercise and anything else that provides for your health and well-being. Block out vacation time on your calendar. Your clients will be inspired when they hear you say that you will not be available because you are taking a break.

> One of the benefits I struggled to give up when I left my corporate job was the four weeks of paid vacation per year I had earned. I set as a goal when I started my business to give myself four weeks of vacation. I have met that goal every year. Each vacation is not necessarily a trip to an exotic location, but I do put aside four weeks each year to recharge my batteries and take a break from client work and other business activities.

You will especially appreciate an occasional reprieve once your business has progressed. You will need time to step back and strategically plan your business. As much as it is important to be committed to your professional goals, it is also important to engage in activities such as exercise or a hobby to energize your spirit and renew your enthusiasm. It is critical to turn to others for support and guidance. Talk with a colleague, family member, or friend that you trust to give you encouragement and validate your aspirations.

Take the time to recognize and celebrate your successes. When you hit a milestone or reach a goal, call a friend or share your delight with a family member or a colleague – someone who truly cares about your achievements. Create a list of rewards and use it to motivate yourself to take on challenges. Some of the rewards on my list are a massage, a bottle of body lotion from the spa, a round of golf, and a pedicure. Rewards really can be motivating. I longed for a certain small briefcase for several years, but I kept brushing aside my wish because the item was so expensive. I finally decided to set a business goal high enough to justify such an extravagant purchase, a goal that I reached within six months.

Start and maintain a kudos folder or box for collecting thank-you notes, recognition, compliments, affirmations, photos, and anything that reminds you that you are in the right business, that you are helping other people achieve their organizing goals. Review it often. Keep it handy so that you can pull it out after having had a bad day. I also keep a scrapbook that shows the history of my company through the way my letterhead evolved and other mementos. Reminders of the progress you have made and special sentiments expressed by people who truly appreciate you will help to sooth your occasional feelings of failure and give you encouragement.

Part III

Working with Clients

Chapter Twelve: Cultivating the Client Relationship

"Correction does much, but encouragement does more." - Johann Wolfgang von Goethe

The organizer-client relationship depends a great deal on compatibility. You will maximize your success if you work exclusively with ideal clients. Find clients you can fall in love with, and who will fall in love with you. Compatible clients create emotional energy, which has a very positive effect on your bottom line.

Converting prospects into paying clients

Create a standard about which clients you will and will not work with, and make it your goal to work only with ideal clients. Make a list of features you would expect to find in an ideal client. Think of the people you enjoyed working with, in the past. What was it about them that distinguished them from others? Think about the characteristics that made them easy to work with. Consider aspects that would make the best use of your talents. What qualities are important to you?

Use this list along with your intuition to create an Ideal Client Profile. Write it down and keep it close to your phone. Refer to your Ideal Client Profile when you are interviewing potential clients. Have the courage to say "no" to clients who do not make your heart sing, referring them to someone else, if possible. Make sure you convey a picture of your ideal client to your friends, family and colleagues, so that they are better equipped to support you by referring ideal clients.

Getting off on the right foot: Your first contact with a prospect usually determines whether the prospect will become a client. Learning how to conduct the initial interview means you must polish your sales skills. Selling is necessary if you are going to do business. Selling is the consummation of your marketing plan. You can spend a fortune in time and money on marketing and not get any clients. Marketing will communicate what you do and get clients into the buying cycle, but if you want to be paid for your services, you must persuade clients to hire you.

Selling is nothing more than conveying information that generates interest in you and your services. If you enjoy the chance to meet different types of people, you will love selling. If you have been conditioned to think badly of people who promote themselves, you may be reluctant to sell. For me, learning how to sell involved a paradigm change. Many people (including me), perceive *sell* to indeed be a four-letter word. For most of us, selling is a violation of the golden rule; "do unto others, as you would like others to do unto you." Who likes to be sold?

Selling carries the negative image of being sleazy, pushy, or deceitful. The focus of formal sales training is on the process of handling objections. Who wants to be handled? There is sort of a used car salesman stigma in most people's minds when they think about selling. Nonetheless, without sales, there will be no revenue. Without revenue, there is nothing to deposit in the bank and your professional organizing business will cease to exist.

Sell became more palatable for me when I learned to substitute another four-letter word, help. Your interest in the professional organizing profession came about because you enjoy helping people. Clients do not want your services and features. They want relief from their organizational anxieties. They want space that is more functional. They want more opportunity to enjoy their belongings. They want a sense of security and peace of mind. They want more time for fun.

As professional organizers, we offer a solution for our client's anxieties. When looking for a solution, our prospects are afraid of making a mistake. Through effective selling, we will assure them and put their mind at ease. The dialogue you have with a prospective client about your services should focus on how you can help them overcome their stressful situation and improve their quality of life.

Emotional connections are the keys to getting and keeping a client. Focus on building relationships and helping people, rather than selling. Reaching out to prospects in a personal way will generate the greatest results. Prospective clients will judge you on how you treat them because they do not really know enough about you to evaluate your knowledge or competence. It will not matter what you know or how you can help them if they do not believe that you understand their needs. Your objective should be to form relationships with clients so that they will want to work with you.

You do not have to be aggressive or use hard-sell tactics in order to get people to buy your services. You do not have to defend yourself, either. Be proud of the value you provide and direct your efforts to serving others in a personal, responsible, honest and professional way. You can be a passionate leader who campaigns for lives that are better organized and more productive. Professional organizing is a very emotional business, and you have to touch people's hearts. Offering your services is an act of kindness.

Get into proactive mode: Make your sales effort a priority. No matter what we would like to believe, a sale is a game of numbers. Set performance goals and keep a daily checklist. Identify the number of prospects you will call everyday and set aside a specific amount of time when you will focus specifically on selling activity. Treat that time as sacred and do not allow distractions.

Give serious thought about what you will say to potential clients and put together a script. Then translate that into an outline and rehearse your script. Before making your pitch to potential clients, do whatever it takes to put yourself in a positive mood, whether that be listening to music or going for a walk. Before you call prospects, make sure that you have the energy that brings out your very best. No matter what, always remember that rejection is an opportunity to learn. Go over your outline and make changes – then try again.

Sharpen your follow-up skills: Calling a prospect a couple of times and then giving up is not likely to gain you many clients. The average sale is made after the fifth call. Converting a prospect into a client might require a series of interactions. After you have begun to have a meaningful conversation with a prospect, be patient and persistent. This work is about helping your prospect to make a decision, so be prepared to articulate answers to his questions.

The harder you work at follow-up, the more clients you will get. Being persistent by trying several times to reach a prospective client and leaving more complete messages will pay off more than leaving a telephone message and assuming it is the client's turn to take the next step. Even if the prospect hired someone else, keep him informed and let him know you are interested in the relationship. You might be the person he calls after the person he hired failed to help him or neglected the relationship.

Once a client has decided to hire you, plan on following up within a few days of talking to him. Contacting him will help to alleviate any doubts he may be having. You may be feeling positive about the outcome of your initial consultation, but your client might be second-guessing his decision to hire you. He may be thinking about other alternatives or even wondering if you deceived him just to get his business. Call or drop him a note to let him know you enjoyed meeting him and reassure him you are confident that you will be able to resolve his problem. Tell him, "I'll see you on Monday at 1:00 p.m. at your house."

If you correspond in writing and email, be sure to use good business writing practices so that you look professional. Since writing is still one of the best methods of communication, you can make or break your business success with good business writing skills. Use the following as reminders:

- Write only when you have something to say.
- Write without inhibition and lay down your thoughts as quickly and completely as you can. Then go back and edit for accuracy, clarity and consistency.
- Use short, simple words, short sentences and short paragraphs to make your writing easy to read and understand. Use the same vocabulary as you use in your everyday conversations.
- Write in the active voice to keep your writing personal and interesting.
- Use the fewest number of words possible. Your prospects and clients are busy people.

Beginning with your very first prospect, capture contact information in a reliable database, even if you do not plan to make regular mailings to your list. Take the time to computerize your list of prospects and clients so that you will be able to keep in touch and build relationships. Manage prospect and client information and sales opportunities in one place so that you can better connect with your clients. Make sure to capture mailing and email addresses.

If you use a contact management system, you will have quick access to pertinent prospect information so that you can take action at the most appropriate time to turn the prospect into a paying client! There is a rule of seven in business, which means that people must hear about you seven times before they will be moved to act. A good contact management system will help you to keep track of the frequency and different methods you use to put your name in front of your contacts.

Choose a system that allows you to track how you know each person and your relationship with him or her. Although I cannot conceive of managing contacts with a manual or paper system, many people still use simple low-tech tools like loose-leaf notebooks and card files. Use whatever system works for you.

With today's technology, you can handle more volume and perform tasks that are more complex with ease, so it is wise to take advantage of the features of contact management software. Contact management programs allow you to not only record the prospect's name, address and phone information, but most programs also enable you to track an assistant's name, birthdays, spouses' names, how he heard about you, and data about the most recent contact you had with the individual.

Contact management programs give you the capability not just to schedule appointments, but also to track calls, letters and email. You will have a complete record of a client's activity with your business. You can track a prospect's needs, interests, and specific challenges. Most programs provide a free-form field for you to track custom information or information about the background of the prospect.

Conduct a qualifying interview: The initial interview is an opportunity for you to learn about the prospect and her needs in order to determine if you and the prospect are well matched. It is also an opportunity to discuss your pricing policy to ensure that the client understands the cost involved.

Pre-qualifying a prospect is the first step in the initial interview. A qualified prospect has a genuine and urgent need for what you offer, can afford it and is willing to pay for it. Until you are satisfied that a prospect fits that description, do not schedule a face-to-face meeting. Taking the time to pre-qualify prospects keeps you from wasting time, yours and your prospects. The key is to focus on the prospect and her concerns, rather than you and what you have to offer.

People often pick up the phone and call a professional organizer out of sheer frustration. They watch home-makeover reality shows and envision an overnight miracle as a team of organizers swiftly turns their disaster into order. They do not always understand the time and effort that will be involved in implementing a solution. Your initial interview should include questions that will help you determine whether they are truly ready to commit the resources necessary to getting organized.

Acknowledge up front that neither of you has enough information to determine whether there is an effective match between her needs and your experience, skill set, consulting style, and methods. This will help the prospect feel at ease and be more willing to be honest. Find out whether she has the authority to make a decision to hire you without having to consult with a spouse, boss, or anyone else. With practice, you can learn to screen prospects over the phone to weed out tire kickers, rate shoppers and curiosity seekers.

Although prospects usually have a list of questions about you, this is not the time to divulge your special knowledge. Resist the urge to launch into your presentation about the merits of your services and do not get into the habit of giving away your consulting free. Your primary objective in the initial interview should be to understand the prospect's issues and concerns. Take the focus off you and your services.

Get the client engaged by having a series of questions at hand to help you discern the prospect's urgent needs, goals and expectations. Your questions should address generalities, as well as details about the prospects' unique circumstances. The more targeted your niche, the more relevant your questions will be. Your prospects will know from the questions you ask that you are already qualified and well prepared to handle their problems.

Asking specific questions demonstrates your expertise, helps the prospect identify her own needs, screens those whose needs are outside of your expertise, and qualifies her as a potential client. By the questions you ask, she will be lead to recognize your capabilities and identify how you help her. Develop a form that you can use to collect information about the prospect and assist you in pre-qualifying. For samples, see Organizing For A Living Workbook at http://www.organizingforaliving.com/docs.

Most people want to share information about their needs, but they may not even be aware of them. They might need prompting, and your specific questions asked in the proper tone will help to stimulate their consciousness. Be careful that it does not seem like an interrogation. Be sincere and authentic. Take the time to listen so that you can identify her needs, both existing and potential. Listening to her establishes a connection and shows you are interested in her. Tell her how you have solved a client's similar needs, and she will want to know more about how you did that.

Make sure she knows that you want to be sure that you are the most qualified person to do the job. By the end of your conversation, she may believe that she has discovered a solution to her problem. That is far more acceptable to a prospect than buying what you are selling.

Develop a client contact sheet to keep near your phone, so that you will not forget to collect all of the pertinent information that you need to know about your clients. Include a section for note taking, so you can jot down specific words and descriptions the client uses to describe their situation. When you echo these words back to her later, she will know that you were really listening.

Customize your client contact sheet to discover information about the client and her environment that could alert you to potential conflicts. If you are passionate about preserving the environment, for instance, you will want to know if the client is willing to participate in a recycling program. If you are allergic to cats or have a fear of dogs, be sure to ask whether the client has pets.

Chapter Twelve: Cultivating the Client Relationship

Have a list of other organizers to whom you can refer a prospect who is not your ideal client or perhaps cannot afford your fee. Do not waste the prospective client's time or yours if she has not aroused your interest. Do not try to turn a poor prospect into a client. If you have a sense that this prospect or the project is not a good fit for you, say, "Based on some of your answers to my questions, I do not believe I am the right person for you. I know just the person who can help," and refer another professional organizer. Stick to what you do best and spend your time and energy where you can really make a difference and succeed.

Finalize an agreement: A sale is closed when the client has made a decision to hire you. People want to get decisions made, but they do not like to make decisions because they are afraid to make the wrong decision. Rather than persuade a hesitant client, offer some choices that will minimize perceived risks and help the client make a decision. Here are some strategies and closing techniques that might help clients move closer to making up their minds:

Ask simple questions, like, "Would you like to work with me?", or "Do you think we are a good fit?" Make the decision for the client, and then ask her to agree with your decision. "Let's (do this). Is that okay?" Have an alternative in case the client does not like the first recommendation. "Okay, then let's (do that). Is that okay?"

Once the client says "Yes," say, "Let's put a hold on my schedule for (day, date, and time). Is that okay?"

Propose several options. Instead of proposing one solution for one fee, come up with a multi-tiered approach and ask the prospective client, "Which solution would you prefer, A, B, or C?"

A. Basic solution: undertake the first step in the organizing project you have identified, with the option of continuing after evaluating the initial progress

B. Intermediate solution: tackle highest priority client concerns, cutting corners on the least critical areas

C. Deluxe solution: provide a solution for every concern the client expressed.

You want to leave the client with the feeling that it is her preference, and she cannot make a bad decision; that no matter what she chooses, she will have your full attention. Even if she chooses Plan A, your client will have the opportunity to appreciate your work, and you will have an opportunity to evaluate whether the client is one with whom you want to continue to work.

If there appears to be hesitancy, offer to do some small, preliminary work for the client that will enable them to see some progress. Small jobs are a great way to prove yourself and test your compatibility with the client before taking on a large project. Recommend that your potential client hire you on a trial basis, and suggest that you schedule an appointment to address one specific problem. Choose a problem that will enable you to show the client immediate and conspicuous improvement.

At the conclusion of your initial consultation, summarize by saying, "My understanding is that you need X, Y and Z. I cannot help you with Y, but I can refer you to someone who is very capable in this area." Then you can talk about your expertise in the X and Z areas, and offer an opening in your schedule.

Once the client has agreed to hire you, schedule the first appointment right away. Waiting for a callback allows time for the client to change her mind. Take the fear out of working with you by communicating the systematic process of working with you. Make the scope of your work clear and comprehensible. Take the surprise out of your invoice by spelling out your fees and payment terms. Talk about the next steps in getting the job done. Immediately after you have reached a verbal agreement, prepare and mail or email a client agreement for her signature and request a deposit, if you require one.

Handle rejections gracefully: You have worked hard to get to know your prospect. You have spent time with her on the phone and listened to her concerns. You were proud of the way you answered all of her questions. You know you can solve her problems and you just know you and she are a good fit. You have discussed possible openings for your first appointment and she has agreed to call you back to confirm later in the day.

The phone rings and you see her name on Caller ID. You look forward to the discussion with eager anticipation. You answer the phone expecting to confirm the appointment, only to discover that the prospect has hired another professional organizer. You do not believe your ears. You were so eager for this project. You have been optimistic and were sure you were the right person for the job.

Any of us who has received such a call can appreciate how you feel. Rejection stings, for sure, but we must learn to accept it as part of business. Realize that the rejection was not about you as a person. All that the prospect is saying is that she has found a situation that she is more comfortable about, whether it be because of a gut feeling, a lower fee, or other variables. Bear in mind that she may discover that she has made a mistake and might call you at some point in the future anyway. Do not be discouraged. Just move on to the next opportunity.

Creating and presenting proposals

Once you have collected data about the prospective client, defined her problems and identified a process for resolving them, you will offer a recommendation, or a proposal. This might all happen in the course of the initial interview and can be verbal or written. Your proposal might simply be to hire you to assist her at your hourly rate. My preferred method is to present a verbal proposal, and then follow up with a written agreement that will serve as a guide for the project.

Before committing to a written proposal, thoroughly evaluate the client and her needs in order to determine whether it is feasible to take the time to write a proposal. In most cases, a written proposal is unnecessary. Written proposals can be quite costly in terms of your time, so make sure the investment is worth it. You may charge a fee for proposal development, but be sure to let the prospective client know beforehand so that your bill does not surprise her.

My advice to new organizers is this: unless you have the expertise to write proposals, and can afford the time, even at the risk of not getting the project, do not waste your time. I have personally spent hours, and even days, writing brilliant proposals for projects that never got off the ground, let alone generated any revenue.

Unfortunately, many (usually commercial clients) in the position to require written proposals already have someone in mind for the job. Many RFP's (Requests for Proposal) are issued only to satisfy an internal policy or requirement. Even where this is not the case, projects requiring written proposals frequently do not justify the investment in time to write a proposal, since the contract goes to the lowest bidder, and not necessarily the most qualified professional organizer in the end. To complicate matters even further, a detailed, written proposal obligates you to complete a project according to a finite time line. You may not be paid, even if you could not meet the production schedule due to circumstances beyond your control.

If a written proposal is required, here are some guidelines. In its simplest form, a proposal is an estimate of the amount of time it will take to complete a project, and how much it will cost. Projects will usually take longer than you expect and cost more than a client expected to pay. When you quote a project, make provisions for extras you might have provided at your hourly rate, such as errands or unforeseen complications. Be clear about the project limits and exactly what you will provide.

As soon as you offer a proposal and accept payment for a project, you are legally bound to the terms of the proposal and/or contract. Keep your risk to a minimum by specifying in your agreement for what the client will be responsible. This may include space, equipment, personnel, sticking to a specific schedule, and direct costs, such as supplies, delivery and trash disposal.

A proposal has several basic components:

- Explanation of the client's problems
- What needs to be done to solve them
- Who will implement the solution
- When it will be completed
- How much it will cost

If you decide to present a written proposal, it should be addressed to the client and printed on your stationery. The first part of the proposal should be a summary of objectives. The next section will itemize the tasks needed to complete the project in the order the tasks will be completed, along with detailed descriptions and expected results. The last part of the proposal will be a schedule with estimated dates of completion.

Laying the groundwork for success

Most professional organizers call the first client meeting a Client Needs Assessment. During this meeting, you will interview the client and gather facts. You will determine whether your potential client has a problem and what the problem is. You will discuss how to solve the problem and who should solve it. At this initial consultation, you have an opportunity to lay the groundwork for your relationship before you get involved in the practical details of organizing.

Under certain circumstances, the needs assessment can be done over the phone. The distance to the client's location may make this a necessity. Conducting the initial consultation at the client's site can be a great advantage, however, as it enables you to assess his environment. It is difficult to determine the size or condition of the space from oral descriptions. A face-to-face meeting also establishes the tone for your working relationship and helps both you and the client determine if the chemistry between you is suitable. You absolutely must hit a home run at this first meeting, by providing your best advice.

During the needs assessment, the client will describe his circumstances. Learn as much as you can about his situation and identify factors that may inhibit the organizing process. The more you can keep the prospect talking about his own situation, the more information you can gather about him that will help you to make an introductory recommendation and offer the appropriate solutions to his needs and problems.

Ask open-ended questions that require you to do most of the listening. A few examples of open-ended questions are "What are your greatest organizing challenges?", or "What are your goals regarding your office productivity for the next 12 months?", or "If you could only change one thing, what would it be?", or "How do you envision me helping you?"

Once you fully understand the prospect's situation and the complexity of the job, you can begin to talk about the details of the organizing project, asking additional questions to make him aware of any needs he might have overlooked. The goal is to establish exactly what the client wants to accomplish. Discuss what is possible and what is not possible. Describe to him how you work, propose your solution and explain what results he can expect. Make sure he understands why doing the job in a less expensive way may not achieve what he wants, or may cost more in the end.

Your value will go beyond ways you can help clients directly through your services. As a trusted advisor, you will build good will by tapping your connections and specialized resources to help your clients. Your sincerity and willingness to help will come back to you in the form of referrals and more consulting business.

Set clear guidelines: Prior to your first appointment, you will want to have a conversation with your client to discuss guidelines for your work together. You must tell the client what you expect of her. If you have not already discussed it, mention your Client Agreement, and deposit and payment policy. This can be done over the phone or during the initial consultation.

Determine how long your client will realistically be able to work. Three hours is a good starting point. Clients rarely have the tenacity and attention span to stick with a project for 6-8 hours, but some clients do prefer to complete a project in one session. In most cases, you should avoid completing large projects in one session and break them up into two or more sessions.

If the client has responsibilities or distractions, such as staff, children, or even pets, discuss with her how you will be able to minimize interruptions in order to maximize your time together. If a client has children, ask her to arrange for childcare so that you can focus your attention on the project.

Develop rapport with your client: Understanding your client will help you to have a positive impact and work toward the client's goals. Establishing trust and empathy is crucial for influencing a client in an effective manner. The sooner you can build rapport with your client, the less stress you will have about the job and its outcome. If you understand the client, you will have confidence as you suggest remedies and solutions for his organizing challenges.

I do not usually watch much television, but in the summer of 2004, my husband drew my attention to a relatively new reality TV organizing program being aired on cable TV. The program opened as the host introduced the client, and gave a brief overview of her situation. The client was an artist who lived in a very small apartment in New York City. In the next scene, the professional organizer knocked on the door, shook hands with the client as if he were meeting her for the first time, and immediately launched into a lecture about what was inefficient about her apartment and how the space should be rearranged.

"Just trust me" was a general theme of the session, and I found myself wondering throughout the program how much of the show had been staged. The client looked uncertain (and even a bit scared) as the organizer chose items to be discarded, stacking them in a corner. She was surprisingly compliant as he assigned homework, introduced new containers, installed shelves, and changed the whole look of her home.

At the show's end, the client and the professional organizer seemed to be in harmony. The client was very happy with the results. I can tell you I would not have been! His approach to interior design was to expose personal items to public view, which does not fit my style. To me, the space looked cluttered. The style and color scheme of the storage containers he chose were gaudy. The client's redesigned apartment might be satisfying to the aesthetic standards of an artist, but I would have hated that apartment when he was finished with it!

To me, something was missing in this scenario. Where was the scene where the consultant builds a relationship with the client? When did the professional organizer develop rapport? The type of trust that was demonstrated in the television show could not have existed unless the professional organizer had time to get to know the client and get a sense of what would appeal to her.

What I expected to see on the television program was a professional organizer walking into a client's home, scanning the room to identify something that the client was enthusiastic about, and starting a conversation around that topic. Rather than telling the client what to do and what needed to change, I expected the professional organizer to ask questions, get the client talking, and build rapport.

Rapport is not a prelude to persuasion and sales. Rapport requires sincerity, empathy, identifying a bond or commonality and taking time to establish a personal connection with the client. Before you discuss how you might work together, get to know the client. Look around the room and notice pictures, plaques, trophies, books, diplomas, certificates, magazines, or other items that might tell you something about the client and be a good point of conversation. What are his involvements? What are his diversions? Encourage the client to share about something of which he is proud. Allow a friendly relationship to begin by getting your client to talk about himself and his interests, rather than proceeding directly into a business discussion.

People are naturally drawn to other people who are like them, so pay attention and observe similarities. If you can discover something that you might have in common with the client, your client will be less defensive, and your conversation will be more natural.

Discuss various implementation methods: The consulting process requires an agreement between you and the client on how you will be providing your services. You are the foundation for hope, but responsibility ultimately lies with the client. If it has not already been made clear, ensure that the client understands your role in the organizing process. There are several methods to choose from in implementing your organizing services:

- Doing hands-on organizing, actively participating in each step of the process
- Organizing without the presence of the client
- Facilitate the planning process
- Overseeing the organizing process
- Participating, as well as involving other organizers in the project
- Delegating the organizing work to subcontractors
- Give expert answers and suggest solutions
- Make diagnosis and prescribe solutions
- Teaching and advising the client
- Coaching the client

Clarify with your client the conditions for success. Your clients do not have to follow these rules but they need to hear them from you. If you perceive that a client is resistant, it probably means that she is feeling lack of confidence. A good approach to this situation is to remind your client that she has a choice, including continuing as she has always done.

Conducting the needs assessment

During the needs assessment, you will take stock of the client's current situation. You will discuss the client's organizing challenges, long and short-term goals, and specific needs. You will determine what he already knows so that you can design a plan around his situation and teach him what he needs to learn. This is your opportunity to use your listening skills to draw this information from the client and offer your most focused advice about how to achieve the desired results.

The first objective of the needs assessment is to discover what is important to the client. Listen to everything the client says; ask questions to clarify if you do not understand, then reiterate in your own words to insure mutual understanding. Listen for themes and recurring patterns. Listen to find out what is meaningful to your client. Listening strategically to evaluate his needs and priorities will prepare you to offer solutions. Here are ten steps for conducting a needs assessment.

Acquaint yourself with the client: You will start out by getting to know your client, reassuring him, developing rapport, and observing him and his environment. Whether or not they are expressed, first time clients usually have concerns that their situation will be the worst you have ever seen. Offering reassurance and calming their fears may be all that is needed to relieve their worries. Some clients have feelings of shame or anxiety about their level of disorganization and need a little confidence boosting. Above all, they need to be reassured that you will be able to help them. Encourage them to talk about what they are most worried about and listen intently and respectfully. By affirming them in a nonjudgmental way, you will let them know you are on their side. To build trust, express concern in your client's best interest.

- What is the client's personality type and style?
- What is the client's dominant learning style?
- How strong is the client's desire to change?
- What is the value to the client of being organized?

Observe your client's situation. The most obvious awareness is what you see in your client's physical space, but your other senses will also help you to investigate what is going on with your client.

- What is on the floor?

Chapter Twelve: Cultivating the Client Relationship

- What is on the surfaces?
- How long does the clutter appear to have been there?
- Do you notice any odors?

Be aware that the physical reality is only a part of your client's story. There may be emotional influences that could be affecting your client's organizing behavior. On an emotional level, your client may associate certain messes, chaos and clutter with such things as an event, a person (living or deceased), or a loss. You should not try to analyze or evaluate the roots of your client's behavior, but you must be sensitive to the possibility of deep personal meaning and significance in your client's inability to make a decision or let go of a possession. Assure your client that you will not criticize him for how messy or how forgetful he is.

Convey a sense of confidence and assure your client that you are capable of helping him meet his organizational goals. Unless your client feels safe with the professional organizer he has chosen, he will not be able to learn the new skills and concepts necessary to becoming organized. Although you probably already discussed your credentials with your client in the qualifying interview, making it clear again in your initial conversation that you are competent and capable will help to build your client's confidence in you and the process you are about to encounter.

Determine the client's objectives: It may be a challenge during your first encounter with the client to uncover his desired outcome of your work together. Although all clients hire professional organizers with the hope of being better organized, each has unique expectations. Clients may be hiring you to save time, make decisions, or achieve a certain status. Take the time to understand your client's expectations and expect to exceed them. See if you can get him to describe his vision for organizing success. Help your client understand that knowledge of his goals helps you to prioritize your activities and make decisions to facilitate his objectives.

- What are the client's goals?
- What does the client wish to achieve through your work together?
- What results does the client believe can be attained?
- What would success look like upon completion?

It is natural for a client to have fears and even question his own decision to hire you. He may question whether having an organized environment is even attainable. Your client may not be able to visualize the outcome of your work together, and it might be helpful for you to paint a picture for him. Echo the goals and desires that the client has stated, so that he knows you understand his objectives. As you explain how you work and describe for him how you expect the result to look and feel, he will begin to trust you and feel more at ease with the process.

Identify organizing challenges: Take time to determine the real problem that your client is trying to solve. It is not always obvious, but defining the real problem is a critical step. Do not leap to the solution before completely understanding the real underlying problem. Ask your clients to describe situations they face on a day-to-day basis. The specific problems that clients want solved may not necessarily be the ones they verbalize. Clarify their most urgent needs for improvement, and try to tune in to their unexpressed concerns. Your challenge is to evaluate their situation and determine their true needs.

- What problem needs to be addressed?
- What are the symptoms?
- What is the history of the problem?
- What solutions have been tried?
- What are the sources of problems?
- Is the problem strategic or operational?

Determine current processes: In order to satisfy your client's objectives, you need to analyze problems and develop solutions. If your work is a replacement for an existing process, determine what the client likes and dislikes about the current process and fully understand how it currently functions. Ask the hard questions and evaluate how the client currently does things.

- What does the client currently do well?
- What techniques are working?
- What techniques are not working?
- Is there a thorough understanding of the current workflow?
- What areas need improvement?

Identify participants who will be involved: Identify and determine the commitment of all individuals that will be involved in the organizing process. This may include family members, interior decorators, and administrative assistants. Alternatively, clients may want you to fix their situation without their involvement.

- How does the client see his role in the project?
- How extensively will you be involved in the job?
- Who else is involved?

- Is there buy-in from all participants?
- Are other key players committed to making changes?

Identify obstacles: The more you know about what might interfere or delay progress, the better you can prepare for contingencies. Ask each participant for his perspective to help you learn about potential obstacles you may encounter.

- What factors are in place that could sabotage success?
- What organizational obstacles exist?
- What do you see as potential obstacles?
- How committed is the client to maintaining an established system?
- How vested are employees in the current system?
- What internal or external pressures prevent the client from being fully effective?
- How committed is the client to getting rid of unneeded items?
- How willing is the client to try a new system?
- Is the client open to acquiring a resource for ongoing maintenance?

Determine parameters: Gather information to help indicate the level of solutions that you should offer and estimate the project scope and cost.

- Are there any budget concerns?
- How much time will you have to spend?
- Where does the job begin and end?
- Is there an established deadline for completing the project?
- What is the time-line for this project in regards to sequence of events?
- What is negotiable and what is not negotiable?

Evaluate existing resources: Take stock of the client's existing resources, in terms of available time, space, money and skills.

- What resources does the client have?
- Are there additional people available to assist with the project?
- What existing skills does the client have?
- What other opportunities exist?

Review client preferences: Determine how your client likes to interact. Learn about his desired frequency and method of communication.

- What time of day does he prefer to work?
- Is there a time or day that he feels particularly hassled or tired?
- Does your client like to have conversations by phone, in person, or by email?

- How does he prefer to receive feedback?
- Does your client like long lists or little bits at a time?
- Does he have any pet peeves?

Decide how to proceed: Begin to demonstrate your competence in the identification of the client's issues. Determine how you can assist the client through your own skills and other resources, or whether to refer the client to another support professional. If you determine that you will be able to help the client reach his organizing goals, come to an agreement on an action plan.

Once you have figured out the prospective client's goals and concerns, you might determine that you cannot meet all of his needs. A combination of your services and other solutions may be required in order to help him succeed. A professional who wants to build relationships will give honest advice, even if that advice is to contract someone else for a portion of the project. As you work with clients and educate them, they will often discover needs they were not aware of until after they hired you. Even though you may have given away some business up front, you have established credibility with your clients and they will be comfortable asking you to assist them with additional needs when they are identified.

Developing an action plan

This is where you get to demonstrate to the client the true value of your expertise. This is also a good time to educate him about the reality of what can and what cannot be accomplished. One of the greatest benefits you provide your clients is your fresh perspective. You are not emotionally attached to their world. You see things differently and can approach the situation objectively and positively. You have the ability to see the areas where change and growth could occur. This is your highest value as a professional organizer.

Disorganization causes difficulty when beginning work on any project, and this is often the source of overwhelm for your clients. Your clients' day-to-day activities may seem like more work than they actually are because of the time wasted looking for what it is they are supposed to be working on. An action plan provides instant relief and helps your clients to see that there is a light at the end of the tunnel.

A word of caution: anxiety can negatively affect the working relationship you have with your client, so be sensitive to your client's feelings about his organizing competence. Meet the client on his level and do not be condescending. During the action-plan development process, be sure to focus on building your client's confidence, not your ego. Your job is to advise the client and help him improve, not to prove how smart you are. Summarize the client's objectives and demonstrate that you can relate to his needs. Affirm that your expertise meets those required to produce the desired outcome. To assure the client of your competence, you may consider discussing past assignments with other clients (without mentioning specifics) and how they were successfully completed.

From the initial consultation and needs assessment, you have determined the client's objectives and priorities. With the client's anticipated outcome as the basis for your action plan, you will define the project and develop a work plan to help the client achieve the desired results. Within the limits of her budget, itemize the tasks to be completed. Prioritizing the tasks and laying out a time line up front can be quite helpful, especially if certain tasks are in the critical path (literally, as well as figuratively) of others. Evaluate existing resources and determine whether additional resources will be required. Finally, develop a detailed schedule for implementing the project.

When developing an action plan, your recommendation should go beyond what you can deliver. One of the biggest roadblocks in professional organizing is the difference between what a client must do to benefit from your contribution and what she is actually willing and able to do. A successful outcome is dependent as much upon client initiative as it is on your effectiveness as a professional organizer. You cannot force her to change; you can only make recommendations. Your expectation with regard to your client's level of commitment should be stated in your action plan.

Discuss what methods will be employed to accomplish the client's objectives. Do you recommend redesigning inefficient systems or even developing new systems? Should a room be rearranged? Do you recommend a shift from paper to electronic? Will a trash dumpster be required? Would the introduction of recycling be appropriate? Would it make sense to plan a garage sale? Would that be something with which you could assist? Outline the strategy, talk about the benefits, and estimate the time and costs involved.

Determine what assistance is needed and develop an implementation schedule. Explain that organizing takes time and encourage the client to plan sessions in advance in order to develop momentum. Be specific with regard to your recommendation about time allocation. For instance, you might recommend that you work together for four hours per week for the next five weeks, or two hours per day, three days per week with a schedule reevaluation after two weeks.

Have a conversation with the client about your working relationship. Do not make assumptions. Take the time to share your expectations and explain to the client how you work. Try to schedule sessions that are convenient and timely for him. Some clients take a very passive role and will expect you to guide them every step of the way. Conversely, I have a client who proposes a thoughtful agenda of our next session by email. We discuss and refine our plans and when I arrive, we go straight to work, having clarified the details of our entire agenda by email beforehand.

Prepare your client for trade-offs. Three variables can determine what is possible for you to achieve. Time + Cost=Quality. Make sure that your client is willing to invest the time and money to establish a level of quality that meets her needs. Reducing any one of the three will affect the other two. Make sure that you understand which of these three variables is most important to your client, and that your client understands the consequences of cutting any of the three.

If you have not already addressed them, discuss your rates and payment terms. You may need to discuss schedules, equipment, information, supplies, or anything else that enables you to give the client the results he is seeking. Let your client know that you have his best interests at heart and that you are there to support him. Come to an agreement on the organizing process, goals, objectives, strategies, fees and schedules. Reach an understanding about what services are being offered, and what is the responsibility of the client.

If possible, give the client something of value at the initial meeting. Determine what you can accomplish right away to enable the client to see immediate results and energize your relationship. Convey to the client that you are on his side; you are his partner. Make sure your client knows that he is important to you.

Chapter Thirteen: Helping Your Client Get & Stay Organized

"We are what we repeatedly do. Excellence then, is not an act, but a habit." - Aristotle

We have finally arrived at the nitty-gritty of being a professional organizer, where we earn our bread. Here is where we share our professional expertise and integrate our knowledge, skills, and talents to transform the lives of our clients. Every day is filled with new challenges that we can overcome to bring smiles to the faces of our clients and give us a sense of satisfaction. You have worked hard to land your first client. So how do you get started?

Preparing for client visits

Call your client the day before to remind him of your appointment and let him know what time you will be there. Your call will let him know he is important to you, and it will help him mentally prepare for your work together. It will also give him a chance to make sure he has eliminated anything that may be a distraction.

Whether you will be advising, coaching, teaching, overseeing, or actively participating in the organizing process, you will likely begin your day with a client by reviewing the client file in your own office.

- Go over your notes from your phone and/or initial consultation.
- Make sure you have clear directions to the client's location.
- Pack necessary tools and supplies

The first few minutes that you spend with your client will set the tone for your work with him. You may be stunned by what you see upon arrival at the client's home/office. In fact, you may feel slightly overwhelmed yourself. That is natural. Pause a moment before opening up dialogue with your client, and try to visualize the hidden treasures within your client's space rather than focusing on all of the trash that needs to be disposed of. It is important to use positive language that will relieve the client's stress and anxiety.

Spend a few minutes assessing the environment and reviewing his goals and objectives. Make sure the client understands that this preparation helps you ultimately to use time wisely. At the beginning, you want to gather information from him to determine his readiness, in areas such as:

- Available time for working together today
- Anticipated interruptions
- Vision/desire for next 6-8 hours, or however long you plan to work

From this information, you will be able to define deliverables and determine how you can best help him restore order to his life.

Purchasing organizing supplies: New clients often ask what they should buy in preparation for my visit, and my advice is to postpone any shopping until I have a chance to assess what they already have. Although they lack a plan and direction, many clients know exactly where they want to go and have already purchased containers. People generally try containerizing first when attempting to get organized, which is why, when you arrive at a client's location for the first time, you will often discover that she already has plenty of containers.

Many office supply and organizing product companies deliver goods within 24 hours, so the preferred method for ordering supplies is for the client to order from the catalogues that you bring to the initial assessment. She can select items, place orders, and pay with her own preferred method of payment. The items will be shipped to the client's address prior to the start of the next session or project. Since the items are ordered directly from the supplier, no money needs to change hands between you and the client, saving you from having to deal with billing her and with sales tax issues. Local super stores also stock commonly used organizing products that the client can purchase in between sessions.

Another method (second choice) of purchasing organizing supplies is to arrange to collect an amount up front as an advance for supplies. After you purchase and deliver the supplies, the client can reimburse you for anything beyond the advance. If you have a solid level of trust between you and the client, you may want to have the client authorize you to purchase supplies. To avoid misunderstandings, make sure this agreement is in writing, includes guidelines for the supplies to be purchased, and includes a spending limit.

Many organizers keep a supply of frequently used items, which they mark up and sell to their clients. When items are used on a project, the client receives an invoice for supplies taken from the supply list. When using this method, be sure to understand the sales tax laws that pertain to your state.

Chapter Thirteen: Helping Your Client Get & Stay Organized

Decide what to bring on the job: What you bring on the job will depend on the type of project you will be working on. Most organizers bring a box or bag with them to every job that contains the basic tools and supplies they usually need. You will not use every item every time, but having crucial items in your kit can save you frustration. To build your kit, start by selecting items from this partial list:

- A-Z file sorter
- Band-aids and Neosporin
- Batteries (camera, label maker)
- Booties (surgical shoe covers)
- Box cutter
- Business cards
- Cable clamps
- Cable corral or wire snake
- Cable ties
- Calculator
- Cup hooks
- Digital camera
- Empty boxes
- Energy bars
- File folders and labels
- First aid kit
- Flashlight
- Folding stepladder
- Furniture polish wipes
- Furniture sliders/moving discs
- Goo-Gone®
- Graph paper
- Hammer and/or mallet
- Hamper (collapsing mesh type)
- Hanging file folders and tabs
- Heavy-duty contractor bags
- Highlighters
- Hole punch (3-hole)
- Invoice or blank invoice pad
- Label maker and labels (½" & ¾")
- Liquid hand cleaner
- Letter opener
- Luggage wheelie
- Markers (permanent)
- Microfiber cleaning cloth
- Multi-purpose wipes
- Notebook
- Notepads
- Over the door hooks
- Packing tape and dispenser
- Pain relievers
- Painter's tape
- Paper clips and clamps
- Pens and pencils
- Pepper spray
- Picture hooks
- Portable trash container
- Promotional items and giveaways
- Protective gloves
- Removable labels or sticky notes
- Rubber bands
- Rubber finger or wetting solution
- Rubber gloves
- Rubber mallet
- Ruler
- Scissors
- Screwdrivers – Phillips/flat head
- Shipping tape
- Staple remover
- Stapler and staples
- Supply catalogues
- Tape and dispenser
- Tape measure (cloth & 25')
- Timer
- Tool belt
- Tote for hanging files

Tote with wheels or rolling bag
Trash bags in different sizes/colors
Velcro
Water (bottled)

Zip-lock bags
(Gallon, Quart, 2-Gallon)

Take before and after photos: Before and after photos can be the best way to illustrate the progress you have made, remind clients of their success, and help motivate clients to maintain order. Pictures are also worth a thousand words when used as examples of your work in your portfolio or on your website,

Ask every client for permission to take photographs, and explain that you offer this to every client (not just the ones with the most obvious chaos). Offer to make a copy for her, as a reminder of her progress. If you plan to publish the pictures, be sure to get an agreement with the client in writing. If your client is reluctant about allowing you to take pictures, assure her that you will not publicize her disorganization (and then do not!). Do not have the client pose for the pictures, unless they specifically ask to be included.

Some clients may be proud to see their success published. Understand that others may feel awkward about having their space exposed, they may be embarrassed about their disorganization, or they may see photographs as an infringement of their privacy. If a client does not want you to take pictures, suggest that she take her own before and after pictures. If, after finishing the project the client is more comfortable with you and the process, she may offer to share them with you.

Set your work schedule: The number of hours you invest will vary each week, and how you spend those hours will vary even more. Some weeks you will do more client work, where other weeks you will see only a few clients and spend the rest of your time reading, doing research, attending continuing education workshops, or working on projects.

It is common to be booked three-four weeks out. You may be able to handle more, depending on the amount of marketing and administrative activities in which you are involved. Resist the temptation to overfill your calendar. Say you receive a call from a new client who sounds urgent and wants to schedule an appointment for next week. You check your calendar and realize that it is quite full for next week and you have just a few hours open to handle contingencies. Do not be afraid to say, "My schedule is booked until the week after next," and offer her a time slot during that week. She may be disappointed, but chances are she will agree to the later time slot. Listen to your inner voice and set yourself up for success. Make sure you can deliver on your promises.

Chapter Thirteen: Helping Your Client Get & Stay Organized

As exciting as it can be to have new clients, bringing on a new client can often be overwhelming. Consider bringing on new clients one at a time, after you already feel comfortable with those you already have.

Learn as much as you can about her as quickly as possible so that you can show your client the value of your services. If you do find that you are feeling overwhelmed with the learning curve associated with bringing on a new client, talk to her. Confide that you are not handling the workload as well as you thought you could, and ask her to help you explore other solutions.

It is better to be honest about your shortcomings than to risk having an unhappy client who may tell others of her displeasure. Remember that your reputation helps you grow your business. You might be surprised at your client's patience and understanding. Collaborating with her will build goodwill and may even reveal a solution that you had never even considered.

Phases of the organizing process

For most organizers, hands-on organizing is the heart and soul of their occupation – digging in with the client, cleaning out closets, going through piles of paper and sorting into file folders, making boxes of stuff for donation centers. The very first projects can become the launching pad for more ambitious efforts, so you want to make sure your progress is visible and obvious. It is important to achieve conspicuous progress as early as possible (during the first appointment, if possible).

Your value as a professional organizer becomes obvious to the client immediately because you focus your work to the client's objectives and can disregard the details and responsibilities that occupy her day. You can direct your full attention to the project you are working on and help direct the client to stay on task. As your client overcomes obstacles, her confidence will soar.

As you begin working, make sure that the client understands that each time you come to visit; her space is going to look worse before it gets better. Allow plenty of time for each project. The scope of each organizing project should be no more than what you think you can finish within the allotted time. Assure her that you will never leave her in worse shape than when you arrived (and do not).

Phase One – Consolidate, sort and categorize: About 75% of your time with a client will be spent consolidating, sorting and purging. Consolidating and sorting is the first step, because you need to determine what you have to work with. The best place to begin is usually with the floor, since that is the most noticeable. Then move to the open surfaces, and then closets, cabinets and drawers. Clear a space on the floor or use large containers and start several groups of items. You and the client will divide and group her belongings and decide on useful categories, which will include:

Containers …	shoe boxes, plastic bins, checkbook boxes, etc. – anything that might be useful later to hold other items that need to be contained
Trash or Recycle…	items that are not useful to the client or anyone else
Give Away or Donate…	items that may be useful to someone else
Move…	items that belong in another location
Keep …	items that the client finds useful or loves that will stay in this space

Touch every item, and have the client make a decision about each item. Use a series of questions to help her.

"Is this important to you?"
"When did you last use/wear/play with this?"
"Why are you keeping it?"
"Would you keep it if you had half the space?"
"Do you love it?"

If the item is in poor condition, ask

"Is it worth fixing?"
"When and how will you fix it?"

The same basic principles apply to paper, except the categories will be handled a bit differently.

Containers …	file folders, blank envelopes, etc. – anything that might be useful later to hold other paper that need to be filed
Recycle …	paper that has no useful purpose
Destroy/Shred …	paper that must be securely destroyed
Move …	paper that belongs in another location
Keep/File …	paper that the client finds useful or important

From each pile, pick up each piece of paper and ask questions to help the client make a decision about its proper category.

"Is this document useful / important?"
"Do you need this for compliance or legal reasons?"

Chapter Thirteen: Helping Your Client Get & Stay Organized

"Is this document up-to-date?"
"Are you the originator of this document?"
"Can you obtain this information from somewhere else, if needed?"
"Can you rely on the originator to provide up-to-date information?"
"What is the worst possible thing that could happen if you destroyed this?"

When handling paper, you will not need a Trash stack, assuming that any paper that can be put in the trash can be recycled instead. Junk mail, old magazines and newspapers, and obsolete records all go directly into the Recycle stack. Put aside to be destroyed any papers with personal information that are not needed for tax accounting. Trash is public domain for identity thieves, so the recommended method is shredding.

The Move stack could actually be several stacks – one for each person in the household or office. The Keep/File stack will be all the paper that has the client's important information. In residential organizing, that would be paper with personal information on it, such as social security numbers, bank account numbers, and credit card numbers.

Phase Two – Purge: The series of questions you ask will help the client eliminate items she does not need, and she may be surprised at the end of the day at how large the Trash, Donate, and Recycle piles have become. Help the client determine how to get rid of the items. It took courage for the client to get rid of those items, and the sooner you remove them, the easier it will be for her to let go. When you are finished sorting, instruct the client to take the Trash pile out to the curb, while you put the Donate items in your vehicle. Wise professional organizers offer to deliver donations as part of their services. When you drop off the donations, be sure to pick up a receipt from the charity organization and mail it to your client.

Put aside the *Move* pile or put the items in a laundry basket. This can be your client's homework. Have the client put the items in their proper places in between sessions while you are not on the clock.

Although you may find it easy to determine what a client should keep and what she needs to purge, prepare to deal with some reluctance on the part of your clients. As your clients begin to make decisions, you will hear comments like "I might need it someday", or "It was my grandmother's", or "It was so expensive". The key to overcoming reluctance is to deal directly with your client's concerns. Help them determine whether their fears are justified by asking pertinent questions about the items that stump them, like "Is it something you can use?" or "does it work?" or "when was the last time you used it?"

Phase Three –Prepare the Space: Even if you have previously done so, evaluate the room and have the client visualize how she is going to use it. Seeing the empty space will give the client a fresh perspective. You and the client may decide to add shelving, reconfigure a closet, replace furniture and cabinets with more appropriate fixtures, buy additional containers, etc. Before putting everything away, prepare the space. Although your job is not to be a housekeeper, you will not want to put things back into a dirty space. Put on rubber gloves and use your multi-purpose wipes to clean cabinets and counter tops and furniture polish wipes to wipe down shelves and furniture.

Phase Four – Containerize, Store, and Label: All that is left now is the pile of belongings the client wants to keep, along with some possible containers. Begin with items that must be stored in a specific location. For instance, in a broom closet that is also home to the water meter and an assortment of pipes and plumbing fixtures, the vacuum may only fit one way in a particular spot. On the other hand, the crock-pot may only fit on the bottom shelf of the largest kitchen cabinet. Make sure to put those items away first. Then deal with flexible items. Put all remaining items into functional containers and store everything in its place.

Stop before you are done, making sure to allow at least 10 minutes before quitting time to clean up and make final changes. Remember that you never want to leave the client's space looking worse than the way you found it. Take pictures and recap your progress to help the client take time to celebrate a job well done. Point out opportunities for the client to continue to make progress until your next appointment.

Maintaining organizing success

When clients call professional organizers for help, they often have a fantasy of finally getting organized. However, organizing is not a one-time final event. It requires ongoing maintenance. Although you will approach an organizing project as a goal, have a plan for maintaining the system you have designed and implemented. If the system does not fit your client, or if the client does not have a plan for maintaining order that works for her, she will fail. Methods and techniques must be sought for each individual client that will be compatible with her lifestyle, preferences and organizing styles.

Maintaining organizing success may be as simple as filing papers into folders on a daily basis, purging clothes' closets at every change of season, or using a tickler system to manage tasks. For many clients, a simple maintenance and follow-up plan is sufficient. For other clients, involving other people in their ongoing organizing efforts will be necessary. In order to keep disorganization from returning, some clients may need a system of accountability. Other clients, especially chronically disorganized clients may need to make organizing a social event in order to avoid feeling overwhelmed, bored or frustrated with the process of maintenance. When developing a maintenance plan for your clients, you can help them select individuals, such as family members, friends, or retirees to assist them with maintenance.

> I set up a system for a client a decade ago who books an appointment with me every year to go through the process of setting up her financial records for the upcoming tax season. To be truthful, she no longer requires my particular expertise, and we spend a great deal of time just chatting and catching up. The certainty of my visit gives her the assurance that she will start out each year on the right track, and she gladly writes a check to ensure this peace of mind.

One of the main roadblocks in maintaining organizing success is going off-task. The client sets out to do organizing, but runs into something that causes her mind to wander. She ends up going from task to task and soon she has run out of time without accomplishing what she set out to do. Before long, she is back where she was before she hired you.

> A colleague of mine has a client who has a standing appointment with her every other week for the purpose of opening mail and paying bills. A weekly project that used to take her client half a day is now accomplished in one or two hours. My colleague, a professional organizer helps the client trash junk mail and quickly pulls out bills to be paid. She does not actually pay the bills, but serves as a body double. She performs other mindless tasks for the client while the client focuses on bill paying. The very presence of my colleague helps this client to get through the tedious task of paying bills.

You may be a resource to your clients on an ongoing basis to help them maintain organizing success by scheduling regular maintenance appointments. Professional organizers often call these clients *maintenance clients*, or recurring clients. You may serve as your client's body double helping your client to avoid distractions and keep focused. You can provide the external discipline for your client to keep her from being tempted by obstacles that draw her attention from her task. You can help her focus on what is important.

Clients who were happy with the systems you implemented get frustrated when they fall apart. They yearn for the environment they experienced just after you worked your magic. They associate you with organizing success and trust you as an ongoing resource to ensure they do not fail. You can be an anchor for this type of client, and these clients can be a great source of ongoing income for you.

Understanding basic organizing principles

Getting organized is not at all a modern concept. For centuries, economists have conducted studies to examine efficiency in labor production and space utilization. Throughout civilization, from the Egyptian Pyramids, to medieval estates, to early American farms, to manufacturing companies, to mammoth business enterprises, systematic approaches to organization have been sought. Reorganization is frequently an attempt to improve efficiency and profitability in large companies. Comparative studies have been conducted to learn the best use of resources. Government grants have been created in the interest of efficiency in the area of natural resources.

People instinctively desire extra time for relaxation and enjoyable activities, and naturally want to know how to do more in less time with fewer resources. Despite modern conveniences, however, our society is more organizationally challenged than ever before. The need to understand how to recognize and remove obstacles, restore balance and create a productive environment has never been greater.

No matter what direction your organizing career takes you, it is important for you to understand basic organizing principles and apply them to the systems you develop and the work you do with your clients. The Suggested Reading list in the Resource section at the back of this book includes a number of books that discuss these principles at great length. Your education, experience, business focus, clientele, and specialty will determine the direction of your studies and help you decide which books to choose. To get you started, here is a condensed version.

Setting goals and objectives: Goals and objectives are the criteria used to judge the success of a project. The clearer you are about your objectives at the outset, the less disagreement there will be at the end about whether you have met them. Objectives should be SMART — Specific, Measurable, Action-oriented, Realistic, and Time-limited.

Action without clarity about goals is often one of the first symptoms of disorganization. Your client can have the sturdiest containers, the most popular day planner, a professionally constructed closet, and the best of intentions. However, if his actions are not focused on SMART goals, he will continue to be sidetracked and disorganized.

Values clarification is the first step in setting goals. The choices you make about how to spend your time and energy are based on your true values.

Being clear on what is most valuable to you helps you to stay focused on the tasks and activities that really make a difference. Unless you are clear on values, you may work very diligently on irrelevant tasks.

It is a natural tendency of every human to take the path of least resistance. Helping your clients develop clarity about their values will help them focus on the most critical and important action that will lead to results with the highest payoff. Clear values lead to clear goals.

Effective time management requires that you organize your goals clearly and direct your efforts to achieve them. Clear goals help you to avoid wasting time and losing sight of what you want to accomplish. Before you design and implement any system for your clients, you must help them determine what they want and why they want it. Systematically help them create and prioritize goals and make plans for their accomplishment.

Setting priorities: Once you have determined values and goals, applying rules of economy and using resources efficiently can guide your priorities. Two well-known principles, Pareto's Principle and Parkinson's Law, are helpful guides for priority setting.

In the Pareto Principle, also known as the 80/20 rule, 80 percent of output or results come from 20 percent of input or effort. Here are some examples of the Pareto Principle:

Eighty percent of revenue comes from twenty percent of clients

Eighty percent of problems come from twenty percent of causes

Eighty percent of the time spent on a project will be spent on twenty percent of the project

The 80/20 rule was named after the Italian economist and sociologist named Vilfredo Pareto around the turn of the 18th Century. He noticed a remarkable concept about how wealth was distributed in his country of Italy. His discovery revealed that 20 percent of the Italian people controlled 80 percent of the wealth. Pareto then tested his principle on other countries and scenarios, by which he was able to confirm that the 80:20 Principle could be used as a reliable model to predict, measure and manage all kinds of situations.

This formula was eventually declared the Pareto Principle, or Pareto's Law. The 80/20 rule has been applied to other economic data and has been used effectively in time management analysis. The assumption is that 80 percent of focused effort yields only 20 percent of the results, while 20 percent of focused effort yields 80 percent of the results. In other words, 20 percent of what you do will generate 80 percent of the value of everything you do.

The essence of effective time management is based on concentrating the greatest amount of time and energy on tasks that will produce the most significant return. Without conscious effort and effective time management, trivial tasks consume 80 percent of your time and effort. Only 20 percent of your time and effort are spent on what is really important to you.

In Parkinson's Law: The Pursuit of Progress, British scholar C. Northcode Parkinson introduced the concept that work expands so as to fill the time available for its completion. This proverb suggests that people usually take (at least) all of the time allotted to complete any task. If you have an hour available to get ready for a date, you will be ready in an hour. If a project is allotted one month, it will take 30 days for its completion. This same principle can be applied to other measurements, such as expense. If given a budget of $1000, most people will spend it.

Parkinson's Law speaks to the importance of setting priorities and understanding what is filling your time. If you do not know what your priorities are, other work will expand to fill in any extra time. In other words, it will take you longer to accomplish less. Responding to interruptions and distractions is not critical to your client's business day, yet you may find that these are the very activities that consume his time.

Differentiating between urgent and important: Often, our activities are directed by whatever is most urgent in the moment. According to Stephen Covey, highly effective people concentrate their efforts on the most important activities. Habit number three in Stephen Covey's Seven Habits of Highly Effective People is to put first things first. To help us understand what he means by first things, Covey presents a Time Management Matrix, which is broken down into four quadrants:

1. Urgent and Important	2. Not Urgent and Important
3. Urgent and Not Important	4. Not Urgent and Not Important

Each of your day's activities can be classified into one of these four quadrants. Covey's studies have found that the most effective people spend most of their time in quadrant number 2, directing their attention on what is important, but not necessarily urgent. Anything that is important has serious impact or potential consequences, but not necessarily in the short term. To leverage our time, we need to be proactive rather than reactive, and avoid the unimportant crises that disrupt our lives.

If eighty percent of your day is spent in urgent not important activities, only twenty percent of your time is spent in the important and not urgent. Helping clients to concentrate their attention and energy on high value tasks to accomplish what is most important will help them to manage their action accordingly and reduce their feeling of overwhelm.

Batching tasks: Doing a series of similar tasks one after another rather than spreading them out throughout the day reduces the amount of time it takes to do each individual task. Each time you do one of these tasks you take advantage of the learning curve to improve your competency and pick up speed, so it takes less time to do it. Many tasks can be batched, like phone calls, errands, and paying bills. Tasks become easier once we are in a rhythm, and they are accomplished with less thought and effort.

Project management: Clients often have a mile long list of intentions. They read books, stock up on containers, and begin to make changes in their everyday activities in hopes of getting organized. Yet despite their best intentions, they are not able to achieve their desired results. They often fail because they do not have a clear and organized path to follow. They lack the skills required to manage the interrelated activities of a project, or the confidence to overcome challenges and pitfalls.

Managing a project and solving a big problem for a client can be one of the most rewarding aspects of being a professional organizer. Though sometimes tedious, project management can be creative, challenging and exciting.

Project management involves a series of tasks and activities designed to solve a problem or accomplish specific objectives. It requires planning and coordination of effort. No matter whether you want to plan an event, develop a website, organize a room, or clean up after a disaster, you cannot do it all at once. Tasks must be completed one at a time and combined in the right sequence in order to reach the desired outcome.

It is essential for a professional organizer to be equipped to manage a project and lead it to a successful conclusion. In your role as project manager, you will teach your client how to break a long list of tasks into logical groups to achieve the desired result. Some organizers teach the salami technique to help their clients manage projects. With this technique, a major job is treated like a loaf of salami. Just as you would never sit down and eat a whole loaf of salami, you should never try to take on a major job all at once. Break it down into manageable pieces and tackle each piece by itself. Stop subdividing when you reach the smallest unit of time you want to schedule.

When grouping tasks, sequence activities into a critical path. Some activities cannot begin until another group of activities is complete. Provide your clients with a systematic process, and identify milestones along the way. In order to ensure that the expected results are achieved on time and within budget, a project will have the following components:

An identifiable endpoint
A shared vision of the desired result
Clearly established objectives
A budget
Committed participants with agreed-upon expectations
Key resources – money, workers, time, equipment and supplies
Assessment of resource limitations and potential obstacles
Defined phases, including planning, start-up, implementation and completion
An effective plan detailing the tasks needing to be completed
Schedules and deadlines with a built-in cushion to deal with obstacles and delays
Progress tracking; review and reinforcement of objectives

As you identify areas for improvement, taking the time to organize tasks into projects will improve the likelihood of your success. Viewing a task as part of a project gives your clients more control and enables them to focus on priorities and overcome obstacles. Although you will want to teach your clients to distinguish, between projects and routine work, in many cases you will be able to incorporate existing processes in your project management. Help your clients schedule tasks and complete work in a logical and realistic manner so that they make consistent progress, meet deadlines and achieve desired results.

Eliminating excess (clutter): Your clients are often overwhelmed with too much stuff and too much information. Your value to them is to help them decide what to consolidate, what to purge, what to discard, what to relocate, what to recycle, or what to donate. You will help them identify the functional value of their time and possessions. You will help them sort out the personal and sentimental value of their activities and belongings. By helping your clients eliminate clutter, you will help them make the most efficient use of their available time and space.

If you plan to assist clients with paper and information, make sure that you are prepared with the proper knowledge and tools. Clients expect professional organizers to be familiar with statutory matters. They trust you to know the best methods of disposing of paper and electronic data securely. They will expect you to know how to properly destroy confidential, proprietary, personal, and sensitive information, as well as how long to keep tax and legal documents.

Be familiar with recycling and shredding services that are available in your area. Even if paper is to be recycled, paper documents are best disposed of by shredding. Unless the client has a high-speed crosscut shredder, be prepared to send paper waste to a shredding service and obtain a certificate of destruction, if needed.

If you assist clients with organizing electronic documents, you must be knowledgeable about the proper methods of permanently deleting sensitive data from a computer system or removable media. A client could hold you responsible if you delete sensitive data that causes a problem later when it is restored from a discarded hard drive.

When you build your resource library, be sure to include a list of recycling facilities, organizations that receive donations, and consignment stores. Be prepared not only to help your client decide what to eliminate, but also to direct them to resources for eliminating responsibly. Your client will feel better about letting go if she knows the item has found a new home, or if the item can be reused or recycled.

Decision-making: Eliminating excess clutter is essential to creating an organized environment and decision-making is key. According to Taming the Paper Tiger author Barbara Hemphill, "clutter is postponed decisions." As a professional organizer, you will discover that an underlying problem with most clients is their inability to make decisions. Clutter manifests itself in the mind, as well as in paper and stuff, and your clients will find that they can concentrate better when they are in an uncluttered environment. Building decisiveness into the work habits of your clients will result in a decrease in all kinds of clutter.

To assist your clients, think about the 80/20 rule in terms of clutter. If a given category of items is sorted in order of value, eighty percent of the value will come from only twenty percent of the items. Eighty percent of our space is filled with stuff we never need or use. Eighty percent of our information comes from twenty percent of the material in our computers, bookcases, and filing cabinets. Eighty percent of the outfits we wear come from twenty percent of the clothes crammed into our closets and drawers. If you can help your clients get rid of eighty percent that is clutter, they will be twenty percent more efficient.

When you walk into a home or office with the idea of helping a client get organized, you instinctively plan to reduce the amount of stuff in the place. Clients will need your help and encouragement to let go of, rather than organize and rearrange, clutter. One of your greatest challenges will be to deal with the client's emotional attachment with all of her stuff so that eliminating some of it will be acceptable. For the client, deciding what to keep is the most daunting step in the organizing process. Developing a list of key questions for dealing with piles of paper or household clutter can move a client to action:

Is this item something you need?
Is this item something you use?
How is this item meaningful to you?
Can this item be discarded?
Can this item be recycled?
Can this item be donated?

Commit a set of questions to memory and ask them repeatedly. After a while, they will become second nature to you. You may think you sound like a broken record to your client, but the entire process of sorting through clutter will gain speed as she anticipates your next question.

In this age of information overload, paper and electronic documents present an extra set of challenges. Again, the 80/20 rule applies in that people will only ever use about twenty percent of what is in their office, desk, or file cabinet. To encourage decision-making, focus on the contents and identify the information contained in the document. You can help the client eliminate the non-essential documents by asking the following additional questions:

Is this a duplicate?
Can you obtain this information from somewhere else?
Did someone else originate this information?
Do you (or anyone else) keep this information up to date?
Are you legally required to keep this?
Is this information job or business-related?
Does this help you to do your job better?
If job-related, are you keeping it for political reasons?

After going through all of these questions, if the client is still uncomfortable letting it go, ask, "What is the worst possible thing that could happen if you no longer had this?" Do not rush this awkward moment. At this point, your client may be wishing that you would make the decision for her. Be prepared to allow a period of silence to enable your client to think this thorough carefully. After a while, the decisions will come more easily and quickly.

Improving space utilization: The density of a space may seem unimportant when a space if half-empty, but space utilization becomes critical when there is no room to function effectively. Optimum space utilization is flexible, functional and maintainable. When analyzing efficient utilization of space and before recommending alternatives, consider the following factors:

Amount of space
Whether the boundaries of the space can be expanded or consolidated
Purpose and objectives of the space
People occupying and using the space
Assets needed in the space
Non-functioning or redundant assets present in the space
Convenience with regard to fundamental functions
Facilitation of the exchange of information
Category of utilization of the space (shared, office, sleeping quarters, storage, etc.)
Projected space needs
Potentially sharable assets (furniture or equipment) and frequency of use
Available funds to provide for changes or renovations
Respect for the environment, neighbors, personal safety and accessibility
Respect for cost, maintenance, and the facilitation of cleaning

Space can be made more efficient simply by making use of dead space. One example is to make use of vertical space with shelves or suspension. Making use of vertical space is an effective solution for crowded spaces. A carousel or Lazy Susan makes use of the full depth of a space by moving items to the back (unreachable area) of a shelf or cabinet.

Grouping similar items together: Gestalt psychologists outlined several fundamental and universal principles of perceptual organization. One of these principles is that of proximity, which suggests that objects that are near to each other are perceived as belonging together. The implication of this principle is that we are more likely to associate items that are close together than those which are further apart. Another Gestalt principle of organization is that of similarity. This principle holds that features that look similar are associated.

To create an organized environment, it is essential to define categories and group like things together. The point is not where things are put, but where they can be found when they are needed. The objective is simplification, not complication, and rules before exceptions. The closer you store an item to where it is needed and will be used, the more likely it will be returned to its original location. You will help your clients learn to identify categories and group similar items, so that they understand why bills should not put in the same drawer as their underwear. When choosing a location to store an item, the nearer an item is to where you will use it, the easier it will be to retrieve the item when it is needed. Teach your clients to store frequently used items in easily accessible spaces, and to store items used less often in out-of-the-way spots.

Grouping is how we typically organize the world of objects, as well as places and information. A child is taught to categorize by color, shape, and size, or to keep Barbie Doll clothes separate from Lego blocks. My children used to watch Sesame Street on TV, and learned a game called "One of these things is not like the others", a basic process that you will use with your clients in determining the relationship between items.

When we write, our thoughts can best be conveyed if we discuss one topic at a time. At home, our clothes are grouped in a different location from the dishes. Like things grouped together become more pronounced and stand out. We are able to locate a bottle of aspirin in a drug store because all pain relievers are arranged on the same shelf. If a farmer put all of his seeds in the same bag and sowed them in the same field, he would have a very difficult time tending and harvesting his crops. Everywhere we go, things are grouped together as opposed to the chaos of individual items being randomly located throughout a room or a space.

Create a place for everything and containerize: To create order and facilitate easy retrieval, every item needs a home. The first thing to consider when selecting a home is ease of access and retrieval. Easy access insures convenience and reliable maintenance. Other things to consider are frequency of use, safety, and item size.

Containers designated for specific use, purpose or theme, are essential to creating order. Containers keep like-things together, turn stacks and piles into convenient storage, and keep small and loose items from spilling out into functional space. Using a container increases the likelihood that items will be returned to their proper place. Using clear containers that allow you to see what is inside and labeling the contents further improves your chances of maintaining order. With practice, you can learn to locate and utilize the right container for the right application.

Balance function with aesthetics: In helping your clients determine the placement of their things, keep in mind that rearranging your clients' things to create a more attractive space will not necessarily help them stay organized. Being organized is not the same thing as being neat and tidy. Conversely, improving the physical appearance of your clients' space will positively affect their mental attitude and motivate them to maintain order.

For this reason, it is important to plan your work with a client so that it has maximum visual impact at an early stage in the organizing process. Ascertain up front the client's preferences with regard to open storage areas versus hidden storage areas. Some clients need to have their belongings out in the open, where they can see at a glance where things are and where to put things away. Others function better when everything is out of the line of site

Teaching organizing principles and skills

One of the most fulfilling aspects of a professional organizer's experience is to learn that a client has maintained an organized environment that was achieved through mutual effort. Most clients do not intend to include the services of a professional organizer in their ongoing organizing strategy. Their intent is to get organized, finally. Unless you and the client are committed to work together on a continual basis, your most valuable role in the life of your client is that of a teacher. The ideal goal is that clients learn to help themselves in being organized.

Even though you may have little or no teaching or coaching experience, you certainly have had those people in your lifetime whose example you can follow. Schoolteachers determine the overall objective of the course, develop lesson plans, and break the lessons down into lecture, exercises, practice, and homework. At the beginning of each lesson, the teacher reviews the previous lesson and makes sure the students have learned the skills and mastered the concepts.

A teacher who teaches the same subject will tweak and reuse the lesson plan year after year, and you can apply this same concept to teaching your clients. Before meeting with a client, take the time to review your own methods and document the steps you take to achieve the best results. Take your notes with you to the client to help you to explain the relevance of each step, and teach her why it is important for her to learn each skill. Keeping notes with you will enable you to make adjustments and improvements to your system as you gain experience. Before you know it, you are an expert teacher!

Teaching a client to be organized requires that she is willing to change her behavior and master new skills. You do not have to be an expert in behavior modification to bring about this change. Life is the stadium where change occurs, and daily practice over an extended period will ensure your client's progress. Offering assignments that are relevant to your client's daily routines will challenge her and give her the opportunity to practice new behaviors that will support her in her life.

Considering your client's styles and preferences: Assessing the organizing style of the client is one of the first steps to bringing about a successful outcome. Everyone has his own way of processing information and responding to what he learns. Since we are all wired differently, we each have a natural way to communicate and work with others. Your goal is to present information to your client in a way that will make the most sense to him.

Task-oriented versus process oriented: The first concept to consider is the individual's preferred orientation to working with others. Some clients will want you to describe what you will be doing and get to the point very quickly. They want to know the bottom line, and expect all other information to be in line with that. They are *task-oriented*. They will only be concerned about the details after they are clear about the essential meaning. Task-oriented people take pleasure in getting results. To task-oriented individuals, digressing or getting off the point is equivalent to wasting time.

Other clients want you to present your methodology in a logical, systematic progression. They are *process-oriented*. They want you to slow down so that they can hear the whole story before they are able to look at a possible conclusion. Process-oriented people want to understand each step and the reason for doing each step. They do not want you to skip over points. Process-oriented people take pleasure from working with people.

Once you get to know your client, you will recognize whether they are predominantly task or process-oriented by nature. Until then, the way you communicate effectively is a matter of sequence. Begin your communication by getting right to the point, which will appeal to the task-oriented person. The process-oriented person may not engage until you build your case. Work in some information or a story that gives your point meaning. As you interact with the client, watch to see how he reacts.

Thinking style: The second concept to consider is an individual's style of thinking. This concept refers to where in the brain your thought processes are most likely to be centered. Although both sides of the brain are involved in almost all thinking, one side may be dominant.

Verbal-oriented left-brain dominant individuals tend to be well organized. Because they depend heavily on left-brain abilities, they are likely to be tidy, rational, sequential, logical, methodical and punctual.

Visually oriented right-brain dominant individuals are characteristically creative, with traits opposite of left-brain individuals. Right-brain dominant people are not all necessarily artists and not necessarily messy. Many creative people have learned to utilize left-brain abilities and have highly developed organizing skills. By nature though, right-brain people tend to be disorganized.

Learning style: Every brain is wired differently, and there are over 100 factors identified by researchers that contribute to a person's preferred learning style. Preference, in this case, does not mean a conscious, willful act, but for whatever reason the individual is wired in such a way that one perceptual channel or another gets preference in the brain.

Most individuals acquire new knowledge and skills most easily through one of four perceptual channels. In the western culture, the most common preferred channel is visual, or learning through seeing. A visual client will find an adequate supply of organizing books and tools designed just for him. Visual organizing methods and tools such as color-coding and transparent containers are effective ways to teach people who predominantly process information visually.

The second most preferred is the auditory channel. Auditory clients learn best through discussions, talking things through and listening to what others have to say. Tactile (touching or handling) and kinesthetic (experiential) learning styles are preferred by a small percentage of the population. Tactile and kinesthetic clients learn best through a hands-on approach involving touch, movement, imitation and practice.

Most traditional teaching methods involve a combination of lecture and textbook or written material, since those methods hit about 85% of the population, in terms of their preferred perceptual channels for learning. Students whose learning styles are tactile or kinesthetic are often labeled learning disabled. This is because schools rarely teach to their preferred learning styles. Conventional organizing methods and tools often do not work well for these individuals and you may need to find innovative approaches.

Most of us can move from one thinking style and learning style to another, but we prefer some methods of thinking and learning. Few people fit exactly into any one style. Just like your fingerprint, your personal preferences and blend of behaviors form your unique organizing style. An effective teacher will appreciate different learning styles and use various teaching methods in order to accommodate them. As you discover the dominant learning style(s) of your client, you can work to develop organizing systems that are most compatible for him.

A multitude of books on the topic can be found at public libraries and bookstores. It will be well worth the effort for you to learn how to identify individual learning styles.

Keys to establishing supportive habits: You will probably discover that clients have already purchased and studied numerous books about getting organized. They may have even tried the suggestions without success. Learning is in doing, and maintaining organizing success requires that you gradually introduce skills that are more challenging, and encourage the client to practice.

> Mike wanted to get better at golf so that he would feel confident entertaining his clients. He went to the bookstore and bought *Golf My Way* by Jack Nicklaus, *How I Play Golf* by Tiger Woods, and *Golf for Dummies* by Gary McCord. After reading and studying for days, he went to the driving range and bought a bucket of balls to apply what he learned. After watching Mike hack and slice for 45 minutes, the golf pro could no longer contain himself. He walked over to Mike and demonstrated one simple technique. Mike tried it and hit a ball 100 yards. The golf pro then asked Mike if he would like to hit the ball 275 yards, and Mike said "yes!" The golf pro said, "Keep practicing that single technique for 15 minutes each day. Come back next week with $50.00 for your first lesson and I will show you the next step." Proficiency at golf requires that you learn and practice one skill at a time, and the same is true of organizing proficiency.

Gradually increase the difficulty: Begin with basics, building on what is already familiar to the client, and then move to tasks that are more complex. Start with small steps and encourage the client to practice the task until she has mastered a new habit. Start with relatively easy tasks before attempting to establish ones that are more difficult. Gradually advance to more difficult steps and processes, reinforcing each step and affirming new habits as they are mastered. Once the client has a habit down pat, congratulate her success. Then you can begin to introduce a more complex skill or habit for the client to practice.

> Ann is an executive who had difficulty managing her task list. Ann was introduced to a rather complex system, part of which was a tickler file. The professional organizer created three documents, each representing one daily task. She instructed Ann to open her drawer each day and select the tickler file representing that day. She was to complete the three tasks, and then move the documents into the next day's file. The process was simple, and it seemed silly to Ann, but she followed the in-

Chapter Thirteen: Helping Your Client Get & Stay Organized

> struction. After several weeks, Ann was introduced to the next step, which was to sort her in-basket into the tickler file every day. Three weeks later, Ann reported that she no longer needed the original documents that her professional organizer created because she had already developed the habit of completing those three tasks. She also expressed complete confidence that this more complex system would work for her.

Your client experiences a sense of accomplishment when she masters a simple supportive habit. This opens the door for you to introduce harder tasks. Success breeds success and before long, the client is able to advance to more complex systems with confidence. As new tasks are introduced, continue to reinforce the original ones. Training your clients to govern their own behavior by following rules can help to reinforce new habits.

Positive focus: Negative messages are counterproductive, so try not to focus on bad habits that need to be broken. Say you tee off your golf ball and it dribbles a few feet in front of the tee. An experienced golfer tells you that you keep picking up your head. So what do you do? You keep picking up your head. Why do you do this? You are focused on that bad habit. A far better approach is for the experienced golfer to suggest that you to keep your eye on the ball. Your focus will be clearer if you are told what to do, rather than what not to do. Keep the client's focus on the positive aspect of building new supportive habits, rather than on the negative expression of breaking bad habits. Eventually, the new habits will replace the old.

Repetition: Repetition is the key to establishing supportive habits, and you can help your clients repeat positive behavior by turning formulas for success into rules. Each time you work with a client, you can repeat a rule. The more often you say it, the more ingrained it is in your client's mind. With repetition, the habit will be established and restating the rule will no longer be necessary. The client will proudly state the rule before you can even get it out of your mouth, as if to say, "I got it!" Here are a few examples of what my clients call *Jackie's Rules,* that have helped them establish supportive habits:

> If you can do it in two minutes or less, do it now
> Fill file drawers no more than two-thirds full
> Reconcile your bank statement the day you receive it
> Recycle or destroy junk mail before you leave the mail center
> Allow only useful documents to pass through your office door
> Use sticky notes for routing slips and story boarding, but not for reminders or internal memos

Some rules work in both an office and a residential environment; some rules work in an office but not in a household, and vice versa. A couple of examples of rules that might apply in a residential setting are:

> If it hasn't been worn in over a year, let it go
> For every gift you decide to keep, you must let something go
> Allow paper only in a designated space
> Store everything within two steps of where you will use it
> Never walk past an item that is not in its proper place

These are just examples of the types of prescriptions I use with my clients. Whether or not you agree with my methodology, remember that your client will be more likely to persist at a new habit if it is at the forefront of her mind. A mantra that you taught her may help to remind her to repeat a behavior. Establishing repetition and accountability will assist your clients in adapting themselves to new supportive habits.

In addition to repetition, sometimes getting the client to sign a contract helps her to take recommended action. An action contract can be something as simple as a sheet of paper with the written words, "I will open my mail every day." A contract establishes accountability, which becomes incentive for the client to take responsibility for taking consistent action.

Each organizer employs his own doctrine with his clients. There really are no written commandments and we do not all necessarily agree on every approach, but the basic concepts work in any scenario. You will develop your own set of rules that are most effective for your clients. You will develop your own patterns and as your unique style comes to the forefront, it will endear you to your client. Your rule will be the basis for a positive change in a client's life, and before you know it, your clients will be quoting you.

Managing large-scale organizing projects

Professional organizers are frequently called on to undertake major projects that transcend traditional hands-on organizing and transference of skills. The circumstances of these types of projects vary, but often come about because of relocation, a decision to downsize, a changeover in business management, merging of two families, or a death in the family. Clients' levels of frustration and commitment are sometimes high enough that they are willing to pay the price for a rapid turnaround rather than persevering for a year or more while they assist with the transformation.

Taking on a project of this magnitude requires a sizable budget, a clear strategy, a tactical plan, and a team of organizers. Your job is that of supervisor, rather than a hands-on organizer. You will be overseeing the entire project. To control costs and maximize time, the needs assessment for this type of project can take many hours. Understand your client's goals and desires before you begin the project. Help him visualize the ideal utilization of his space. In response to your recommendations, the client will decide how the space will ultimately be used and you can then communicate this information to your team.

Along with the client, you will develop a strategy and determine broad categories in which to pre-sort his belongings. Each category will be assigned a new home, according to your client's ultimate objectives for his utilization of space. Your team of trained organizers will be doing the pre-sorting, without the assistance (or possibly interference) of the client. In addition to the predefined categories, you can expect to have a category that is titled *Do Not Know* and a category titled *Potentially Discard*.

The tactical action plan will include a time schedule, a floor plan identifying staging, and reloading areas. Having a sketch of before and after usage of the space is also helpful. Prior to the start of the project, prepare large signs, one for each predefined category and one for each of the following: discard, recycle, give away/donate, and sell. Post large category signs in the client's location to assist your team in sorting the client's belongings, and hold the rest of the signs for after the sorting.

Make sure that ample trash and recycling bins are available. If shelving and containers will be needed, it is best to buy these in advance. Choose an outlet that is return-friendly so that you can over-buy and return for a refund any items that do not get used. This strategy maximizes the time of your organizing team, who will not have to pause while purchases are made. Also, include on your shopping list supplies and items that will ensure the safety of your team, such as work gloves and masks.

Once you assemble your team of organizers, give them clear instructions with regard to the client's objectives and the ultimate purpose for each room or space. With the right knowledge and skills, your team of organizers will be able to get right to work immediately upon their arrival at the client's location with minimal direction from you. Your job during the pre-sorting process will be to clarify your client's objectives, make supplies and containers available as needed, and ensure the team progresses according to schedule.

The *Do Not Know* category can be used for items that do not have an easily identifiable purpose. The *Potentially Discard* category often takes up the largest space in this type of project. The team of organizers is instructed to use the category for items that seem to lack a useful purpose, are broken or damaged, stained, redundant, moldy, insect-infested, etc.

Once the pre-sort is complete, the client will be called on to direct the team and make decisions with regard to uncategorized items and items to be discarded, donated or recycled. You or a member of your team can serve as a body double during this process. The team of organizers should be ready to label items that the client decides to keep and use, discard, recycle, give away, donate, or sell. Once the decisions have been made, the items should promptly be moved to new staging areas marked by the signs you prepared ahead of time. Items to keep and use can then be arranged in their new home and containers clearly labeled.

Although you can expect to adjust the placement of items, clients usually feel greatly relieved at this point, sometimes to the point of euphoria. The final step in the process is to create a follow-up plan for the client and schedule any necessary assistance he has requested.

Understanding clients with special needs

You may occasionally arrive at a client's location for the initial assessment to find a completely unmanageable environment. It may be difficult to find a clear tabletop or even a free square-foot of floor surface. Piles of paper are everywhere. Closets are stuffed with more clothing than can be worn in a lifetime. There is not just clutter, but clutter that has been dormant for years. The client wants to be better organized, but cannot imagine getting rid of anything.

It is important to understand the essence of the clients' disorganization. You may find, in your initial consultations with clients that they simply lack basic organizing systems, or their systems fell apart after major change in their life. Alternatively, the situation may be more serious. They may have physical or mental health issues. Your clients may have special challenges, and their disorganization may be long-suffering. Conventional methods of goal-setting, de-cluttering, sorting and systems implementation may not work for clients with special needs.

Without preparation and training, you may find yourself in over your head with a chronically disorganized client. It takes careful planning and consistent progress to achieve organizational success with a chronically disorganized client. There is often significant client anxiety and you must fully understand her situation and be able to empathize. The client is usually so embarrassed about her disorganization that it has taken a Herculean effort just to ask for your help. Once you have begun the organizational change process, learn to recognize the signs of approaching challenging situations. You must be prepared with a plan to support her through the entire process, especially during times of backsliding.

Chronically disorganized people accumulate clutter and have difficulty getting rid of possessions. Many have a fear of filing. They have poor time management skills and have difficulty making decisions. After working with this type of client, you may get discouraged when you see that the progress you made became undone between appointments. Chronically disorganized people do not respond to traditional, conventional, or logical organizing methods. Sensitivity to emotions and individual learning styles is critical in working with chronically disorganized clients.

If the client has a history of disorganization, forbearance on your part is critical. A chronically disorganized client has a special need to be reassured that you will be able to help her and that you will stick with it and improve her situation. You may find that you need the assistance of a colleague who specializes in chronic disorganization. Whether or not you have the inclination to work with chronically disorganized clients, it is imperative that you learn how to recognize chronic situations and identify the various causes and traits of chronic disorganization.

Chronic disorganization and hoarding tendencies are often associated with Obsessive-Compulsive Disorder, or OCD. There is also a link with Attention Deficit Hyperactivity Disorder, or AD/HD. There may be a materialistic or cultural component, or even a link to emotional deprivation. In some cases, psychological intervention may be required.

If you are not trained in working with chronically disorganized clients, knowledge of distinguishing traits will help you to refer the client appropriately to other professionals who can help them. The National Study Group on Chronic Disorganization (NSGCD) offers a facts-sheet titled *Are Your Clients Chronically Disorganized?* (http://www.nsgcd.org/gp/factsheets_gp.html), which will help you to recognize chronically disorganized clients. Another powerful resource is a 70-page book written by Judith Kohlberg, What Every Professional Organizer Needs to Know about Chronic Disorganization.

AD/HD clients are generally intelligent and creative, as well as often being impulsive, easily distracted and highly disorganized. AD/HD clients have difficulty staying focused on a task. According to medical data, approximately 4% to 6% of the U.S. population has AD/HD, or Attention Deficit Hyperactivity Disorder, a clinical term also referred to as ADD. Treatment of AD/HD varies from patient to patient and may include diet modification and supplements, or medication. Some professional organizers themselves have learned to overcome the challenges associated with AD/HD, and have helped to discover specific techniques that work especially well with AD/HD clients.

OCD (Obsessive-Compulsive Disorder) is a behavioral and emotional condition that is often diagnosed when patients are being treated for other conditions, such as anxiety and depression. OCD clients suffer from irrational impulses, or obsessions, which often give rise to persistent urges (compulsions) to relieve the distress associated with the obsession. OCD clients are often emotionally attached to their possessions, and have a tendency to accumulate excess, often to the point of hoarding.

In desperation, OCD hoarding clients may call a professional organizer for help. Unless you are trained and qualified to handle these issues, the likelihood of a successful outcome is doubtful. A high level of skill and experience is essential to working effectively with OCD clients, as well as knowledge of the complexity of emotional attachments and difficulty in letting go. Because OCD is a psychological condition, simple clutter reduction is ineffective. Until the underlying issues are addressed, clients will not be able to maintain the systems you have implemented. Treatment involves cognitive-behavioral therapy.

Although most of us are not therapists, we can be an effective part of a team of counselors, coaches, organizers and other services known as collaborative therapy. Our work side by side with a client can bring about the environmental improvements that support behavioral change and emotional healing. Collaborating with other professionals who have your client's best interests at heart may improve the effectiveness of current therapy programs. While work with a therapist may address your client's deep emotional issues, your work with the client deals with organizational logistics.

Being trained to deal with chronically disorganized clients can help ensure success with clients who have difficulty focusing or maintaining the systems you have put in place. You may want to pursue the many educational opportunities offered through NAPO (National Association of Professional Organizers) and NSGCD (National Study Group on Chronic Disorganization) on chronic disorganization. Through these programs, you will learn tested strategies and organizational approaches. NSGCD is a great resource for guidance in developing strategies for working with special-needs clients. NSGCD can also introduce you to finding appropriate and effective mental health professionals and support groups matched to your clients needs.

Working with business clients

The first distinction to make in working with business clients is whether you will be paid by the company or an individual. In other words, who is the client? The way you approach an organizing project in a company can be very different from working with an individual.

When your client is an executive or a support staff member who wants to improve her personal productivity, she is happy to pay your fee because she is likely to benefit financially from working with you. The individual gains, not so much the company. The financial benefit may be in the form of a raise or promotion, or simply helping to secure the existing paycheck. I once received a call from a manager in the former position. When I asked to whom I would be sending the invoice, she said, "I will be paying you. If I do not find a way to clean up my act really quick, I'm out of here."

Most individual business clients inquiring about organizing services say they need to learn, as opposed to residential clients who often say they need to "clean up this mess." Individual business clients consider their investment in an organizing consultant to be continuing education. In the process of working with a professional organizer, clients receive instruction in areas that are typically not included in college curriculums, such as:

- Goal setting and priority planning
- Establishing supportive work habits
- Effective time management
- Using advanced technology to organize data and automate tasks
- Making efficient use of space
- Paper management and filing systems
- Records management
- Designing a functional work area
- Project management
- Workflow management
- Procedure documentation

These skills often give employees the skills and confidence to seek promotions or a better position in a different company.

Unless the company you are working for is an independent professional or a solo entrepreneur, you will be presented with special challenges when the name on your paycheck is a business, rather than an individual. When creating an effective system for a corporate client, it must be able to accomplish the intended outcome without wasting time, effort, space or expense. In a corporate environment, the grading curve is high and the results must be measurable. The way success is defined is distinguished by the fact that a business will expect that the company and not just one employee will benefit from the changes you implement.

When you are hired by a business to implement companywide change, you must understand the psychology of business. Regardless of who hired you or who signs the check, a successful outcome is dependent upon cooperation from all of the people involved. The person who initiated the change process within the company may not have taken the time to create buy-in from upper management or from those who are involved in day-to-day operations. It will usually fall on you as the consultant to take on the challenge of persuading other team members that they will benefit from productivity and efficiency improvements. You can expect resistance.

Management itself can present obstacles. Corporate structure and rules can restrict your progress, since management must approve every move you make. If you have worked in a large corporation, you are familiar with the bureaucracy, and you know the challenges of moving forward with the most simple and logical modifications. Your success is contingent upon management approval, support and a commitment to provide the necessary resources to implement new systems within the company.

It is essential to involve those who will be using the system in every aspect of its design and development. The introduction of a productivity expert often gives employees the impression that management sees them as unproductive. Hard-working employees may resent you and take on an attitude of defensiveness, sabotaging your efforts. Unless you engage participants in the process of creating, implementing and maintaining a companywide system, they will not take the time to ensure its success. Your objective should be to facilitate, rather than direct or control change. Rather than resisting, you can get the participants to take ownership of change and champion your recommendations.

Chapter Fourteen: Retaining Ideal Clients

"The secret of joy in work is contained in one word - excellence. To know how to do something well is to enjoy it." - Pearl Buck

The clients that are already in your database are your most valuable clients. They are more profitable, and the most loyal of them provide an ongoing stream of business. According to business analysts, the time and money you spend retaining existing clients has four to eight times the value of cultivating new clients.

Marketing activities consume both time and money, and retaining existing clients is a powerful marketing strategy. It is more expensive to get a new client than to keep an old one. Client retention can lead to increased profits, since the reductions in marketing expenses go straight to the bottom line. Your time can also be spent more efficiently when dealing with familiar clients, making them cheaper to serve. Focusing the majority of your marketing time, effort and resources on existing clients will have the greatest return.

When you present an agreement to a client, you should be focusing on the lifetime value of that client, and not a single transaction. Be dependable and consistent, treat your clients with honesty and respect, and always follow through on your commitments. Do what you say you will do, whether you have agreed to call them on a certain day, do research, or send them information.

You might be hired for one organizing project and be called back repeatedly to provide organizing solutions as the client is ready to take on additional projects. You may be asked to periodically come back and do adjustments or even an overhaul of a project you have organized. A great deal of energy is spent in building mutual understanding and trust with your clients, so it can be a relief to work with clients with whom you have already developed rapport.

Although clients may not need you every year, you will provide new services to existing clients. Once your business is established, you will get at least

50% of your business from past clients and their referrals. If this is not the case, take a good look at the quality of your customer service.

Gaining satisfied clients

The best source of repeat and new business is a satisfied client. A sales director for Mary Kay Cosmetics told a group of professional organizers at a chapter meeting that she moved five times in seven years and hired a professional organizer for each move. Repeat business and referrals will be your best source of new business, so client goodwill and word of mouth must be carefully protected. Your success as a professional organizer depends on generating business through referrals and your customers returning for additional projects. One unsuccessful project can ruin your relationship with a client and destroy the prospects of getting any referrals from them. It is crucial to treat each project as if your career depended on it. It does.

The best approach is to have a sharp awareness of the client's needs and objectives. Your goal should always be to help him succeed, which requires that you see the reality of the situation from the client's perspective and respond with empathy and sensitivity. Probe and listen to what is important to him. Be aware of his tone of voice and facial expressions. Nonverbal clues such as nervous fidgeting alert you to areas where your client may be concealing his true feelings to hide his embarrassment or anxiety. Sensing and responding to your client's unspoken concerns will help you to deal with the issues that are behind his feelings. Put aside your own agenda and stay attuned to discern how you can best satisfy the client.

Your clients see you as the authority. They will gladly pay a reasonable rate for assistance in getting their life in order. As the business owner, you must personally review every job, resolve client disputes and do everything in your power to make your clients satisfied. If they are satisfied with your work, they will hire you again. If their life is improved because of your help, they will praise you enthusiastically to their friends and associates.

Be sure that you understand your client's expectations and that you can expertly perform the requested services before you accept an assignment. If you are unsure, find another professional organizer who can handle the job expertly. Do not risk damaging your reputation and losing potential new business by accepting an assignment for which you are not prepared. Refer the job to someone else and offer to assist with the project. You will build solid relationships with your associates, have the opportunity to learn from an expert, protect client goodwill, and make money in the process.

Chapter Fourteen: Retaining Ideal Clients

The way you handle complaints can be critical in retaining clients. Dissatisfied clients who are treated with respect can sometimes become your most loyal clients. If a client voices a complaint, let him know you care by asking questions, letting him vent, and listening attentively. Take full responsibility for whatever concerns the client expresses, and do everything you can to get clarity on the issue. Thank him for bringing the issue to your attention, and apologize for the inconvenience. Suggest a solution, or let the client choose between several options. Act immediately to make sure he is satisfied.

Occasionally, you will find a situation where it is not mutually beneficial to continue a relationship. The client may not be a good fit, the job might not be as expected, or you do not believe you will be able to resolve a dispute to the client's satisfaction. It is not worth any price to retain a client that it is not possible to please. My recommendation is to tell the client that continuing a business relationship is not in the best interest of either party. You are not required by law to work with any client. Make provisions for completing any work in process, collect the final payment, and cease the business relationship in as professional a manner as possible. Refer the work to another service if feasible. You may have to absorb the cost of client dissatisfaction occasionally, but it is crucial to the future of your business that you preserve your reputation.

Set yourself up to win, and make sure that you are positioned to provide first-class results for your clients. If clients complain, let them complain about your prices, because your fee does not matter if your quality is substandard. Providing consistently high quality work will generate consistent income for years to come, as long as your clients are satisfied with your work.

Special treatment: Unless you are without competition, having a client who is satisfied with the service you provide is not good enough. The relationship you build with your clients, how often you contact them, how well you treat them, and the extras you give them are equally as important. To have loyal clients who will do repeat business with you and tell others great stories about you require that your clients are ecstatic with you and your service. They must enjoy working with you. You have to give extraordinary service. You have to treat them special.

Special treatment of your clients involves not only doing a great job for them, but also connecting with them at a level that is deeper than strictly business. Develop a sense of friendship and find out what you share in common. Understand what is important to them, and get to know their goals and dreams. Share resources, like books, websites or someone that can help them, so that you can help them reach their desired outcomes.

Here are a few ideas for ways you can reward your clients for their loyalty and treat them special:

An arrangement of holiday greenery
A bottle of their favorite wine
A certificate for a free car wash
A complimentary ticket to your seminar
A vial of essential oils
Their completion photo in a classic picture frame
Write about your client's achievements in your newsletter

Do not assume your client's level of satisfaction. Create an instrument to gauge your approval rating and measure client satisfaction. Ask your clients directly how they feel about working with you. Continuously monitor your client's perception of value derived from the relationship. Send out satisfaction surveys and ask for input and suggestions to determine how well your client perceives your performance. Thank your clients for both positive and negative comments. Showing that you care about their opinions by asking for feedback will boost your odds of retaining clients.

Managing client expectations

Your clients are always right, even if they are wrong in your mind, so you must regulate their perceptions. Your initial meeting with your clients is the time to set the tone. Understand what the clients want and for what they are willing to pay. Let the clients know when you are available, your limits regarding telephone contact, how you respond to voicemail and email, and what they can expect at the conclusion of the project. Carefully manage you clients' expectations and they will be much more likely to be satisfied.

Clients have a set expectation that your service will meet their perceived needs. This expectation may or may not be achievable. You could fall short if there is a disparity between what the clients expect and what you deliver. Do not be so eager to please the clients and get business that you promise them the world. Colleen Barrett, President of Southwest Airlines said it best, "If you promise a client you'll do something tomorrow and don't do it for three days, you've got a very unhappy client. If you tell somebody you'll get it done in a week and you deliver in three days, you're a hero." The best policy is to always under promise and over deliver.

Organizing projects present a unique challenge in that the results are often short-lived. Unless a client has followed through and learned new habits, his situation frequently will begin to degrade as soon as you walk away. It is up to you to help him understand up front that it will degrade over time if he does not commit to developing new habits and adopt the standards you put into place.

As in all areas of life, there will be some bumps. Clients may complain and criticize your efforts. Though you believe the criticism is unjustified, becoming defensive may make him more determined to make his point. The best approach is to thank him and ask for clarification about how you might serve him better. If a client is unhappy and wants compensation in the form a refund, additional consulting, or adjustments to payment terms, you will have to appraise the situation. Be honest in evaluating where the problem lies and think through your options. Do not let your ego get in the way.

You may decide not to charge a valuable client for an extra hour or two every now and then to show goodwill, compensate them for an error on your part, or simply because you want the satisfaction of finishing the project and have exceeded the time allowed in the contract. Be sure to show this on your invoice and make it clear that it is a one-time occurrence. Make sure the client knows that you are giving him extra time and why.

If you feel that you have let the client down, give him the opportunity to provide you with a resolution. You may make less on the project, but you will maintain your reputation. If the client decides to terminate your contract, do not burn bridges. Figure out how much of the delivered work has value to the client, and offer to refund the balance that has been paid to you, or waive the remaining fees due.

Treating your clients with dignity

A professional organizer is a trusted advisor to the client. You will be assessing some of the most personal elements of your clients' lives. When a client invites you into her home or office, she is exposing the most intimate dealings of her life. Your client has likely gone through some great discomfort before getting to the point where she is willing to be vulnerable and call you to ask for help with whatever in her life is unmanageable. It is vital that you vow to protect your client. Your concern, compassion, empathy, encouragement and nonjudgmental attitude are critical.

> I recently watched a Los Angeles area organizer promote her upcoming messiest home contest. The video showed her as she entered a couple's home for an initial assessment. Her immediate reaction was to shout, "You should be ashamed of yourself!" I was horrified. It is inconceivable to me that some people are actually entertained by such behavior. It brought the Jerry Springer show to mind. I was

embarrassed to think that people might expect this kind of reaction from a professional organizer. My heart went out to that couple.

When a client calls you for help, it is likely her situation has become unmanageable. After being introduced to people, you will often hear, "Oh, you are a professional organizer? You wouldn't want to see *my* home/office, etc.!" Being in a dysfunctional situation can be very embarrassing for people, and it will be your job to put them at ease.

Even before new clients bring you into their homes or offices, they may warn you of the chaos you will experience. As they show you their clutter, piles of paper and disorder, they may express curiosity as to whether you have ever seen such a disaster before. Even if you cannot comprehend how they got into this situation, remember that they already feel self-conscious and uncomfortable.

It is vital that you have a nonjudgmental attitude toward clients and their situation. Be compassionate and empathetic and treat the situation as objectively as you can. Emphasize your hope about the potential for change and improvement. Focus on the positive action clients can take to move forward.

Avoid crossing intimate boundaries. Professional organizers often enter the most intimate areas of a person's life, particularly when the job involves the client's home. Make it a practice to be friendly, but do not pursue a personal friendship with your client. Do not ask personal questions of the client that are not necessary for you to maintain a cordial relationship and perform your service.

Do not probe or inquire about personal matters unless your client is comfortable. Take the cue from your client as to how friendly to be. Listen for verbal clues and watch for body language. If the client asks, "How is your family?", or "What are you doing this weekend?", then it is fine to go there with your client as well. Do not get too personal, such as complaining about your sister-in-law's bad habits or your teenage son's driving record.

Handling difficult situations

The following scenarios are included here to make you aware, so that you can recognize difficult situations before they negatively affect your practice.

Client dependence can be risky: There is a danger in depending on one or two clients for your source of income. The risk in throwing all of your business into one client is that the checks that come regularly from the same client (without any sales effort on your part) can be enticing. Your sales efforts slow down, and you risk losing a lot of money if the one client has financial problems or the client simply decides that he no longer needs your services. A wise professional organizer will create a marketing objective that builds and sustains an expansive client base that will give your business a constant, reliable source of income.

Twice in my career, I have been employed by companies that were overly dependant on a single customer. Both companies suffered tragic outcomes when their customer pulled the rug out from under them. I learned a valuable lesson from these experiences (not). Actually, despite having firsthand knowledge of the consequences, during my early years in business I also fell into the trap of having too few clients. It is easier to get into this situation than you might expect. It can happen without your awareness. You may start out working together on a project, and before long, your client recognizes your value and begins to find other ways to benefit from your expertise. Her admiration and gratitude are intoxicating and make you eager to help her. Before you know it, your client has come to depend on you – and you on her.

At one point, my business revolved around one long-term client to the extent that not only my professional time and attention, but also my quality of life was impacted from the intensity of her influence. Once I became aware that a single client I was beginning to depend on for business was virtually controlling my fate, I managed to step up my marketing efforts and expand my client base before it was too late.

I am not alone in this foolishness. Three of my closest colleagues have been caught in a similar situation. One found herself without an income practically overnight when her client abruptly decided to terminate a long-standing agreement. As tempting as it may seem to build your business around what seems to be one or two lucrative, dependable clients, please do not make the mistake of becoming overly dependent on one or two clients. Keep your eye out for the possibility that a major client can move away, sell his business, or have a serious medical issue.

Continue your valuable long-standing relationships, and put them in the proper perspective. Balance one or two major clients with several smaller clients to protect yourself. Make your major clients understand that you have other clients and must balance your time and attention. Be the director of your own security and make it your priority to expand your client base beyond one or two steady clients.

Setting boundaries: Do not allow a client to play on your sympathies and convince you to do something that is too time-consuming, too far away from your specialty, or free. The Policies and Procedures Manual for your business should have a section that pertains to fee setting and how you deal with your clients. This would include things such as:

> Do you collect a deposit?
> What level of commitment to the organizing process do you expect of your clients?
> What happens when the client feels free to call at all hours?
> Do you set your phone to voicemail at the end of your workday?
> What are your ethical guidelines?
> What is the scope of your practice?
> What is your cancellation policy?

It is up to you to manage your time and your business, and setting healthy limits is a primary element. Putting your policies in writing can be very powerful, and can be a buffer for you when there is conflict. For instance, if you have a policy that you charge $25.00 for every 15 minutes of phone support, you will have a much easier time explaining to a client that you do not work free and you will be happy to schedule a phone consultation to continue the conversation.

Dealing with client cancellations: Even with a well-drafted cancellation policy, client cancellations are sometimes unavoidable. I once had three clients in one week cancel with proper notice, leaving me with an open schedule and no revenue for that week. The worst part of the deal was that I had turned away three clients due to a full schedule that week. It happens. You reserve a slot of time for your client, but that time slot will not generate revenue for you if your client cancels.

Cancellations sometimes occur because clients do not plan properly or do not manage their calendars effectively. You can greatly reduce cancellations if you make it a practice of sending an email one week prior to the appointment. The email will remind clients to look at their calendars and make sure there are no conflicts. Then call them the day before to confirm and to remind them to turn on the answering machine, make certain preparations, have supplies available, etc.

You can minimize cancellations by scheduling the appointment as soon as it is mutually convenient. The sooner the appointment, the less time there is for the client to back out. Cancellations can occur when clients are not prepared, so to avoid cancellations, try not to make the session contingent on the client taking action beforehand.

Have a cancellation clause in your Client Agreement and ask for a deposit up front. If you take charge cards, this can easily be done over the phone.

The client could also send a check for the deposit along with the signed copy of the agreement.

Security concerns: Every now and then, warnings circulate throughout our professional community about potential clients who may be a personal safety risk, particularly to women. The typical story that circulates is about a deviate so desperate for attention that he attempts to hire a professional organizer to soothe his desolation.

Situations like this bring to mind such fictional scenes as the one in the HBO series The Sopranos where Tony Soprano makes a sexual advance at his psychologist. Unfortunately, life does hold such perverted realities, so do take heed. The movie Patch Adams is based on a true story. If you have seen this movie, you recall the scene where Patch finally wins his girlfriend over to his way of thinking, about giving and sharing of personal time, attention and humor with needy patients. In the next haunting scene, a mentally ill patient murders Patch's girlfriend during a house call.

There are serious and potentially dangerous risks in every helping profession. Every professional organizer should be on alert and implement protective guidelines. Certain measures can be taken to ensure your protection. For instance, when you go to a client's home or office, always leave a number where you can be reached. Let someone know where you are going (the specific address), and how long you expect to be gone. If you are the least bit suspicious, have someone call you on your cell phone at one-half-hour and one-hour intervals.

Dealing with difficult clients: Making your clients happy can be satisfying and rewarding, but some clients are just destined to be difficult. Every now and then, we all have one. There are many types of clients. Be prepared for handling clients that are more challenging.

As a business owner, you must decide whether each client is a good fit and that a long-term relationship will be successful for both parties. You will occasionally find a client or a specific job that you do not value enough to make it worth the aggravation. At times, you will need to fire a client who takes too much of your time and wears you out. Despite your best efforts, the client continues to demand more than is realistic. Over time, you will learn to predict who will be a time-consuming draining client and avoid them.

Sometimes there is just not a personality fit between you and the client. Some jobs turn out to be very different from what was originally thought, or evolve into projects that do not fit your interests and abilities. Some clients exhibit annoying and inappropriate behavior that just has no explanation. As tactful and nonjudgmental as you have been in approaching a client's situation, an occasional client just cannot cope with the reality of the consequential truth she has been avoiding. Some clients are desperate for attention. It may seem that you are their last hope, but your options for helping them are limited. You want to get new business, not turn it away, but sometimes a client is just not worth keeping.

Be tactful and do not burn bridges when you do dismiss a client. Try to help her find another solution. In some cases, you may want to refer the client to a specialist. Maintain a list of professional organizers and their specialties, along with a list of other consultants, therapists and counselors. Refer business to them when it is appropriate.

Of course, you cannot fire every difficult client, but you must draw the line when the client's needs are beyond your capabilities, when she becomes a daily annoyance, or when a client's demands begin to take control of your business. Sometimes you may find a client that just cannot be pleased. The longer you work with her, the more her demands escalate. She calls every day, leaves voicemails and sends repeated emails. She expects you to leave other client projects to attend to her emergencies.

As much as you may hate to turn away business, a client is not worth keeping and needs to be fired if you are no longer making money on the relationship and that client is not bringing you other business that would be profitable. It is not beneficial for you, your business, or the client to go forward with these types of relationships. Do not allow self-doubts about walking away from income hold you back. Without being indignant, let her know that it is time for her to seek other professional help. If you are concerned about the client badmouthing you, consider that ridding yourself of the negativity will open you up to attract and retain the right kind of client that will boost your reputation.

Occasionally, you may even encounter a prospective client who is rude or confrontational. The person might just be having a bad day, or it may be her personal style. I once received a voicemail message that went something like this, "I was calling to see if you could help me with my clutter, but if you were capable of that, you would certainly have answered your phone." I was grateful to have missed that call. Fortunately, she did not leave a call back number, but if she had, I likely would have given myself permission to ignore it. Before investing your time and energy, ask yourself if you really want to work with someone who is testy or provocative.

You are not a failure because you cannot make a business relationship work. Having your own business is hard enough work without clients making it tougher. Your talents are valuable and working with difficult clients is a drain on your energy. Unhappy clients do not enhance your self-esteem or your reputation. When a client hires you to work for her, be sure to consider how she works for you.

Ethics and integrity

Ethics and law are similar in that they both offer guidelines. Whereas law represents minimum standards set by the government, ethics represents a set of ideal standards set by a profession. The common usage of the word ethics means the acceptable and right way to behave. The primary reason that professional associations adopt a code of ethics is to protect its members and the public from dishonest and incompetent practitioners.

We are living in an era of moral decline, and it seems as if our society has developed a tolerance for questionable behavior. The negative side of business ethics is in the news every day. Employees have lost confidence in executive management, and the public has lost trust in the legal system.

There has been a good deal of notable scandals in recent times. More serious than the loss of money, those involved in well-known scandals have paid the price in the form of lost reputation and self-respect. Their entire life's reputation has been overshadowed by a single mistake. A world-famous entrepreneur and billionaire, highly esteemed by many professional organizers, Martha Stewart's reputation was irrevocably tainted by one seemingly insignificant event affecting a small portion of her net worth. Baseball's all-time hits leader, Pete Rose was denied Hall of Fame consideration after betting on the game while managing a Major League team. Instead of her magnificent performances on ice as an excellent figure skater, Tonya Harding may always be remembered for masterminding an attack on her competitor, Nancy Kerrigan, a month before the 1994 Olympic Winter Games. Bill Clinton's accomplishments during two terms as President seemed almost insignificant when he became involved in a brief relationship with a White House intern.

Approached from a positive viewpoint, ethics is behavior that is in harmony with the best of us as individuals. Ethics goes beyond complying with laws, professional standards and codes of conduct. Ethics is about doing the right thing with your client and being true to yourself. Ethics is contagious behavior. If you have high moral values, if you are honest, accurate and sincere, others will admire you and follow your lead.

As an entrepreneur, always assume you are being observed. Your clients and associates are watching your actions and forming opinions. Every move you make affects your reputation. Every choice you make has consequences.

Even a petty rumor could mean serious damage to your credibility. You are being evaluated for playing by the rules, being honest and trustworthy, making fair judgments, being on time, and doing what you say you will do. Make sure that all of your actions, if seen on the Five O'clock News, would make you and your family proud.

Consider the potential consequences of every step you take. Pay attention and listen, look people in the eye, practice patience and respect, show up on time, keep your word. Tell the truth, especially when it hurts. Call your client personally the moment you realize you have erred and admit your mistake. Always intend to under promise and over deliver. If you say you are going to do something, do it. Clients will notice, even if it is something small. If something is outside of your area of expertise, help the client find another professional. Building your practice on these very things will enrich your personal life and strengthen relationships.

In addition to following your association's Code of Ethics, put your own Code of Ethics in writing to help you define the basic ground rules for your business. Your Code of Ethics will clarify what specific business policies your company has adopted, and to what behavior you and your employees will be expected to adhere.

Your clients are most likely to go with their gut when choosing you. They will trust you with their time, their belongings, their money, their information and their life. While you are busy earning your fee, they will be carefully and thoroughly examining you to ensure that you are earning their trust. Build your reputation on a solid foundation of moral principles and integrity so that you can confidently say to your clients, "trust me."

Ethical dilemmas: As a professional, you are accepting the responsibility to operate within the ethical guidelines of your profession. You will likely face ethical dilemmas in your business. Use your association's Code of Ethics and your own Code of Ethics as your guide. Make revisions as new issues present themselves.

One of the most common ethical issues faced by professional organizers is a situation where helping a client means doing harm to others. This issue could present itself in many ways. Always live and work within your moral-ethical framework, and commit to do no harm. If you know that what you are involved in is wrong and may harm another, you must conclude that you cannot help this client and end the relationship.

Another common ethical issue is staying within your knowledge and qualifications. You have an ethical responsibility to offer only services for which you have been trained and are competent to perform. You have certain strengths, but there is no way you can do everything well. Keep your strengths and limitations in mind when deciding whether to accept new clients, or when working with a client as new issues develop in the organizing process. Be aware of your skill and training. Know when to refer to another professional who is better able to assist your client, and do not practice outside the boundaries of your competence. It is okay to try new things in your interaction with clients, especially if you are in training or working with an experienced organizer, but add new services only after you have accomplished new technical skills or obtained knowledge that is more comprehensive.

Getting repeat business

Getting repeat business is all about enhancing your client's experience and making additional business irresistible to current clients. Develop a close relationship with your clients through regular contact. This goes beyond sending a thank you note after you have deposited their check, or going through your client list and making calls during slow times. It means picking up the phone every now and then and calling your clients just to see how they are doing.

One of the secrets to business growth is to have steady communication with clients even when they no longer need your advice or services. Many organizers work hard to earn their client's business, and then disappear from the client's view after the first project is complete by not keeping in touch. They not only miss opportunities for repeat business, but referrals to the client's friends, relatives and business associates, as well.

Most satisfied clients are happy to refer business to you, but they often forget about you after your work with them is complete. It is common for professional organizers to lose touch with a happy client, only to find years later not only has the client hired a competitor. Unless you inform your clients that you are still available, they may not hire you again, nor will they refer their friends to you.

A great way to keep in touch with clients is to send greeting cards. Try to find out your clients birthdays and anniversaries, as well as other holidays that are important to them, so that you can send them a greeting card to help them celebrate. The remembrance inspires loyalty.

> A great way to generate client loyalty is to send a photo of them in their newly organized environment. I got this idea when I bought my first Saturn. After the paperwork was signed, the salesperson took a picture of me in front of my new car. A

> few weeks later, he sent a thank you card with the photo enclosed. It was a nice touch, which I did not forget. With this tradition, the clients appreciate the photos and I keep a copy to remember their smiling faces.

Gather personal information about your clients, such as their spouses and children's names, their hobbies, recreational activities or athletic teams they support. Organizing this information in your contact management system will help you to get quickly past small talk and give you material to stimulate a conversation. Your conversation may eventually turn to your client's challenges, and provide a chance for you to suggest strategies to resolve problems. Potential organizing opportunities may come up, but even if they do not, your client will remember that you cared enough to call.

When you call, you might talk to your client about interests you have in common or the success of your local football team. Be alert and aware of issues and events that may interest your clients. If your client is a college alumnus, find out whether he supports his alma mater. Then call him when you hear that his team won. If your client likes Irish Dancing and you read that River Dance is touring in your area, give her a call to make sure she knows about it.

If you find a website that might be useful, send an email to your clients with a link. If you read an article that would be of interest to your clientele forward a copy to them (assuming you have obtained permission). Invite clients to read an electronic newsletter that you find useful, so that they can subscribe if they choose.

Write notes and send cards. Keep track of your client's birthday and send him a card. Sending thank-you-notes is a very powerful communication strategy. Everyone should send thank-you-notes, but very few actually do. A timely thank-you shows gratitude and makes you stand out in the client's mind.

Here are some ideas for following up with your existing clients:

Send the client a thank-you-note.
Call the client to find out if he was satisfied with your service.
Communicate with your clients through a newsletter or by sending relevant news clippings or articles.
When clients are pleased with your service, ask for a testimonial letter.
Send a survey to keep in touch and find out how your clients are maintaining the systems you implemented.
Write personal, handwritten notes to clients that you have not seen for a while.

If a client comes to mind, write them a note or give them a call. It is okay to say, "I have been thinking of you. I have not talked to you in a while and I just decided to call even though I did not have any particular reason."

If you run into an old client somewhere, follow up with a note that says it was great seeing him.

Find a way to follow up with your clients on a regular basis. Whether you make occasional phone calls, send organizing tips, or put out a newsletter; being visible, showing you care, and continuing to ask for business will get you results. Let your clients know you have not forgotten about them, you care about their needs, and you are there to help them.

A client does not stop being a client just because you have completed a project. You put a lot of work into converting prospects to clients. Develop a system for communicating with your clients on a regular basis. Keep them in the client category in your database, and help them to remember you. Talk to at least one existing client every day. Keep your focus on the clients and show them genuine concern. Never forget that your clients are the reason you became a professional organizer.

Afterword

The potential for success in the professional organizing field has never been better. Believe in yourself and in your ability to help make the world a better place through being better organized. Your confidence will lead to success, which will lead to increased confidence. Success breeds success. That is exactly how successful professional organizers have approached their careers.

The advice in this book comes from the experiences of professional organizers who earn money in the marketplace. Their knowledge combined with my own experience and my work with struggling organizers should increase your chances for success in this exploding field. Yet the content of this book is certainly not all you will ever need to know. Take full advantage of the opportunities available to you.

Whatever you do, keep learning. Read everything you can get your hands on about organizing, productivity, time management, simplicity, and other related topics. Take classes to learn about building your business. Join the National Association of Professional Organizers and its affiliates.

The advice in this book can only show you what others have done to make their mark in this exciting world of professional organizing. No one has the secret recipe that can guarantee your efforts will produce a successful organizing business. There are many intangibles, such as luck, timing, and intuition. Your success will be in direct proportion to your persistent determination and positive attitude. Avoid the naysayer who discourages you about making a living through organizing. Do not listen to that nagging internal voice that urges you to get a real job.

Hold on tight to your dream of doing work you love. Even if everything seems to be in proper alignment, you are still taking a step of faith into the unknown. You will experiment. Try things out until they fit. You will make mistakes. Treasure the valuable lessons in them. You will have Humpty Dumpty days. You will have days you are on cloud nine.

Honor your deep desire to help others. When you see your name on a check from a client, celebrate! You have earned it and you deserve it. I hope this book has helped you to plan your life, achieve your desires, and fulfill your purpose. I wish you success in everything you do.

Resources

Business Resources

Association for Records Managers and Administrators
ARMA provides information about retention guidelines
4200 Somerset Drive, Suite 215, Prairie Village, KS 66208 USA
Telephone: 913-341-3808
http://www.arma.org

Attention Deficit Disorder Association
ADDA provides information, resources and networking to adults with AD/HD and to the professionals who work with them.
http://www.add.org

Board of Certification for Professional Organizers
BCPO administers the CPO® Certified Professional Organizer exam.
2494 Bayshore Blvd. Suite 201, Dunedin, FL 34698 USA
Telephone: 800-556-0484 or 727-738-8727; Fax: 727-734-9578
http://www.certifiedprofessionalorganizers.org

Business and Marketing Plans
http://www.bplans.com

CCH Business Owner's Toolkit
Business Owner's Toolkit™ offers free cost-cutting tips, step-by-step checklists, real-life case studies, startup advice, and business templates to small business owners and entrepreneurs.
http://www.toolkit.com

Entrepreneur
http://www.entrepreneur.com

Freecycle Network
A network to promote waste reduction and help save landscape from being taken over by landfills, this is a resource for listing items no longer needed for the purpose of finding a new home.
http://www.freecycle.org

Internal Revenue Service
Federal tax information and assistance for small businesses
http://www.irs.gov

Limited Liability Company
http://www.llcweb.com

National Association of Insurance Commissioners
NAIC provides information about risks and protection offered by insurance in six categories: Worker's Compensation, Group health and disability, Business property and liability, Commercial auto, Group life and key-person life, and Home-based business insurance.
http://www.insureUonline.org/smallbusiness

National Association of Professional Organizers
NAPO is the original association dedicated to the professional organizing industry.
15000 Commerce Parkway Suite C Mount Laurel, NJ 08054
Telephone: 856-380-6828; Fax: 856-439-0525
http://www.napo.net

National Study Group on Chronic Disorganization (NSGCD)
4728 Hedgemont Dr., St. Louis, MO 63128 USA
Telephone: 314-416-2236
http://www.nsgcd.org

Nolo
Self-help legal information including books, software and forms
http://www.nolo.com

Professional Organizers In Canada (POC)
P.O. Box 59004, 728 Anderson St. N., Whitby, Ontario L1N 0A4
http://www.organizersincanada.com

SCORE - Counselors to America's Small Business
(Formerly Service Corps of Retired Executives)
SCORE is a national organization of volunteer business executives who provide free counseling, workshops and seminars to prospective and existing small business people.

Telephone: 800-634-0245
http://www.score.org

Small Business Administration
http://www.sba.gov

United States Business Advisor
http://business.gov

United States Copyright Office
Information and updates about copyright registration
Telephone: 202-707-3000
http://www.copyright.gov

United States Department of Treasury Internal Revenue Service (IRS)
Information for operating a business with employees, deductions and credits, recordkeeping and accounting methods
PO Box 25866 Richmond, VA 23260
Telephone: 800-424-3676
http://www.irs.gov/businesses/small/

United States Patent and Trademark Office
Information about intellectual property options
Telephone: 571-273-8300
http://www.uspto.gov

United States Small Business Administration (SBA)
Small Business Development Centers (SBDC) provide assistance, counseling and training to prospective and existing business people.
Telephone: 800-827-5722
http://www.sba.gov

Donation Resources

American Cancer Society	www.cancer.org
AMVETS	www.amvets.org
Disabled American Veterans	www.dav.org
Catholic Charities	www.catholiccharitiesusa.org
Goodwill Industries	www.goodwill.org
Habitat for Humanity	www.habitat.org
Salvation Army	www.salvationarmyusa.org

Recycling Resources

Batteries	www.batteryrecycling.com
Batteries: rechargeable	http://www.rbrc.org
Bicycles	www.ibike.org
Blankets and towels	www.pets911.com
Books	local libraries & hospitals
Cell phones	www.wirelessfoundation.org
Christmas trees	www.christmastree.org
Clothing	www.dressforsuccess.org
Clothing	www.glassslipperproject.org
Computers	www.dell.com/recycling
Electronics	www.sony.net
Eyeglasses	www.lionsclubs.org

National public workshops and seminars

American Management Association http://www.amanet.org
Dale Carnegie - http://www.dalecarnegie.com
Franklin Covey - http://www.franklincovery.com
Fred Pryor – http://www.pryor.com
Kenneth Blanchard – http://www.kenblanchard.com
National Seminars Group - http://www.nationalseminarstraining.com
Padgett-Thompson http://www/findaseminar.com
Skill Path - http://www.skillpath.com

Suggested Reading

Allen, David, *Getting Things Done*
Aslett, Don, *Clutter's Last Stand*
Baker, Sunny, *The Complete Idiot's Guide to Project Management*
Bruce, Andy and Langdon, Ken, *Essential Managers: Project Management*
Cantor, Jeffrey A., *Delivering Instruction to Adult Learners*
Crouch, Chris, Getting Organized: *Learning How to Focus, Organize and Prioritize*
Covey, Stephen, *First Things First*
Covey, Stephen, *The Seven Habits of Highly Effective People*
Culp, Stephanie, *How to Get Organized When You Do not Have the Time*
Edwards, Paul and Sarah, *Getting Business to Come to You*
Edwards, Paul and Sarah, *Working from Home*
Felton, Sandra, *The Messies Superguide*
Fishman, Stephen, *Consultant and Independent Contractor Agreements*
Fishman, Stephen, *Working for Yourself*
Gerber, Michael, *The E Myth*
Gilmore, James, *Authenticity: What Customers Really Want*
Gitomer, Jeffrey, *Little Red Book of Selling*
Gladwell, Malcolm, *The Tipping Point*
Glovinski, Cindy, *Making Peace With the Things in Your Life*
Goldberg, Donna, *The Organized Student*
Hemphill, Barbara, *Taming the Paper Tiger at Home*
Hemphill, Barbara, *Taming the Paper Tiger at Work*
Holtz, Herman, *How to Succeed as an Independent Consultant*
Izsak, Barry, *Organize Your Garage in No Time*
Kanerek, Lisa, *Organizing Your Home Office for Success*
Kingston, Karen, *Clear Your Clutter with Feng Shui*
Kolberg, Judith, *What Every Professional Organizer Needs to Know About Chronic Disorganization*
Kolberg, Judith, *Conquering Chronic Disorganization*
Kolberg, Judith, *Organize for Disaster*
Kolberg, Judith and Kathleen Nadeau, Ph.D. *ADD-Friendly Ways to Organize Your Life*
Kotler, Philip and Gary Armstrong, *Principles of Marketing*
Lehmkuhl, Dorothy and Dolores Cotter Lamping, *Organizing for the Creative Person*
Levinson, Jay Conrad, *Guerrilla Marketing*
Lockwood, Georgene, *The Complete Idiot's Guide to Organizing Your Life*

Lonier, Terri, *Working Solo*
Maple, Stephen, *The Complete Idiot's Guide to Law for Small Business Owners*
Mandino, Og, *The Greatest Salesman In The World*
McCorry, K.J., *Organize Your Work Day in No Time*
McKeever, Mike, *How to Write a Business Plan*
McQuown, Judith, *Inc. Yourself*
Meyer, Jeffrey, *If You Haven't Got the Time To Do It Right When Will You Find the Time To Do It Over?*
Morgenstern, Julie, *Organizing From the Inside Out*
Ricci, Monica, *Organize Your Office in No Time*
Robak, Mary, Gerald F. Brown and David Stephens, *Information and Records Management*
Roth, Eileen and Elizabeth Miles, *Organizing for Dummies*
Sapadin, Linda, *It is About Time*
Sgro, Valentina, *Organize Your Family's Schedule in No Time*
Skupsky, Donald, *Recordkeeping Requirements*
Smallin, Donna, *Organizing Plain and Simple*
Stanley, Debbie, *Organize Your Home in No Time*
Stanley, Debbie, *Organize Your Personal Finances in No Time*
Taylor, Harold, *Making Time Work for You*
Waddill, Kathy, *The Organizing Sourcebook: Nine Strategies for Simplifying Your Life*
Winston, Stephanie, *Getting Organized*
Winston, Stephanie, *The Organized Executive*
Wood, Robert, *Home-Office Money & Tax Guide*
Ziglar, Zig, *Selling 101: What Every Successful Sales Professional Needs to Know*

Index

80/20 rule 253, 257, 258
accountant 116
accounting ....41, 59, 191, 194, 207, *See* also bookkeeping
   software 184, 185, 190, 191, 207, 209, 210
action plan 240–42, 267
ADD, AD-HD (Attention Deficit Hyperactivity Disorder) ..... *See* special needs clients
address
   choosing your e-mail 96
   list, clean-up 147
   using your home 214
advantages of professional organizing 18–30
advertising .... 141, 140–45, 158, *See* also marketing
agreements
   client contracts and 127, 184
   Partnership 105–6, 111
   subcontractor 202
Angie's List 156
antitrust laws 166
appearance 43, 46, 47, 89
appointments 193, 194, 227
articles, writing 141, 147, 162
Association of Professional Declutteres and Organisers (APDO) 57
associations, professional 55, 57, 59, 63, 143
attorney 103, 115, 116, 119, 127, 192
auditory learning style 263
Australasian Association of Professional Organisers (AAPO) 57
Barrett, Colleen 276
bartering 179, 185, 195
benefits
   employee 109, 110, 121, 201
   of professional organizing 18–30
   of your services 149, 150, 159
   tax 121, 122

billable hours 172, 174
billing 184, 209
bookkeeper 191
bookkeeping 112, 203, 210
books 58
boundaries 218, 278, 279, 285
branding 89–90
break-even analysis .... 82, 83, 173, 174, *See*
brochures 95, 146, 147, 192
business

    alliances 29, 64, 85, 129, 155, 228
    cards 94, 95, 96, 145
    clients, working with 271
    coach 62
    colors 92
    entity structuring 103
    expenses 211, 212, 213
    funds vs personal funds 211
    getting repeat 285
    hours 22
    identity 89, 94
    license 117, 118–19
    logo 93, 94
    name 91–92, 97, 119–20
    owner 41, 42, 79, 104, 122
    plan 79–86, 133, 173
    stationery 95, 96

business organizing 72, 271
cancellation policy 185, 280
cash flow .... *See* money management
certification 62–67
charge cards, taking for payment 98, 212, 280
checking account 211, 212
client(s)

    cancellations 280
    database 194, 226, 273
    referrals 71, 155
    retaining 273, 275, 276

 satisfaction 156, 184, 276
 special needs 268–70
 working with 223, 269, 270, 271
coach, hiring a 62
code of ethics 205, 283, 284
collecting money due 184
color, business identification 92
commercial organizing .... *See* business organizing
community
 and zoning 118, 119
 organizations 58, 61, 62, 63, 138, 139, 151
competition 27, 28, 73, 166
computer 189, 190, 192, 207, 213, 214
contact management 194, 226, 227, 286
contractor .... *See* independent contractor
contracts .... *See* agreements
copy machine 191
copyright 130, 131
corporate clients 75
corporation .... *See* incorporating
Covey, Stephen 81, 254
credit cards, taking for payment 98, 212, 280
credit, business 52
database, client 191, 194, 226, 273, 287
DBA (doing business as) 120
deductions .... *See* taxes, income
deductions, tax 107, 109, 211
depreciation 123, 213
desktop publishing 190, 192
determination 37–40
direct mail 140–41
disability insurance 217
Disney, Walt 80
domain name 92, 95, 96, 97
dress 46
Drucker, Peter 80
earnings potential 23–25
education 55, 59, 270

e-mail 96, 97, 147
employee

    benefits .... *See* benefits: employee
    hiring and supervising 194, 195, 196, 197, 200, 201
    versus independent contractor 198–200
    working as an 112

Employer Identification Number (EIN) 125, 126
employment taxes .... *See* taxes
entrepreneur .... *See* also business owner

    versus freelance contractor 42

errors and omissions insurance 215
estimated taxes .... *See* taxes
estimating jobs 180–83
ethics 283–85
experts, hiring 62, 103, 116, 137, 214
Federal Employer Identification Number (FEIN) 125, 126
fees

    establishing 165–87
    hourly 171–73
    raising 186–87

fictitious name 120
financing, funding 52–55
firing a client 281, 282
flyers 95, 146, 192
follow-up with clients 225
freelancer 112
gatekeeper 76
Gates, Bill 80
Genco, Figen 87
generalist 69, 70
gift certificates 139
goal setting 81
growth, business 75, 285
health insurance 216, 217
Hemphill, Barbara .... viii, 28, 142, 257
Hill, Napoleon 87
hiring

employees .... *See* employee
experts .... *See* experts, hiring
history of professional organizing 30–34
home office 123
homeowner's insurance 214
homework, assigning 249
hourly rate .... *See* fees
household organizing .... *See* residential organizing
ideal client profile 223
identity, business 89–101
image, professional 43–47
improving skills 55–62
income potential 23–25
incorporating 107–9
independent contractor

    hiring 195, 196
    operating as 51, 104, 112, 113, 129
    versus employee status 195, 198

initial consultation 175, 176, 177, 175–77, 223–29, 232–40
insurance 214–18
insurance agent 214
intellectual property 129–31
Internet presence 96–100
Internet promotion 141
invoicing clients 180, 184, 186, 209, 212, 230, 244
isolation 19
Ivie, Cynthia 23
Kay, Mary 80
kinesthetic learning style 263
Kohlberg, Judith 269
lawyer .... *See* attorney
leads groups 153
learning style 263
leasing equipment 208
left-brain 262, 263
legal and regulatory issues 117–19
legal documents 257
letterhead 94, 95

liability
- insurance ... 215, 216
- limiting ... 103, 104, 106, 107, 109, 110, 201, 215

license, business ... 117, 118–19
Limited Liability Company (LLC) ... 106–7
logo ... 93–94
maintenance clients ... 251
market research ... 135
marketing ... 133–63
marketing plan ... 133–38
mastermind group ... 86–88
mentor ... 59–60, 86
merchant accounts ... 212
Meyer O'Dowd, Lynn ... 42
mission statement ... 79–81
money management ... 206–13
motivation ... 20, 37–40, 41, 218, 219
naming your business ... 91–92, 97, 119–20
National Association of Professional Organizers (NAPO) ... 33, 56
National Study Group on Chronic Disorganization (NSGCD) ... 56, 57
Nederlandse Beroepsvereniging van Professional Organizers (NBPO) ... 57
needs assessment ... 175–77, 232–40
networking ... 148–53
news release ... 159–60
newsletter
- being included in ... 142, 162, 163
- distributing your own ... 147–48

newspaper advertising ... 142–43
niche ... 69–78
OCD (Obsessive-Dompulsive Disorder) ... *See* special needs clients
organizations, professional ... 55–57, 63–64
organizing principles ... 252–61
packaging your services ... 174–80
paper trail ... 184, 211
paper, choosing for stationery ... 96, 147
Pareto Principle ... 253
Pareto, Vilfredo ... 253
Parkinson, C. Northcode ... 254

Parkinson's Law 254
Partnerships 105–6
Patent and Trademark Office 130
permits 104, 118
phases of organizing 250
phone .... *See* telephone
policies and procedures 204–6, 204–6
portfolio 83–84, 246
post office box 191, 214
pre-qualify clients 176, 227
press release 137, 159–60, 159–60, 160
pricing

    break-even analysis 173–74

    flat fee 178–79

    hourly rate 165, 177–78

    initial consultation 175–77

    project 179

    strategies 165, 167, 168, 174

principles of organizing 252–61
process-oriented 262
professional image 43–47
professional organizations 55–57, 63–64
Professional Organizers in Canada (POC) 57
professional organizing

    advantages 18–30

    associations 33, 55–57

    history of 30–34

    qualifications for 35–43

profit 23, 25, 80, 83, 123, 165, 167, 168, 172, 174, 175
project management 255–56
project planning 180–83
promotional products 141
promotional tools 148
proposals 231–32
prospects, pre-qualifying 227
protecting

    assets 213–18

intellectual property ... 129–31
publicity ... 135, 162, 163
qualifications ... 35–43
radio advertising ... 143
rates ... *See* fees
reading ... 58
recordkeeping ... *See* bookkeeping
referral fees ... 157, 158
referral groups ... 154
referrals
    from clients ... 155
    from colleagues ... 156
    word of mouth ... 154–55
registering a business name ... 119–20
registration ... 118, 119, 120, 126, 129, 130, 131
regulations ... 117–19
residential organizing ... 72, 266
retaining clients ... 273–88
right-brain ... 263
safety, personal ... 267, 281
sales
    closing ... 229–30
    defined ... 223–31
    follow-up ... 227
    tax ... 126, 127
saving money
    on equipment and furniture ... 208
    on printing ... 209
security ... 213, 214, 217, 281
self-discipline ... 37–40
self-employment tax ... 105, 112, 121, 125
seller's permit ... 127
seminars, teaching ... 162
service mark ... 119, 120, 129, 130
skills
    business management ... 41–43

developing	55–67
improving	55–62
marketing and sales	42–43
resources for building	55–60
Small Business Administration (SBA)	26, 53
Smith, Jeff	24
Social Security	105, 112, 121
sole proprietorship	103–5
speaking	138, 139
special needs clients	268–70
specialist	70, 71
specialties	71–74
start-up costs	25, 55
stationery	92, 94–96
strategic alliances	29, 64, 85, 129, 155, 228
strategic business plan	82
strategic partners	27
Subchapter S-Corporation	107, 109
subcontractor	*See* independent contractor
supplies to bring on the job	245
support team	86–88
support, getting	55, 86–88, 149, 219
tactile learning style	263
task-oriented	262
taxes	121–25, 127
employment	108, 112, 195, 197, 198, 213
estimated	104, 105, 108, 125
home office deduction	123, 211
income	105, 108, 112, 121–25
municipal	119
sales	126–27
self-employment	104, 105, 112, 121
teaching organizing principles & skills	261–66
telephone	
answering	100–101, 148, 193
lines	193
listing	31, 144

television advertising 143
testimonials 62, 155–56, 286
time management 253, 254
trade shows 143–44
trademark 120, 129–30
training

    acquiring 55–62

    employees 200

travel expenses 180
URL 96, 97
value of your services 60, 70, 71, 72, 73, 135, 166, 169, 170, 174
values clarification 252, 253
vision for your business 79–81
visual learning style 263
voice-mail 148, 193
volunteering 61, 62, 151
Website, developing 96–100
word of mouth marketing 154–55
worker's compensation 216
working with clients .... *See* Part III
writing articles 141, 147, 162
Yellow Pages 31, 73, 144–45
zoning laws 117–18

About the Author

Jackie Tiani entered the world of professional organizing from her successful career in corporate accounting. She is one of the country's foremost authorities on business organization. For a living, Jackie teaches clients how to take control of their workday and have more time to focus on their most important work. Her dream is that everyone could leave the office earlier to go home and spend more quality time with family and friends.

As a respected industry leader, Jackie is frequently a spokesperson for the organizing industry. She contributed her expertise as technical editor of Organizing for Dummies®, and has been quoted in publications such as The Wall Street Journal, Chicago Tribune, and Chicago Daily Herald. Jackie is a Certified Professional Organizer®, a Certified QuickBooks ProAdvisor®, and a Paper Tiger Authorized Consultant®.

Since the founding of her Glendale Heights, IL-based consulting firm, Organizing Systems Inc., Jackie has been a speaker, trainer or consultant for over 250 companies, and has helped thousands of men and women become more organized and productive.

Jackie lives with her husband, Dan, in Glendale Heights, Illinois. They have two grown sons, a grown daughter and four grandchildren, all of whom are very organized. In their spare time, Dan & Jackie love to camp, golf, and travel.

Jackie Tiani Would Like to Hear from You
How did you like this book? Did it help you launch or grow your organizing business? How can this book be improved? Please share your feedback and success stories with Jackie. She can be reached:
Organizing Systems, Inc.
PO Box 5085
Glendale Heights, IL 60139
Her phone number is 630-681-9080
Her email address is jackie@organizingforaliving.com
You can visit her Website at www.organizingsystems.com